Music

Books of the Theatre Series

H. D. Albright, General Editor

Number 3

A Rare Books of the Theatre project of the
American Educational Theatre Association

FRONTISPIECE—Adolphe Appia before the setting for the sacred forest in *Parsifal*.
Painting by René Martin. From *Art Vivant ou Nature Morte?*, Milan, 1923.

ADOLPHE APPIA'S

"Music and the Art of the Theatre"

translated by

Robert W. Corrigan and Mary Douglas Dirks

with a

Foreword by Lee Simonson

Edited by Barnard Hewitt

UNIVERSITY OF MIAMI PRESS
CORAL GABLES, FLORIDA 33124

Printed in the United States of America

CONTENTS

EDITOR'S NOTE

THE AMERICAN EDUCATIONAL THEATRE ASSOCIATION is particularly pleased to be able to publish a translation of "La Musique et la Mise en Scène," Adolphe Appia's best known work, during the centennial year of his birth. Although the essay was completed in 1898, the original has not yet been published.

A few persons have read the original manuscript in Berne, Switzerland, or the incomplete copy in the New York Public Library. However, its contents have become known largely through the German translation, *Die Musik und die Inscenierung,* published by F. Bruckmann in Munich in 1899, now a rare book. Although Appia approved this translation by Elsa, Princess von Cantacuzène, wife of Hugo Bruckmann of the publishing firm, it is not always faithful to the original.

Both the original French and the German translation have been used in preparing this English version, and it includes the two diagrams in Part I and notes on the designs, which are found only in *Die Musik*. The Table of Contents, extremely detailed in the original and in the German version, is here greatly reduced. The designs are those in the German version, except that the final one for *Tristan and Isolde,* Act II, has been omitted because it is too dark to reproduce. The Preface which Appia wrote in 1918 for an English version which did not materialize is here included.

This volume, like its predecessor, *Adolphe Appia's "The Work of Living Art",* could not have been prepared without the wholehearted co-operation of Adolphe Appia's nephew, Edmond, who unhappily did not live to see it in print. We are indebted also to Dr. Edmund Stadler of the Schweizer Theatersammlung, Landesbibliothek, Berne, Switzerland, for essential materials and information. We are extremely grateful to Walther R. Volbach of Texas Christian University, who, with the aid of his wife, Claire, and Walton H. Rothrock, carefully checked the translation for the Adolphe Appia Foundation and for the American Educational Theatre Association.

BARNARD HEWITT
University of Illinois

FOREWORD

THE THEORIES THAT ELUCIDATED the basic aesthetic principles of modern scenic design, analyzed its fundamental technical problems, and formed a charter of freedom under which scenic designers still practice, appeared in two volumes under quasi-musical titles: *La Mise en Scène du Drame Wagnérien* (The Staging of Wagner's Music Dramas) and *Die Musik und die Inscenierung*. The first was published in Paris in 1895, an inconspicuous brochure of fifty-one pages, the second as a full-sized volume, translated from the French script, in Munich in 1899. Both the book and the booklet are now so difficult to procure that they have become collector's items. But their influence was immediately felt, for Appia was that rare combination, a creative artist of exceptional imagination and a rigorously logical theorist. *Die Musik und die Inscenierung* contained eighteen illustrations of projected stage settings for Wagner's operas which embodied Appia's aesthetic principles with such finality that they became a revelation of a totally new kind of stage setting and stage lighting, then as strange as the outlines of a new continent seen at dawn and now so familiar. These drawings revealed a unity and simplicity of design that could be made an inherent part of stage settings in a way that no one had hitherto conceived, Wagner least of all. Practitioners of stagecraft were converted by a set of illuminations to a gospel which most of them never read.

Appia expressed in dogmatic form much of what the Duke of Saxe-Meiningen had demonstrated pragmatically. But in promulgating his theory of stage setting he completed its unification by insisting on the plasticity of light itself, which no one before had conceived. He demonstrated in detail, both as a theorist and as a draftsman, how stage lighting could be used and controlled so as to establish a completely three-dimensioned world on the stage.

In Appia's theories, as well as in his drawings, the light which in paintings had already been called dramatic, was for the first time brought into the theatre where its dramatic values could be utilized. Chiaroscuro, so controlled as to reveal essential or significant form, with which painters had been preoccupied for three centuries, became, as Appia described it, an expressive medium for the scene designer. The light and shade of Rembrandt, Piranesi, Daumier, and Meryon was finally brought into the theatre, not splashed on a backdrop as romantic scene painters had used it, but as an ambient medium, actually filling space and possessing actual volume; it was an impalpable bond which fused the actor, wherever and however he moved, with everything around him. The plastic unity of the stage was made continuous.

If one looks at reproductions of stage settings before Appia —and the history of stage setting might be divided by B.A. as history in general is divided by B.C.—they are filled with even radiance; everything is of equal importance. In Appia's drawings, for the first time the stage is a microcosm of the world. It moves "from dawn to noon, from noon to dewy eve" and on through all the watches of the night. And the actors in it seem living beings who move as we do from sunlight or moonlight into light and shadow. Beneath their feet is not the floor of a stage but the surface of the earth, over their heads not a backdrop but the heavens, as we see them, enveloping and remote. There is depth here that seems hewn and distance that recedes infinitely further than a mathematical vanishing point.

In attacking the conventions of scene painting Appia created an ultimate convention. For the transparent trickery of painted illusions of form he substituted the illusion of space built up by the transfiguration that light, directed and controlled, can give to the transient structures of the stage carpenter. The third dimension, incessant preoccupation of the occidental mind for four centuries, defined by metaphysicians, explored by scientists, simulated by painters, was re-created in terms of the theatre, made actual. The stage more completely than ever became a world that we could vicariously inhabit; stage settings acquired a new reality. The light in Appia's first drawings, if one compares them to the designs that preceded his, seems the night and morning of a First Day.

The art of the theatre today finds its full freedom within the boundaries of Appia's original concepts in a stage setting that is completely plastic — plastic in the sense of being infinitely malleable;

plastic also in the sense of being consistently three-dimensional. More recent experiments in production continue to play with our sensations of space and our emotional reactions to projections, either actual or implied, of the third dimension. We accept the dynamic relations of a three-dimensional actor moving through the third dimension.

Appia, designing for opera, evolved a type of stage setting so compact, so directly related to the emotional flux of drama, that he anticipated the development of scenic design in the theatre. Light fluctuates in Appia's drawings as it does on the stage of a theatre, and gives to canvas forms just such simplifications of mass and outline as Appia indicated in his light-plot for Act II of *Tristan and Isolde*. Such a light-plot is now an accepted part of every modern production. It is separately rehearsed, memorized by the stage electrician, and is part of the stage manager's prompt book. The fewest of its changes are dictated by actual stage directions such as the extinguishing of a torch; the vast majority are an accompaniment to action and aim to emphasize the atmospheric qualities of a stage setting in a way that can project variations of dramatic mood and thereby intensify the emotional reaction of an audience.

It was the singular limitation of Appia's temperament that he could find no basis for the interpretation of drama except that dictated by the tempo and timbre of a musical score. His imagination could be stimulated in no other way. But in indicating both theoretically and graphically the complete mobility of stage lighting he has made it possible for any play to be accompanied by a light-score that is almost as directly expressive as a musical accompaniment and can be made as integrally a part of a play as music was in Wagner's music dramas.

LEE SIMONSON

xiii

THE TRANSLATORS' PREFACE

Eric Bentley once wrote, "If life begins on the other side of despair, the translator's life begins on the other side of impossibility." We can think of nothing more appropriate than this remark to describe the almost impossible task of translating Adolphe Appia's "La Musique et la Mise en Scène."

First, there was the problem of text(s). Appia wrote the work in French but it was published only in a German translation which is not always faithful to the original. We have used both French and German, relying principally on the original French in the New York Public Library's typed copy, supplemented by sections from the copy in the Schweizer Theatersammlung, Landesbibliothek, Berne, Switzerland, kindly supplied by Dr. Edmund Stadler.

Our second problem was that this was of necessity a work of collaboration. The four people who worked on it lived in totally different sections of the country and the work was spread over several years. The procedure went something like this: one of us translated the French text and the other the German, and then our efforts were combined into a new version that stayed as close to the French as possible but which also included some material from the German. This version was then sent to the Editor, Barnard Hewitt of the University of Illinois, and to Walther R. Volbach of Texas Christian University, the American representative of the Adolphe Appia Foundation, each of whom checked the translation and sent back to us a large number of suggested revisions. Some of these suggestions were incorporated in the text and a somewhat altered version was sent to them for their final revisions. Thus the translation published here is our version as revised by Professors Hewitt and Volbach.

The other big problem was the question of literal as opposed to free translation. In order to make the book more readable, several alterations were made in the form of the text and these still stand. But the question of style was thornier. Appia's style is highly personal and difficult to translate—in fact it is almost impossible to render his convoluted and florid phrasings into smooth and easily readable

xv

English. For this reason, we took our stand on the side of a "free" translation, being in complete accord with Eric Bentley's position on this issue: "Accuracy must not be bought at the expense of bad English. Since we cannot have everything, we would rather surrender accuracy than style . . . . The clinching argument in favor of this principle is that, finally, bad English cannot be an accurate translation —unless the original is in bad German, bad French, or what have you."

Up to a point we were right, but we became aware that we had fallen into a trap that awaits the free translator—we had produced more of an interpretation of Appia than a translation. From this we were rescued by Professors Hewitt and Volbach, and we trust that the version here published is true to Appia's text in content, form, and tone, and is at the same time readable.

ACKNOWLEDGMENTS

The translators wish to acknowledge their debt to Ulric and Frances Moore, Viola Oliver, and Hugh Barnes whose earlier unpublished translations of this book were exceedingly helpful in the present undertaking. Acknowledgment is also due Mrs. Karen Haller who typed the many versions of the manuscript, and the Tulane University Council on Research for a grant supporting this project. We also wish to express our gratitude to John Dirks and Esther Jane Swartzfager who so patiently put up with us while we were trying to find our way through the labyrinthine ways of Appia's prose.

It is impossible for us adequately to express our indebtedness to Barnard Hewitt and Walther Volbach. Without them this book would not exist, and in a very real sense they have been co-translators rather than editors and advisors.

Finally, we should like to acknowledge our debt to the late Alexander M. Drummond of Cornell University. Although Professor Drummond won't see this volume, we feel certain he would have been pleased at its publication. All his life he encouraged students to read and study Appia, and it is probably safe to say that without his stimulation, enthusiasm, and encouragement this translation would not have been done. Nearly everyone in this country who has ever been involved with the translation of *La Musique et la Mise en Scène* can trace his or her involvement back to this common source of inspiration—so no publication of the book would be complete without acknowledging this debt.

R.W.C.
M.D.D.

ADOLPHE APPIA'S

"Music and the Art of the Theatre"

TO

Houston Stewart Chamberlain, who alone knows the life which I enclose within these pages.

ADOLPHE APPIA

"Music never expresses the phenomenon but only the inner essence of the phenomenon."

SCHOPENHAUER

"When music reaches its noblest power, it becomes form."

SCHILLER

Preface to an English Edition (1918)

This work was written during the years 1892-1897 and published in 1899. It may perhaps seem strange that after twenty-five years it still has sufficient significance to merit translation. As a matter of fact, *mise-en-scène* has remained ill-defined, subject as it is to changing tastes and fashions, and its practical application has remained purely empirical. Music, on the other hand, has enjoyed a far greater development.

The purpose of this preface is to indicate briefly why, in order to be understood, ideas of general significance had once to be related to a particular artistic creation, the work of Richard Wagner—and how these ideas have a value independent of Wagner's work, which justifies their publication today.

At the time when I wrote and published this volume, the problem of production, and consequently of dramatic art, was of concern to no one. The audience, as well as the specialists in the field, was preoccupied solely with innovation through an ever increasing sumptuousness in setting, or else through an ever more complete realism: this attitude toward stage setting condemned the dramatist to mark time. (Incidentally, I trust we are no longer deluded by productions of adulterated Greek dramas performed in sacrilegiously factitious ruins.) In that period, only the exceptional nature of the productions at Bayreuth and the Festival Theatre itself were truly significant attempts at reform. Still, when the curtain was raised, the settings *on stage* offered nothing whatever to correspond with what was wondrous in the score. This continual and ever-renewed conflict, this painful dichotomy, made the work at Bayreuth, as we shall see, the fountainhead of one of the most fruitful of all artistic revolutions. And that is why Wagner's work will always remain inseparable from the dramatic and scenic reforms which are in the process of being realized.

For some, Wagner's work has transformed the Idea of drama itself by virtue of the fact that it locates the center of gravity in the *internal* action, to which music and *only* music holds the key, but of which, nevertheless, the actor must remain the corporeal embodiment on the stage. Later, we shall note the unexpected developments which arose from this concept. So it came about that the stage was most decisively enriched, if not in actual practice, at least in its potential, and Bayreuth will always stand as the classic example of this advance.

Such excessive interiorization caused others, who, moreover, followed much later in the development, to turn in the opposite direction, to the cultivation of the human body as an expressive medium in its own right. The first school of thought, declaring that Wagner's drama was addressed primarily to our aural sense, sought to make a legitimate aesthetic correlation between what the music brings to our ears and what the setting, in order to be meaningful, must offer to our eyes. It was to this concept which I subscribed; and the crude distortion inflicted by contemporary staging upon Wagner's magnificent work impelled me to this study.

As I delved deeper, the evidence forced upon me the realization that an inescapable contradiction exists within the Wagnerian drama itself; that during performance, there is a continual compromise between the music and the actor, between the art of sound and rhythm and the art of plastic and dramatic movement, and any attempt at traditional stage setting for this drama can rest only on a compromise, a compromise which must somehow be transcended if aesthetic truth is to be attained. The more I sought to transcend this compromise, the more urgently was I assailed by the vital question: Which of the elements must be sacrificed, the music, or the actor?

On the other hand, some who were not enthralled by the overwhelming power of the music, and consequently could not plumb the dramatic depths of Wagner's work, found the compromise far less trying: the diminution of the scope and intensity of the music was a matter of indifference to them; the harmonious glorification of the human body suited their aesthetic aim, although in pursuit of it they little suspected the problems they were to raise for themselves.

Approaching each other from almost completely opposite

directions, aroused by the only work at that time whose form was sufficiently powerful to push affirmation as well as contradiction to extreme limits, these two groups of artists met—and I should better say, collided head-on—at the crossroads . . .

And here at the crossroads, we find ourselves today, in direct confrontation.

Wagner's urge to create in homogeneous form the integral expression of the human drama in all its purity and profundity was infinitely more compelling than the influence of opera. Still, the Master could not encompass everything; it did not occur to him to sacrifice even a modicum of his prodigious musical genius, and hence could not resolve the cruel conflict in which he struggled, even with some degree of awareness: the conflict between music for which there was no suitable expression in the living body of the performer, music which *could not achieve such externalization* without the risk of having its own identity suppressed—and the necessity, nevertheless, of presenting the music and the human body *simultaneously*.

One like me, who has felt this tragic conflict in his own soul, will never disavow Wagner the man, or his works, for they inspired me with compassion, thus setting me free. Wagner's work itself has preserved me from presenting an arbitrary case, for it has pointed out the way and constrained me to follow it almost involuntarily.

In 1895, as I was writing the chapter on the Actor (I), I felt intuitively that some kind of rhythmic movement which would serve as link and intermediary between the actor and the music must be brought to light. It seemed to me that although there was unfortunately little possibility of resolving the Wagnerian compromise, this concept might prove to be a means of making it less obvious, and perhaps even serve as a device for orienting the actor (and, with him, the dramatist) towards a more effective dramatic form for the coexistence of actor and music on stage. Eleven years later, I became acquainted with the Eurythmics of Jaques-Dalcroze, who was just beginning his experiments; and there I found the answer to my passionate desire for synthesis! By closely following this musical discipline of the body, I discovered the living germ of a dramatic art, in which music is no longer separated from the human body in a splendor which is after all illusory, at least during performance, nor subjugated to it, a dramatic art which will direct the body towards an externalization in space, and thus make it the primary and supreme means of scenic expression, to which all other elements of production will be subordinated.

This was a marvelous voyage of discovery! Although I went further and further afield in my explorations, nevertheless I returned frequently to my starting point—the Wagnerian compromise—and realized with pleasure that all of the essential ideas contained in this old work of mine had found confirmation in the discipline of Eurythmics, and in its results. By freeing the music from its self-centered and unnatural isolation, and by joining it with the dramatist in a fruitful union, Wagner took the first, the decisive step. But he neglected the role of the body: he regarded it simply as the visible carrier of the dramatic action, little suspecting that between the rhythm and duration of the music, and the activity of the body as it preserved in spite of everything its own life independent of that rhythm and duration, there existed an impassable abyss. And because of this lack of understanding, he subjected the human body to manifest violence from beginning to end of the productions. But now, with the liberation of the body, music is once again free. No longer will the poet be a separate and conflicting entity with regard to the music: This *vital* step has at last been taken. The poet will become the prime focus; *he alone* will consecrate the divine union of music with the human body.

Today, the resurgence of the body as an expressive medium essential to our aesthetic culture is a concept which possesses many minds, animates the imagination, and gives rise to diverse experiments, doubtless not all of equal value, but all directed toward the same reform. We now feel that the performer tends, almost implicitly, to come closer to the spectator; we also feel (some more deeply and sensitively than others) a mysterious involvement on the part of the spectator with the performer. Our modern productions used to force us into such miserable passivity that we veiled our humiliation in the shadowy recesses of the auditorium. But now, as we behold the body's effort finally to rediscover itself, our emotion is almost a fraternal collaboration: we wish to be that body on stage; our role of spectator is now a responsibility; the social instinct awakens in us, an instinct which has been heartlessly stifled until now, and the barrier between the stage and the audience now strikes us as an unpleasant and unfortunate disassociation, the result of our own egoism.

And here we face the most critical factor in theatre reform.

Incontestably a reciprocity exists between the dramatist's original conception and the methods of scenic realization upon which he can depend. It would be more accurate to say that this reciprocity should exist, for in our time, unfortunately, with very few exceptions, the determining influence lies on one side only: quite simply, what forces the dramatist to limit his concept, to restrict his vision, is our modern concept of stage and theatre; there is no reciprocity possible for the dramatist when it comes to the staging of his work.

Let us proclaim it strongly: the dramatist will never be able to liberate his *vision* if he insists upon projecting it in a space rigidly separated from the audience. This may be desirable on occasion, but it must never be taken as the norm.

It is hardly necessary to point out that the construction of our theatres should evolve toward a freer, more flexible concept of dramatic art. Sooner or later we shall achieve what will be known as the *Salle* [hall, auditorium], cathedral of the future, which, in a free, vast, and flexible space, will bring together the most diverse manifestations of our social and artistic life—the perfect place for dramatic art to flourish—*with or without an audience.* There is no art form in which social solidarity can be better expressed than in the drama, particularly if it returns to its noble origins in the collective realization of great religious or patriotic feeling, or simply of human feeling, transforming them into our modern image.

The Eurythmics initiated by Dalcroze is still the only discipline which first awakens the will and vital aspirations of the human

· 5

body, and then offers the means by which they can be expressed freely and joyously in space. In this, beauty is not the aim, but the result; thus beauty assures us of the purity of our aspirations.

We have seen that the harmonious culture of the body, as it obeys the profound commands of the music created for this purpose, tends to overcome our passive isolation as spectators, changing it into a feeling of mutual responsibility, of collaboration somehow implicit in the very fact of a production. The term *production* will gradually become an anachronism, and finally even meaningless. We shall wish to act in harmonious unity. The dramatic art of tomorrow will be a *social act,* in which each of us will assist. And, who knows, perhaps one day we shall arrive, after a period of transition, at majestic festivals in which a whole people will participate, where each of us will express our feelings, our sorrows, our joys, no longer content to remain a passive onlooker. Then will the dramatist triumph!

ADOLPHE APPIA
October, 1918

Preface (1898)

It is always dangerous to attempt to deal with an aesthetic question without reference to the work of art itself. Indeed, the criticism never means much, the description is completely imaginary, and there is no need to sustain the concept by abstract reasoning. I find myself here doubling as critic and theoretician, and from both standpoints, exposed to the deserved scorn of the artists for whom I am writing. Therefore, I wish to assure them that I undertake this study with unusual reluctance. I am by nature not a writer and, moreover, my thesis includes a discussion of music, that element most elusive of critical analysis. Finally, I cannot develop my thesis, without pointing out some lack in the dramatic work of Richard Wagner, and many readers will deem this an uncalled-for pretension.

If I have not been dissuaded by these considerations, it is only because I know of no other way to communicate those beliefs which seem to me to have considerable significance for the art of the theatre.

To the discussion of a work of art, one need bring only knowledge of the effect of a given age upon the artist and his work; except for that, the simple presence of the work itself is more meaningful and more convincing than any subtle analysis; besides, reverence commands silence, and the work of art needs above all to be surrounded by reverence. The influence of the age manifests itself in many ways; it can affect not only the making, but also the very conception of the work, subjecting the artist to positive tyranny. When that happens, the relevant theoretical considerations become indispensable and have direct applicability without reference to the art work which necessarily will always remain irrelevant. The theatre has always been bound strictly by the special conditions imposed by the age, and consequently, the dramatist has always been the least independent of artists, because he employs so many distinct elements, all of which must be properly united in his work. If one of these elements remains subject to the conventions of the age, while the others free themselves to obey the will of the creative artist, the result will be a lack of balance which alters the essential nature of the dramatic work.

The use of music, as revealed to us by Richard Wagner, has completely transformed the elements of expression at the dramatist's command; on the other hand those elements not strictly dependent upon the personal will of the dramatist have been subject to the crippling influence of the theatrical conventions of the period. The former have developed without conflict; whereas the latter have remained unchanged. In a work of art where harmony must reign supreme, this defect is all the more serious and necessarily produces a kind of inner dislocation in our receptivity which disturbs our judgment and by the same token must extend to other manifestations of modern art. It is therefore necessary to free those now outmoded representational elements of production from the constraints which have hindered their vital progress in the general evolution, and to that end, to allow them a fruition comparable to that achieved by the elements of poetic-musical expression: this is the task I have endeavored to accomplish.

The question of reform presents three different aspects which correspond to the principal parts of my study:

1. Can the existing elements furnish, independently of any particular dramatic work, a principle applicable to the *mise en scène*? And if so, what will be the effect of that principle on existing theatre techniques?

2. What obstacles prevented Richard Wagner from exercising this creativity on the visual elements of the drama?

3. What effect will the theory of production developed in the first part of this book have on the artist of the theatre and on today's audience?

Since the question directly related to Wagner comes second, it is obvious that an aesthetic principle does exist, independent of the great German master's dramas, which is applicable to all forms of theatrical production. This principle will eliminate those subjective

8 ·

and arbitrary elements so incompatible with the manifestation of genius and will even oblige us to relate directly to the work of art because it is an integral part of it. Armed with the ideas thus gained, we can consider the situation today and discern the opportunity for a reform in theatrical production, whether for Richard Wagner's dramas or for later works. We shall see that this reform will bring others in its wake and thus take on a much greater importance than appeared at first glance.

Music has been the inspiration of this book. And evolution in music, though it cannot be reduced to an abstraction, has nonetheless provided the sole motivating force for that evolution in theatrical production, the nature and results of which I seek. I must, therefore, ask my reader to contribute to the reading of this book all the sensitivity to music that he possesses. Naturally I do not mean that he should be himself a musician, in the usual sense of the word: above all, music is an emotional inclination which one may possess without necessarily being a master of musical technique or even an appreciative audience of the crude exhibitions of our concert halls and our operatic stages. Sensitivity to music requires a special aptitude for contemplation, which makes one quick to grasp the aesthetic significance of certain proportions and to respond spontaneously to their content of intensity and harmony.

It is in this sense that I appeal to the reader's sensitivity to music. This is the only demand my study makes, and if I were not convinced that in undertaking it I was in accord with the secret desires of many of my readers, I should never have had the courage to begin it.

ADOLPHE APPIA
Montbrillant (Bière)
March, 1897

PART I

THE *MISE EN SCÈNE*
AS A MEANS OF EXPRESSION IN THE ART
OF THE THEATRE

Chapter I. THE *Mise en Scène* AND MUSIC

The Mise en Scène

IN EVERY WORK OF ART there must be a harmonious relationship
between feeling and form, a perfect balance between the idea which
the artist wishes to express and the means he uses to express it. If
one of the means seems to us clearly unnecessary to the expression
of the idea, or if the artist's idea—the object of his expression—is
only imperfectly communicated to us by the means he employs, our
aesthetic pleasure is weakened, if not destroyed.

The greater the number of media necessary for the realization
of the work of art, the more elusive is harmony. The *drama* (by
which I mean all works written for actual production on the stage)
is the most complex of all the arts because of the great number of
media the dramatist must use in order to communicate.

If the poet, painter, and sculptor see the form of their work
develop and always have it in their control, because the content of
their work is identical with its form, and so the object of expression
and the means employed to communicate it to us are in a way
equivalent, this is not the case for the dramatist. Not only does he
not control the final form of his art, but that form seems relatively
independent of his dramatic intention. This is so because there are
two stages in the making of a drama. First, the dramatist must transpose his idea into a dramatic form; then the resultant text must be
transposed to meet the demands of production for an audience.

Unfortunately, this second step in the process, the creation of the *mise-en-scène,* is not controlled by the dramatist.

The means by which the text is realized in the theatre are of utmost importance to those who distinguish dramatic art from literature; that is, for whom drama is inseparable from its production.

What is this form so indispensable to the dramatist and over which he has no control?

What do we mean when we speak of the *mise en scène?*

Until now it has been thought of as the means of realizing on the stage for the eyes of the audience any dramatic conception. However, the dramatic conception of an author is revealed to us by a written work containing only that portion of the drama which is directed to our understanding. The action of course is therein determined in its continuity and its proportions, but only from a dramatic standpoint and without determining the formal process by which these elements are to be shown on stage. The result of this is that production is subject to all sorts of whims and tastes. This is why the same drama may be produced in the most divergent styles according to individual tastes or those of the times. It follows therefore that the drama (as produced on stage) is not only the most complex of all arts, but also the only one of which one of the basic elements may not be judged as a *medium of expression* in the dramatist's control, a condition acutely diminishing the integrity of drama as an art form and relegating it to an inferior status.

It may be argued that although the dramatist has no control over the production, it still performs an expressive function, and often to great advantage, for by constantly accommodating itself in new ways to the taste of the audience, it gives the dramatic text a far larger scope and a far longer life than if the mode of production were definitely and inexorably attached to the written work; this is obvious, but the fact that the scenic form of the drama *cannot* escape the ever-changing tastes of the time is proof enough that the *mise en scène* is not and cannot be an *expressive medium.*

From the point of view of form, a work of art is not a reproduction of some aspect of life to which everyone can contribute his experience and ability; rather it is the harmonious union of various technical devices for the sole purpose of communicating to many the conception of one artist. Our aim here is not to discuss the nature of artistic conception, but to establish that the inspiration and expression of a work of art are the product of a single mind. So it follows that the devices necessary to that mind's communication cannot be divided among several individuals, for these devices are a part of the artist's original intention. It can be stated then that a work of art can preserve its integrity only when all its expressive elements are under the control of its creator. Once the dramatist has *definitively* prescribed the proportions and relationships of each of the elements of production, his text can be realized on the stage by theatre artists who had no part in the creator's original intention; the elements of production have the character of means of expression, which I am going to define, for the term can be applied properly only to *technical devices* which the dramatist can prescribe absolutely, and thus those artists alien to the work's conception are what the canvas is for the painter, what printer's type is for the poet.

If we mean by the expressive media of an art form, those techniques directly under the control of the artist, then, by definition, the *mise en scène* as we know it in our theatres today is not a *means of expression* for the dramatic artist. The dramatist may envision the production as he writes, and even plan for much of his idea to be expressed by the production alone. He may write a detailed description of how his drama is to be staged. He may even direct each production of it during his life time; still his *mise en scène* will not be an artistic medium of expression, and he must feel in his soul how arbitrary is his will and how vain his hope of being obeyed after his death; that is to say, in spite of everything, how separate his drama remains from the *mise en scène* which he has prescribed in such detail. If he fails to feel this consciously, he will be satisfied to regard the *mise en scène* as a secondary agent, unworthy of so much effort, and in his particular case he will be absolutely right. In truth the will of the dramatist is not enough to unite one of the dramatic factors with the drama. His will can achieve only a juxtaposition, more or less successful, not at all the organic life which is characterized by the *necessity* of such a development of form, being so much a part of the prime conception that only the original idea seems to have been arbitrarily chosen by the brain of the creator, while all the rest flows naturally from that conception. No honest dramatist can claim such necessity for a *mise en scène* whose form is not effectively dictated by his text.

Therefore, in order that the *mise en scène* become an integral part of the drama, in order that it become a medium for artistic expression, *a principle, deriving directly from the drama's original conception, without passing again through the will of the dramatist, must be found to prescribe the* mise en scène.

What can that principle be?

Music

In order to develop this study securely, it is important to determine what the situation of music is at the present time and to understand the significance ascribed to this art form. A question of this nature can easily seem full of paradoxes when, as in this study, it is of necessity treated in a rather summary fashion. Because the writer must assume that much of this subject is well known to his readers, he will allude to certain aspects of it merely to illuminate and to strengthen his thesis. Inevitably, then, his point of view may at times appear prejudiced and limited. He begs his readers' indulgence, therefore, in not attributing to him errors due to ignorance in places where he has simply had to limit his discussion.

The revelations in Wagner's dramatic works with regard to the scope and nature of musical expression as applied to the drama are generally well known today. One who has been stirred to action by these revelations, and who bases his entire thesis upon the Master's work, obviously has no need to inform the reader of things already definitively treated by other writers. He need only present that aspect of them whose radiance illuminates his present subject. But in so doing, he tacitly expresses his convictions and brings them before the reader to be judged, without having to explain them in detail.

Our inner life, therefore, provides music with the form through which music expresses that life. Every contradiction ceases from the moment that the form and the object of the expression are identical.

This assertion would seem to pose a formidable problem: how can our inner life dictate precisely its form to music; or, conversely: how can the musical expression manifest itself *clearly* in the form of this inner life?

Such a problem never confronted the musician as his art rapidly developed, because he had to take care merely to preserve the music itself while increasing its technical resources. Today, these accumulated resources far exceed the maximum needed for the variety of musical forms in themselves. Therefore it became necessary for the musician to approach the dramatic poet whose language by itself no longer answered our needs for expression: with Beethoven, music came close to the drama; Wagner completed the process by uniting poet and musician, thus solving the problem. Henceforward, the poet can express the inner life of his characters and the musician can surrender himself without trepidation to the expression of this life because his mode is inspired by it.

The drama fulfills the conditions indispensable to the existence of music today by providing it the means of manifesting itself clearly in the form of the life which governs its expression.

In this new realm, music is found to be tightly linked, not only to the word, but also to that portion of the drama presented to our eyes by the scenic elements of production. It should therefore be possible to abstract the expressive role of music and to consider it now in its relationship to the *mise en scène*.

From this exclusively visual viewpoint, how can music function?

To understand how music can control the elements of production, let us look briefly at pantomime—that prototype of drama in which, because language has no place, music and the visual elements of theatre are most prominent. In pantomime, music determines the time-durations and the sequence of action. No doubt in the lower forms of pantomime the musician provides no more than flourishes, repeated as often as the length of each episode requires, and the music is no more than a pleasant accompaniment to the show, as at the circus or in a quadrille. But in the true pantomime, music prescribes the duration and sequence of the episodes and necessarily molds the show with mathematical accuracy. Obviously, if we now add words to this music, the relationship between the music and the production remains unaltered. Even in opera, although this falsification of the usual time sequences of life is in no way motivated by any adequate dramatic intention, the music nevertheless measures the time just as in pantomime, only less obviously because it does so destructively.

Let us turn now to the drama of the poet-musician, in which, as we have seen, music finds its form in the object of its expression. This amounts to saying that the musical duration is dictated by the original dramatic conception, so that from the point of view of theatrical production music not only regulates the time, is not merely a length of time, but it is the *time itself,* since its pattern is an integral part of what it expresses.

Let me explain this seeming paradox more fully. When the dramatist seeks to realize his intention in the theatre, he must combine all the elements of production with so much balance and achieve such harmony that the form he uses disappears before the clarity of his communication. Thus the drama achieves in performance an organic life which defies analysis. The dramatist who uses only the spoken word appeals only to our understanding. The life of his work then becomes organic through a continual re-creation by the spectator, and this re-creation does not depend on analysis of the means employed by the dramatist; it results only from the fact that the dramatic action is presented through word and movement only in *appearances.* But life furnishes us daily with just such exterior manifestations and we are therefore accustomed to the work of re-creation; we do it unconsciously, and we can experience the organic life of the spoken drama without suspecting the active role we play in creating that life.

On the other hand, the poet-musician, thanks to the music,

presents us not only with external effects of emotions, the appearance of dramatic life, but with the emotions themselves, the dramatic life in all its reality, as we can know it only in the most profound depths of our being. There is no need for re-creation; each character, according to his dramatic enhancement, presents himself to us as coming from ourselves.

But music, this all powerful medium, if it is thus to express the life of the soul, must give to the form which it receives from the soul a time pattern very different from that of daily life, so that, in order fully to appreciate its expressiveness, we must lose ourselves so completely in that time pattern that our entire personal life is transposed to respond to the emotions of the drama. For this divergence from the pattern of ordinary life, we accept readily enough as long as it affects only time and does not lead to alterations in the visible scene so marked that we cannot accept them, as long as the resultant expression finds its supreme justification in our own hearts.

Thus we have not one pattern of time, that is, a fictional pattern of time on the stage, for an audience living in another pattern of time in the auditorium, but in performance, music in the word-tone drama is *Time* itself.

We shall see later the considerable aesthetic advantages that accrue from this.

16 ·

Chapter II. MUSIC AND THE *Mise en Scène*

Theoretical Principles

WE HAVE SEEN that if the *mise en scène* is to be totally expressive of the playwright's intention, the means of controlling it must exist within the text.

The *mise en scène,* as a design in space with variations in time, presents essentially a question of proportion and sequence. Its regulating principle must therefore govern its proportions in space and their sequence in time, each dependent on the other.

In drama, the playwright seems to have this power through the quantity and order of his text. However, this is not the case because the text itself has no fixed duration; and the time not filled by the text is impossible to calculate. Even if one were to measure the relative duration of speech and silence with a stop watch, this duration would be fixed only by the arbitrary will of the author or the director, without *necessarily* having its origins in the initial conception.

The quantity and order of the text alone, therefore, are insufficient to govern its staging. Music, on the other hand, determines not only time-duration and continuity in the drama, but, as we have seen, should actually be considered from the visual point of view of dramatic action as being time itself.

It is the word-tone poet, then, who possesses the guiding principle which, springing as it does from the original intention, inexorably and of necessity dictates the *mise en scène* without being filtered through the will of the dramatist—and this principle is an integral part of his drama and shares its organic life.

Thus the production attains the rank of an expressive medium in the drama of the poet-musician; but note that it cannot achieve such rank except in this kind of drama.

By means of dramatic representation, music is transported into space and there achieves a material form—in the *mise en scène* —thus satisfying its need for a tangible form, not just illusively in time alone, but quite *actually* in space, a need it has sought to fill in other ways, to the detriment of its very essence. Thus, in a way, musical space which is the setting for the poet-musician's work must perforce be very different from that space in which the poet alone seeks to realize his dramatic action; and since music creates this space, it is from music that we shall receive all information pertaining to it.

One might find it logical that the time pattern of a drama should be transposed into space, without perhaps understanding exactly *how* music has the power to do this. Since this study has no object other than this transposition and a meticulous investigation of its consequences, we shall abandon the more or less abstract argument which has served us up to now, and attempt, by using known elements, to evoke a kind of drama, examples of which are as yet nonexistent.

In the spoken drama, the drama in which the poet employs only words, the external appearances of daily life provide for actors yard-sticks for the time and continuity of their playing. The actor must carefully observe the external effects of his emotions on himself; he must then associate with quite different kinds of people, observing their behavior in the same way in order to discover the hidden springs of their actions, then set himself to reproduce whatever is typical; and finally he must with discretion and taste apply these discoveries to the situations furnished by the poet.

No doubt the length of the text allows the author to impose

on the actor the approximate duration of his role, but it is precisely within this approximate time span that the actor molds the proportions which life has taught him. For the meaning and length of the dramatic poem can only suggest to the actor his mime and his actions; they cannot dictate them precisely.

In the word-tone drama, the actor receives not merely suggestions for his playing, but also the exact proportions which he must observe. He cannot introduce the variety of intensity he has learned from life, for the musical expression itself contains the necessary variations in intensity. Thus, the length and the meaning of the poetic-musical text (by which I mean the complete score of the drama) represent *life* for the interpreter of this work of art; and just as the actor in the spoken drama must acquire the versatility necessary to reproduce those elements which his experience of daily life has supplied him, so the actor in the word-tone drama must acquire the same kind of flexibility in order to obey the explicit orders imposed upon him directly by the life contained within the score.

We now see how music on the stage can be carried into the mime of the characters and into their actions.

But how can music be carried over into the painting, the lighting, the arrangement of the drops and flats?

In order to persuade ourselves that music can do this as well, we must enter even more deeply into the mysterious realm of musical expression.

When, for example, in the spoken drama an actor has to express his suffering over the memory of a lost happiness, he cannot communicate this feeling to us directly except by his facial expression, since his words can only explain the cause of his suffering, thus presenting the logical meaning of the scene without *expressing* its inner content. Gestures and actions are therefore meaningless unless supported by the contents of the text, either as a simple statement of a real situation, or as the meaningful result of the character's innermost suffering. Obviously, then, it is the variety of facial expression which, underscored by the text, will communicate to us most directly the emotion we are meant to feel; and the other means of representation should be subordinate to this. It is for this reason that visibility is a major consideration in production; if the audience is to experience the play, the faces of the actors must be clearly seen.

If the actor in the drama of the word-tone poet wishes to communicate the same kind of suffering to us, of what means shall he avail himself? Music, in any symphonic combination whatever, will make clear the very matter of his memory without such precise expressions; so that before we understand that the fact of recalling lost happiness is painful, we will feel sad within ourselves for the loss of this happiness — with the result that we no longer need the actor to convey this emotion to us.

Moreover, the actor, in allowing the music to paint the images of his suffering, can keep his pain buried in the depths of his soul and express to us emotions that have to do only with his present existence. Here too the music will support him, not only through contrast, but also by expressing with equal precision both the living moment and the memory of the past. The union of music with words allows it to establish the expression of happiness at the time when that happiness existed; now it can let this expression flow into pure music and converge once more with the poem in order to convey the immediate expression demanded by the scene.[1]

The actor thus plunged almost in spite of himself into the atmosphere of the drama's inner life no longer plays so important a role as he does in spoken drama. He realizes that we do not need him to interpret his suffering; he even suspects that we know that suffering better than he.

In a production of spoken drama, the presence of the actor is absolutely necessary to any communication, and consequently he takes an abnormal importance, as the visual requirements we have mentioned prove. But for the author of word-tone drama, the actor is not the sole or even the most important interpreter of the poet's

---

[1] Of course, the actor of the spoken drama may count on the audience's awareness of what has gone before in the action to enhance its appreciation of each new situation. But this is an indirect means of expression, and I am concerned only with those means which at a particular moment make the spectator directly conscious of what the actor is attempting to express, without the intervention of thought.

intention, he is rather but one medium, neither more nor less important than the others, at the poet's disposal. Once the actor ceases to be the dominant element in production, having no longer to "make a speech," he recedes into the background to take his place among his co-workers, the various other poetic-musical devices, ready to follow the convolutions resulting from the momentary importance of any one of them as they are brought into play. He thus becomes part of an organism and must submit himself to the laws of balance regulating this organism. As we have seen, his facial expressions and gestures are prescribed by the music. Furthermore, we see that these are no longer isolated on the stage, for the actor has *become the intermediary* between the music and the inanimate elements of the production.

But, you will say, how can the actor's mime and his movements by themselves determine the proportions of the scenery? In the word-tone drama, should the actor be the measure of the setting in every sense?

To answer this question it is necessary that one understand the nature of those *technical* elements which make up the stage picture. I shall attempt to discuss them here so that they may be readily grasped by the layman.

The inanimate elements of production (which include everything but the actors) can be reduced to three: lighting, the spatial arrangement[1] of the scenery on the stage, and scene painting. How are these interrelated?

The painted scenery must be placed so that it can be lighted effectively; the spatial arrangement thus serves as an intermediary between the painting and the lighting. The lighting must make the painted scenery fully visible, otherwise its arrangement in space is simply aimless; it cannot ignore the painting in favor of the spatial arrangement, for its whole purpose in illuminating the painted canvases is precisely to justify their placement according to the scenes they represent. It would seem, therefore, that these elements are of equal importance, but they are not. Lighting and painting on vertical

---

[1] *Plantation,* by which Appia means both ground plan and elevation. Ed.

canvases are two elements which, far from enriching one another through mutual subordination, are in fact altogether incompatible. The arrangement of painted canvas to represent the setting demands that the lighting be exclusively at its service in order to make the painting visible, a relationship having nothing to do with the active role played by lighting and quite distinctly in conflict with it. The spatial arrangement, because it is in three dimensions, permits light a little of its active function but only to the detriment of the two-dimensional painted drops. If we introduce the actor onto the stage, the importance of the painting is suddenly completely subordinated to the lighting and the spatial arrangement, because the living form of the actor can have no contact and consequently no direct rapport with what is represented on the canvas.

Of the three elements of production, painting is without any question the one subject to the narrowest conventions. It is incapable of revealing any living and expressive reality by itself, and it loses its power of signification to the extent that the rest of the setting plays an active part in the scene; that is, to the extent that lighting and the spatial arrangement are directly related to the actor. Therefore, lighting and the spatial arrangement of the setting are more expressive than painting, and of the two, lighting, apart from its obvious function of simple illumination, is the more expressive. This is so because it is subject to a minimum of conventions, is unobtrusive, and therefore freely communicates external life in its most expressive form.

The obvious inferiority of painting as a means of theatrical expressiveness no doubt seems strange to more than one reader, since contemporary productions, far from keeping this fact in mind, seem instead to deny it systematically by sacrificing everything else to the effects of painted scenery.

Why is it that this element has come to occupy such an important position in the theatre, when by so doing it has hindered the development of those other elements which are far more essential?

There are two very distinct reasons: the nature of spoken drama and the opera. The essential purpose of painted scenery is to present to the eyes what neither the actor, nor lighting, nor the spatial arrangement can accomplish. If painted scenery has come to have an exaggerated importance in the spoken drama, it is simply because the audience needed the help that it alone could provide.

The laws governing sight and sound, which together control the conventions of stage decor, make it impossible to present actually in a production the place of the action with the same plastic truth as characterizes the language of the actors. One must therefore employ *signs* with which to indicate and suggest the scene, but which can never come into direct contact with the living actor. These signs can appeal to the audience only as some kind of highly developed hieroglyphs whose meanings are obvious. The present role of scene painting in the theatre consists in the ostentatious display of these hieroglyphs.

Now one could offer the objection that the illusion so admirably attained by today's scenic artists is well worth consideration. But that illusion has no artistic value unless it fulfills its purpose — which is to create a setting, a viable atmosphere on stage; for everybody knows that as soon as the actors make their entrance, the handsomest painted setting suddenly turns into an ineffectual combination of painted canvases, unless one sacrifices all or at least some of these hieroglyphs to the active role of lighting.[1]

The very nature of spoken drama has caused the excessive development of scene painting. Nowadays, when the needs for expression are considerable, the playwright is forced to substitute decorative suggestion for that which only music could give him. This results in a constant discord between the pretensions of the production and the real content of the dramatic text; and the actors oscillate painfully between a kind of articulated charade and a drawing-room comedy in a ridiculous setting.

If the dramatist sacrifices the painted hieroglyph to living light, he gives up the notion that nothing else in his drama can take

---

[1] In *Parsifal* at Bayreuth, when the curtain went up on the scene of the interior of the Grail Temple, the painted scenery had to be sacrificed to the darkness necessitated by the scene change—imparting a marvelous life to the setting. As the lights started to come up, the illusion was continuously dispelled until finally, in the full glare of the border lights and the footlights, the knights made their entrance into a pasteboard temple. To be sure, the painted setting was then fully visible.

· 23

the place of painted scenery, as long as the text itself does not supply it; on the other hand, if he does encumber his text with descriptions of place, he is stealing from the actors the dramatic life which calls forth the activity of light. Then it is understandable that he disavow a form of production prejudicial to the integrity of his work and that he prefer the dominant use of painted scenery.[1]

The origins and development of opera are sufficient explanation of why the visual aspects of production in this particular genre have developed without dramatic motivation and exist only for the satisfaction of the eye. Since this satisfaction was the result of a desire for more and more marvelous spectacles, and because scenic conventions placed severe limitations upon the three-dimensional realization, it became necessary to resort to painting. Because living light was not used, the audience became accustomed to using its imagination to interpret the flat painted perspectives of the vertical canvas; it came to enjoy having life presented by means of signs, whose easy manipulation permitted great liberty in the choice of subject matter. And so the real life which only lighting and a three-dimensional setting can give is sacrificed to the desire to behold in *indication* many fascinating and spectacular things.

The extent to which production in the spoken drama and the opera could have influenced each other is of historical interest only; therefore I shall not dwell upon it, but simply say that this mutual influence still persists because a common scenic principle joins them together under the same conventions. Of what use will these hieroglyphs, these signs which scene painting seems impelled to provide, and which are in fact the very foundation of all contemporary principles of production, be to the word-tone dramatist?

By noting the three factors which make up the inanimate

---

[1] Only he ought to state that the *realism* of his text, demanding as it does the active roles of lighting and a three-dimensional setting, diminishes the effect of the painted scenery and to the same extent impoverishes the contents of his drama. Later on we shall declare that decorative realism in the theatre has received its death blow from the existence of the word-tone dramatist.

setting, we try to convince ourselves that the music is translated not only into the mime and movement of the actor, but into the whole inanimate setting as well. By analyzing the relationship of these three factors, we were able to demonstrate how inadequate painting is as a means of expression, when compared to the three-dimensional setting and light. Despite this manifest inferiority, painting is still the predominant element in modern stage scenery. This strange dominance must be attributed to the basic nature of the spoken drama and opera. It remains for us to discover how the word-tone dramatist, if he wishes to obey the requirements of the music, must use these three elements, from which it will become quite naturally apparent how the music is translated into the stage space.

All those parts of the setting which are not painted but are actually built and hence come in direct contact with the actor are called "practical."

Whether properties, furniture, and other objects of stage decor are usable or not is a secondary consideration. The main thing is to arrange the space not to suit the painted "signs," or in other words to design the *fictive* form of the inanimate setting so as to relate as much as possible to the real form of the actor. Only if the use of painted scenery is limited and its importance diminished, will the *practical* scenery have the necessary freedom. Once this is achieved the scenery will be brought into a more direct relationship not only with the actor but with the drama itself.

As a result of this newly established relationship, the dramatist's text will be able to dictate the nature of the actor's role more precisely, and this, in turn, will permit the actor to demand that the setting serve him more effectively. This will inevitably increase the already existing conflict between the three-dimensional *practical* scenery and the painted scenery, since the latter by its very nature is, and always will be, in conflict with the actor. Ultimately, this conflict between stage painting and the more dynamic forces of the theatre will reduce the importance of painted scenery. Thus, lighting, finding itself for the most part freed from the drudgery of merely illuminating the painted canvases, recovers its rightful role of independence and

· 25

enters actively into the service of the actor.

The word-tone drama is the one dramatic form which dictates most accurately the actor's role in all its proportions. It is therefore the only drama which empowers the actor through his use of the setting to determine the relation of the spatial arrangement to the lighting and to the painting, and thus to control, through his role, the entire visual expression. But basically it is music, by virtue of its duration in time, which determines the role of the actor; so that this visual expression is already contained in the first concept of the drama and is not only outside the scope of the scene designer, but also of the actor, and to some extent even of the dramatist himself.

The necessity for organic harmony, which is the absolute condition for the integrity of a work of art, thus attains its fullest realization in the drama of the word-tone poet.

The reader will now understand that if music does not reveal itself on the stage quite so obviously as he had perhaps anticipated, it is still intimately bound to the visual element by indissoluble laws.

By way of summing up: a dramatic idea requiring musical expression in order to be revealed must spring from the hidden world of our inner life, since this life *cannot be expressed* except through music, and music can express only that life. By means of the spoken word, [the dramatist] endows it with a practical dramatic form and composes the poetic-musical text, the *score;* this text imposes an already living role upon the *actor,* a role he has now only to take on. The proportions of this role determine the form of the setting through *three-dimensionality* (the point of contact between the living actor and the inanimate setting); the nature and extent of the three-dimensionality determine the *spatial arrangement* of the setting which in turn controls the *lighting* and *painted scenery.*

This hierarchy is organically composed: music, the soul of the drama, gives life to the drama, and by its pulsations determines every motion of the organism, in proportion and sequence. If one of the links of this organic chain breaks or is missing, the expressive power of the music is cut off there and cannot reach beyond it. There could be instances, of course, when the dramatic intention would require such mutilation. In such cases the life of the drama will not

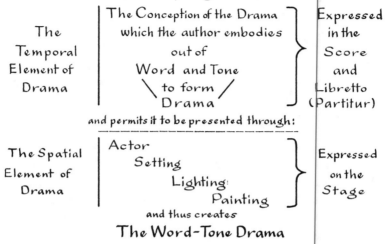

Out of Music
(in the widest sense)
springs

| The Temporal Element of Drama | The Conception of the Drama which the author embodies out of Word and Tone to form Drama | Expressed in the Score and Libretto (Partitur) |

and permits it to be presented through:

| The Spatial Element of Drama | Actor Setting Lighting Painting | Expressed on the Stage |

and thus creates

The Word-Tone Drama

[The above diagram is found only in the German version. Ed.]

suffer in any way, but any attempt made to animate those parts from which life has been cut off will result at best only in an appearance of life, and will have no relationship with the vital core of the organism. Since the actor is the sole intermediary between the score and the form in which it is presented,[1] the production could never dispense with him for the sake of revealing its own life. But once the actor is evoked, the life of the drama is assured, and the use of the other means of expression is no longer regulated except according to the demands of the poetic-musical text.

Just as the theoretical principles concerning the nature of the action in the word-tone drama entail for the dramatist extremely weighty technical problems in the use of poetic-musical methods,

---

[1]Not between the author and the audience, as in the spoken drama.

problems which could not have been foreseen before the existence of this dramatic principle itself, so the hierarchy of production, which is determined by the musical score through the medium of the actor, produces a complete overthrow of existing technical procedures such as no arbitrary caprice could have effected. Nevertheless, what distinguishes these two reforms from one another is the fact that the discovery of the principles involved with the first is the natural result of an expressive power superior to existing dramatic forms; whereas the verification of hierarchal order among the representational means of expression is the result merely of observation. Therefore, the tangible realization of the latter order requires no independent creative power.

Without Richard Wagner, this present study could not exist, because without him we should have no means of experiencing the scope of music in the drama. The specific circumstances which prevented this incomparable genius from logically pursuing the consequences of his creation all the way to the scenic form, as well as the influence of this failure on the very conception of his dramas, will be treated in detail in the second part of this work. But here, before investigating the technical effects brought about by the representational hierarchy, I should, since I have put off justification of my thesis until the following section, inform the reader that Richard Wagner's dramas cannot serve as examples of the normal use of the inanimate elements of theatrical production: this will be the subject of the next chapter. The formidable power of expression revealed to us in his dramas is in its essence independent of the form they happened to take; and while this quality in his dramas may well inspire us in this study, it does not always lend itself to immediate application.

Practical Application

Introduction

The constituent elements of word-tone drama fall into two distinct groups: the words and tones as they are transmitted by the actors' voices and the instruments of the orchestra, and the visual elements of the production. The existence of words and tones outside the drama is quite unlike the unified ideal life conferred upon them by the poet-musician. Whereas the living, moving form of the human body and the continually changing appearance of objects in space, light, and color are things that we observe daily united. Nothing can change or distort their expression. Although music brings these elements together in a new unity — the unity of art, it deprives them of only so much of their independent life as is necessary to transpose itself into space: it does not endow them with life; it only determines their proportions in the drama.

The virtuosity necessary to the dramatist in the employment of poetic-musical methods is not enough by itself to produce a living score. Such an accomplishment will be meaningless unless it is in complete submission to a higher principle, and for the word-tone drama it is the object of expression, the special action which alone can determine the composition of the poetic-musical text. On the other hand, the visual aspects of production, by their very existence in the word-tone drama, are already so subordinated. They must obey, and in obedience attain the greatest virtuosity. Does this mean that they can develop independently? How could light, form, and color do that? Only if they become immobilized in a *fiction* (painting, sculpture, architecture) which divorces them completely from the actor. Hence no experimentation, no virtuosity is possible for any of these elements outside their common life. Only the living form of the human body is capable of such an independent development.

The technical study of production methods is therefore divided into two parts: (1) the actor — the living form of the human body; and (2) the inanimate setting — both the inert and the movable elements.

The virtuosity of the actor of word-tone drama consists of an abnormal versatility and flexibility that is independent not only of the actor's individual temperament, but also of those proportions which he shares with every other human being. Therefore, except for the elementary study of voice and diction, it is training in gymnastics which will allow the actor to follow the demands of the poetic-musical text. Virtuosity seems difficult to achieve in the inanimate setting; nevertheless it is infinitely simpler than in the actor, since it does not encounter active resistance but only the inertia natural to objects. Since management of objects is facultative, it is only a matter of proportions, and in order to determine those proportions, one has only to know as exactly as possible the various methods of reducing the elements of our everyday vision to constructions which correspond to those of the word-tone poet.

Once virtuosity in setting and in acting have been achieved (and I am going to investigate how this can be done), how can the potential of such virtuosity be realized on the stage in an actual production? Theoretically, it should be through the poetic-musical text, but actually the text alone can neither give life to the mechanics of production nor make the actor convincing.

On the one hand, we have the still unrealized drama hidden in the pages of the poetic-musical score; on the other, the actor, with all the resources of his training and personality, together with the producer controlling all the inanimate elements of production. However, putting all of these together does not make a production. The actor may not understand the demands of the poetic-musical text, and consequently may distort the proportions in such a way that the true meaning of the text will not be communicated through him. If this happens, the producer — who usually derives his sense of proportion from the actor — will create stage pictures in an arbitrary fashion. In the event that the producer understands the true proportions of the text — he will design proper settings which the actor will disregard. I have not taken into consideration here the possibility of one or the other's ill will toward the dramatist.

It is therefore indispensable that the score contain a transcription of the poetic-musical requirements in a language accessible to all. The essential portion of that transcription will concern the actor, and just as the poetic-musical notation of his role is achieved through conventional musical and language signs, so a similar method of notation must be found for the visual expression. Graphic signs whose object is purely technical are accessible to all as soon as their convention is adopted; it is sufficient to study the language they constitute. Perhaps it will be possible to give them a form which contains implicitly — but obviously — the essential effects of the actor's role on the inanimate setting. A system of hieroglyphics seems indicated for that purpose. And the development of the electrical sciences, whose numerous possibilities today can find no serious application in our utilitarian civilization, will probably put at the disposal of the poet-musician resources which only he can use.

It is impossible to foresee or invent such a system; it must be born of *necessity*. But since such a system is essential to the word-tone drama, the dramatist of the future will have to invent it. However, the problems and the needs of the future cannot be profitably discussed until we have first studied the drama of Richard Wagner from the point of view of production.

In Part III of this work, which is devoted to those problems and needs, I shall return to the subject of a system of notation for the visual elements of production and of the effects of such a system on the poetic-musical score. For the present we shall simply draw a distinction between the technical considerations that are derived from the theoretical principles we have just established and the particular problems of a given production.

As for the former, the poetic-musical score prescribes the form of the production, but when one considers this or that drama in particular one finds that responsibility for the realization of the drama in production devolves nonetheless on the dramatist, because the language of the score is not intelligible to everyone. This fact does not deny the theory, but it is empirical and therefore has no place in the present chapter. We can only mention it until an analysis of Wagner's dramas enables us to determine its laws.

The reader should not however consider the following discussion of how the poetic-musical score is to be realized on the stage as purely theoretical; it has great practical value. In fact, it is the *primary responsibility* of the word-tone poet. The manner in which he communicates the demands of the poetic-musical text to the common understanding is of secondary importance, to be considered only when the essential act has been accomplished.

In order to establish the hierarchy of production prescribed by the music, I have used commonly accepted theatrical terms, terms which are at best only approximate, since we associate them with current scenic practices, the concepts of which will inevitably force themselves upon the imagination of the reader and in so doing will distort, if not actually destroy, the very ideas which I am so anxious to establish. As a result I must first dispel our theatre's most deeply-rooted prejudice, a prejudice so powerful that it is tenaciously supported, or seems to be, by all existing production principles. I am referring to the necessity which is attached to the search for *scenic illusion.*

Scenic Illusion

In the spoken drama where the means used by the playwright do not involve all of our faculties, each of the means of expression can develop in an indeterminate space, in a space which the place occupied by the others does not necessarily delimit. For this reason the visual elements of production are not only denied a part in the organic life of the play, but also, because of the varied tastes and needs of each member of the audience, they can never communicate with complete expressiveness to the audience as a whole. Without the controlling principle of music, the playwright cannot persuade everyone in the audience to see the inanimate elements of production in the same way. For this reason the spoken drama is invariably produced on the principle of the lowest common denominator: we determine what visual effects will strike all of the spectators in the same way and then reproduce these on the stage. Now, in this kind of theatre—and here I am not taking into account those physiological differences which cause each of us to see things somewhat differently — the designer's only task is to provide a space in which objects can be placed. The audience — unconsciously and through force of habit — will take upon itself the job of discovering the proper relationship of these objects. Then each of these objects is given a suitable color, and finally, light is used only to make them more or less visible.

When we see things in this way, obviously we see *nothing*

at all. It reduces our sense of sight to the same level as our sense of touch, and fails to take into account the fact that there is a vast difference between the meaning of objects as perceived by the inner eye and the actual scene which we observe with the physical eye. But it is this external and superficial way of looking at a play that we have in common with everyone else in the audience. It is the demand of this kind of vision—and this alone—that must be satisfied through *scenic illusion.*

A production which did not obviously seek this illusion would not be accepted by the average audience. This is understandable for we know that if the playwright does not provide the producer with a formal principle that will govern the mounting of his play on the stage, the audience must do it for him. Consequently, our present theatrical conventions have developed not so much to satisfy the dramatic needs of the play—or to provide the means whereby these needs can be successfully realized in production—as to satisfy the tastes of the average audience.[1] But such an audience as we have just pointed out, looks at things in only the most literal and elementary way.

True art never tries to deceive the eye. The illusion created by a work of art is not to delude us regarding the nature of emotions or objects in their relationship to reality, but rather to draw us so completely into the artist's vision that it seems to be our own. This requires a certain refinement of aesthetic perception on the part of the audience. Otherwise our need for illusion is displaced and crude appearance of reality becomes for us the goal of art.

The average audience will always ask to be deceived, and to be given what the ordinary man enjoys most, that is, the most exact replica of what he is *capable of seeing* in the outer world, and the drama, of all the arts, is best suited to satisfy such a desire.

In the first part of this study we saw how the increasing desire for the spectacular in production led to the development of stage painting and decor to the great detriment of the lighting. Here again, audience taste has shown its inferiority. Not content to sacrifice

---

[1]Cf. p. 11.

• 33

the play's artistic expression to a living picture, it must also sacrifice even the latter to a form of still life, a lifeless picture. This illusion, which is so highly valued, is obtained only at the expense of all life in the visible scene. Our eyes function so falsely in this matter that the illusion seems dangerously weakened if the movement of the actors or the light interferes with the deception of the scenery. Yet if this deception remains intact we completely disregard the grossest lack of realism in the acting and lighting.

Since the elements of production cannot be maintained always in the balance necessary to scenic illusion, and since, if such illusion is intermittent it does not exist, we must conclude that *there can be no such thing* as scenic illusion. Whenever we do use the term we are refering either to the illusion of reality produced by the setting or that which is created by the actors. But it cannot be both at the same time, for although they are not always mutually exclusive, these two sources of scenic illusion have nothing in common.

In the word-tone drama this problem does not exist, for if one aspect of production were to become too prominent it would immediately come into conflict with another. Everything is controlled by a superior will which measures from minute to minute the changing proportions of the elements of production. This poetic-musical intention controls with great flexibility every aspect of the production—even the writing of the text itself—and has nothing to do with scenic illusion. In the word-tone drama the visual aspects of production are a *means of expression* available to the dramatist. This does not mean that scenic illusion cannot be as useful to the dramatist as any other tangible production device, but it should in no way determine the form or be the sole aim of any production.

From this important fact we may conclude that just as the word-tone drama frees music from its isolation, so music extends the theatre's vision by revealing a new life far richer than everyday reality. The music unites the audience as one entity; music cares nothing about the audience's needs or tastes; it sweeps the audience along with the sheer force of its own rhythm. And in so doing it fulfills man's need—a need in most cases impossible to satisfy—to escape from himself in order to find himself again. Where is man's image more wonderfully reflected than in the expression of music?

Now we can understand the tragic conflict that develops when we attempt to use music in the contemporary theatre. The great potentials of music seek passionately to be realized once they are introduced, but we turn a deaf ear to its explicit language. Our everyday vision seems superior to the unknown world music wishes to reveal to us, and like children who insist on having our own way, we ignore the advice of those much wiser than we.

But music is eternal. Music can bide its time, patiently lavishing gifts upon us, until the time arrives when we understand that what it has been trying to reveal to us about the nature and form of sound can enrich our life for all time.

The word-tone poet is a *creator;* in fact, he is the only living being deserving of that title because he alone imposes his vision upon us; and that vision is from a world far superior to that which we bring with us when we enter the theatre. For him the ever insoluble problem of the diverse ways of *seeing* no longer exists; he forces us all to see as he does. But he can do this only after he has purged his vision of all that is personal and nonessential, and music bestows upon him the means of achieving this. It transfigures his original conception and permits to pass into the poetic-musical text only the universally expressive, the purest essence. Then, when the drama is produced it will contain nothing that is forced upon it by arbitrary conventions. Instead of trying to satisfy the tastes of everyone—even the most insensitive—it will create a *new* vision for all, which the spectator will no longer be able to shape according to his own desire, but which he will of necessity vividly experience through the vibrations which the music sets up in his entire being.

The Actor

One might argue that it is impossible to achieve such harmony, because even if we were successful in eliminating the demand for scenic illusion in the inanimate elements of production, the very presence of the actor on the stage would maintain that illusion.

As we have seen, music, by virtue of its own time and

sequence, alters the time and sequence copied from life by the actor of the spoken drama. Furthermore, the *time* given by music to the expression of the inner drama (*i.e.,* to our emotions and the complex effects of these emotions) does not correspond to the time of the purely reflex manifestations of our emotions in our everyday life. The actor's physical being is involved in an artificial activity corresponding in his physical organism to the demands of musical diction.

If music did not so profoundly alter the natural time-durations of life, it could not force the actor to renounce his ordinary activity in order to become a means of expression. And unless we were persuaded that the superior world revealed by the music was not factitious, but indeed the *supreme illusion,* which rational analysis cannot enter, we would have no right to be thus transformed by music and hence would derive no pleasure from the transformation. But this very transformation, which deprives the actor of his personal, arbitrary life, brings him closer to the inanimate elements of the production, and those elements are forced by the music to furnish a degree of expression proper to their close relationship with the living actor. The illusion created by the setting and that created by the actor—illusions heretofore irreconcilable and mutually destructive—have both made the sacrifices necessary to a life in common and thereby gained an unsuspected strength. What the actor loses in freedom will be gained by the stage designer; and the setting, in giving up all pretense at scenic illusion, becomes an atmosphere in which the actor can be totally expressive.

Thus, musical duration has considerable aesthetic importance, for only by means of it can the living and *moving* human body become a medium for art. The moving body in an appropriate milieu would no doubt constitute a work of art in itself. The Greeks succeeded in creating such a milieu, because the elementary but perfectly harmonious development of their expressive media and their inborn taste for such media—particularly for those which appealed to the understanding—preserved them for many years from the inevitable mistakes to which an excessive concern for expression leads.

The overwhelming power attained by music in our time makes impossible any artistic role for the human body as it functions in daily life. The Greek considered his body as the very pattern of harmony, and this harmony—this perfect relationship of all the parts of the human body—informed the whole of his life. This is no longer the case. Not only have the entangled and almost insurmountable complexities of modern civilization made this impossible, but more important, the insistent need for musical expression (a need which is itself a product of this civilization) compels us to treat that expression as the norm.

In the realm of the imagination, only music has the power to create a milieu in which the body can have an artistic significance. To be sure, the body can be deprived of music and still, by means of words and gestures, serve as a means of communication between the dramatist and the audience. But it will do this only as a channel through which the poet's expression can more or less successfully pass and not as a form or integral part of that expression. When music is added to the words, we *see,* as a result of the establishment of new proportions, the living human body cast off the accidental covering of its individuality and become the instrument consecrated to the expression of what is common to all human beings. It is not yet the whole expression, but it is already a *visible* part of it.

However, only by altering the natural time-durations can such a metamorphosis be effected, because the expression, taken as a norm, cannot communicate itself through the body except by lending it fictitious proportions.

Whereas a superior degree of intensity, if it does not alter the proportions, communicates to the living form a far more intense *personal* life, still without depriving it of its fortuitous character. But there is yet another means of involving the living body in the expression: and that is by communicating to the actor the basic proportions of music, without necessarily having recourse to song—in other words, by means of the *dance.* By dance, I do not mean those light parlor entertainments or what passes for dance in the opera, but the *rhythmic* life of the human body in its whole scope.

In the dance the body creates for itself an imaginary world. To do this it must sacrifice all the rational aspects of its life to the time value of the music; in return, it gains the living expression of its *forms*. Dance is to the body what pure music is to our feelings: an imaginative, nonrational form. When dance approaches pantomime it does as pure music does when it approaches drama: it seeks in its original form, and in spite of it, to appeal to the intellect. But in doing so, music must permit the emotions to find definite form in words (hence the poetic-musical text) and dance must allow the body to render its life intelligible. But the poetic-musical text needs the actor, and dance cannot deprive the actor of the music's time pattern, the prerequisite of living expression; it must therefore give this time pattern an intelligible base from which the actor can appeal to our understanding. Only in this way can he regain that rationality which he has sacrificed to the dance for the sake of his bodily expressiveness.

Thus dance and symphonic music, starting from the same point, have developed in opposite directions: the first seeking a way to discard its expressive content in order that the body might be more fully expressive, and the second seeking a way to disengage itself from bodily forms in order that the musical idea might be more fully expressive. The development of these brought them together again at a point opposite to that from which they started to form the word-tone drama, and thus the circle is definitely closed.

Is it possible for the actor to approach the word-tone drama by the same road followed by the symphony?

Obviously not, for the free and indeterminate expression of pure music can no more be communicated to the living body than the latter can prescribe symphonic proportions. There is no formal relationship between them. Just as music has had to disregard plastic expression in order to attain to the expression of the inner emotions, so must the actor abolish all overt emotional activity if he is ever to attain that latent plasticity demanded of him by the dramatist.

The dance, then, prepares the human body for the intelligible expression of the word-tone drama by developing the living forms for their own sake and in arbitrary proportions, in the same way the symphony does for sounds. The actor's art in spoken drama is one of imitation; he evokes in his soul fictive emotions through observation of himself and others. When the text omits the accidental and personal details of character in order to attain a more universal

MUSICAL EXPRESSION

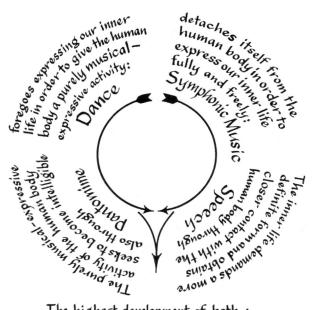

The circular diagram reads:

Dance — foregoes expressing our inner life in order to give the human body a purely musical—expressive activity:

Symphonic Music — detaches itself from the human body in order to express our inner life fully and freely;

Speech — The inner-life definite form demands a closer and obtains human body more contact with the through

Pantomine — The purely musical or the human activity of the body seeks to become intelligible also through expressive

The highest development of both :
The Word—Tone Drama.

[The above diagram is found only in the German version. Ed.]

meaning and to enlarge the scope of the actor's interpretation, the proportions thus augmented are none the less tentative. So the actor is still forced to pattern his playing on the solid foundation of his personal observation, while at the same time detaching himself from the very experience in life which gave intensity to his acting and presenting the conventionalized character called for by the text. But the degrees of that conventionalization are varied, so that the actor can bring the desirable harmony to his role only by means of continual bodily flexibility.

This bodily flexibility cannot be an end in itself because, for the actor of spoken drama, such activity is a *language* which reveals inner motivations, but does not express them. By generalizing the

· 39

hidden motives of an action, the character of their visible manifestations is weakened; the actor's flexibility should therefore consist in the exactitude of the *relationship* he establishes between this inner activity and the reflexes resulting from it. The outward manifestations of these reflexes will have no value unless this relationship is exact; and the tangible experience implied by the actor's external execution of them is merely an accessory. In the word-tone drama, the actor has nothing to do with establishing this relationship—the search for inner motivations, the observation of the resulting reactions, their infinite variety—all this is the business of the word-tone poet. He establishes in the score what is *interior* in his drama (by means of music); what is exterior (by means of musical duration); the degree of concentration or of diffuseness of the expression (by means of the respective values of the poetic text and the musical score).

By thus freely ordering the life-evoking media, he does not require that the animated elements of his production have the plastic activity we find in the spoken drama, but rather that they possess the malleability of sculptor's clay.

If the living body is subject to the empire of real or fictive emotions, it takes on a life, the proportions and continuity of which are determined by the relationship of these emotions with the body's motor system. The actor in the word-tone drama will come to effect his sacrifice, then, by avoiding the study of the emotions. Otherwise, he will develop even more fully and consciously a method of portraying feelings which, for the word-tone drama, must be shunned. In giving himself over to the word-tone poet, not only does he sacrifice the creation of his own role, but also that *natural* emotion the role would elicit from him if it were divorced from the music. The word-tone poet communicates emotion to the actor *by means of the extraordinary forms he imposes upon him.* Only by means of plastic forms developed outside of strong emotional expression could the dance, as it joins symphonic music to create the word-tone drama, receive its dynamic force.

Lyric song and the dance—these are the actor's two masters in the word-tone drama: singing allows him to develop his diction within a fictive time span and his voice so it can project over the music; the dance allows him great rhythmic suppleness without appealing to his personal emotions. Having attained the greatest possible "depersonalization" through these two media, with his body spontaneously obeying the most complex rhythmic patterns, and his voice subjected to musical sequences altogether foreign to his inner life, the actor can now bring himself into direct rapport with the three-dimensional setting, the lighting, and the painting, and share their common life. These last three elements should also be in a position to offer the highest degree of perfection to the actor: but they are inanimate, and the artists and craftsmen whose business it is to put them onto the stage have no more skill in determining the actor's craft than he has in controlling their products—taken all together, they are merely devices awaiting a superior will to make them efficient.

In the word-tone drama, the director, instead of guiding the production according to the time-honored and rigid conventions, as is usual nowadays, assumes the role of a despotic drill-master as he presides over the preparatory dynamics of the stage scene. He does his utmost artificially to effect a synthesis of the representational elements by animating the more flexible elements at the expense of the actor, whose independence must be destroyed. And his methods will naturally be exceedingly arbitrary; he must play *fictively* with the scenic materials, taking care at the same time *not* to create a scenic deception. Therefore, only an *artist* of the first rank can carry out such a mission. He will examine the play of his own imagination in order to strip it as much as possible of convention and, above all, of prevailing tastes. The essential aim of his directing will always be to persuade the members of the production staff that their mutual subordination alone will produce a result worthy of their efforts. He must possess a kind of magnetic influence, much like that of a genial *conductor*.

As soon as the actor comes to feel a close dependence upon his inanimate collaborators, and when, in full awareness of the reasons, he has sacrificed himself to rhythmic and emotional depersonalization by forever renouncing his primary importance, then and then only will he be able to approach the word-tone drama.

And it is the only drama he must ever undertake to perform, for fear of losing the fruits of his preparation. All spoken drama, of no matter what type, is deadly poison for him, because the tendency to carry over the proportions of his inner life into fiction has already become so tenacious, so difficult to conquer, that a deliberate return to those proportions may be enough to render his struggle futile.[1]

There is no practicable transition between the actor's preparatory studies and his effective co-operation in the word-tone drama. Clay cannot take on plastic shape without the sculptor's thumbs: between its raw and malleable state and its final form there is only the artist's will.

For the actor, the will of the *word-tone poet* is life-evoking, and is the actor's intermediary between the poetic-musical text and the inanimate setting. There is no other volition so powerful that would not at the same time destroy the means and reduce the end to mere illusion.

Is such an exclusively *formal* education possible today, and are its elements yet within our power? Alas, even the existence of the word-tone poet himself is just as problematic as that of his interpreters and his audience. All the elements of the supreme work of art are there—sounds, words, form, light, and color—but how shall we light that spark of life which fires the dramatist to expression, the actor to subservience, the spectator to devout and silent reflection?

If Richard Wagner could do no more than inspire us with an infinite yearning for this supreme work of art, and if in so doing his all-encompassing genius was incapacitated and miserably sacrificed to the clarity of his revelation, who then will be able to achieve this impossible desire of which he has made us the responsible heirs?

But for the moment we are considering the representational elements of the drama from their technical aspect only: the fact that one among these happens to be a living entity, and for that reason subject to social conditions independent of the work of art, does not invalidate the normal and legitimate function he must perform. "Art

---

[1] I realize that here I am in direct opposition to Richard Wagner and can only offer as justification Parts II and III of this work, whose comparison with this section may allow the reader to judge whether my boldness is justifiable or not.

establishes its own laws and reigns over time," said Goethe. Later on.
as we examine the possibilities for the existence of the word-tone
drama today, we shall see how this art form must function in relation
to our present state of culture and from what point of view certain
compromises must be an integral part of its independence.

I have said that the word-tone poet communicates the actor's
role to him *by means of the extraordinary forms he imposes upon
him.* One of the great advantages of the kind of theatrical notation
we mentioned earlier will thus be to do away with any personal
responsibility on the part of the interpreters, permitting them to
approach the drama from the standpoint of its total production only.
Granted that the ever incommensurable (or if you prefer "transcendental") nature of the poetic-musical expression renders sterile any
initiative on the part of the actors; still, lacking the theatrical notation,
they will be thrown back on their own resources and forced to seek
the dramatist's implied intention before they can enter into the
formal proportions laid down by the music. But to introduce the
subjective emotions aroused in the actor by the dramatic situation
into the extraordinary proportions of the poetic-musical text is to
perpetuate the kind of travesty offered on all of our lyric stages. On
the other hand, if the actor achieves the expressive content of his
role solely by the formal proportions of this role, then will the
marvelous mystery of the word-tone poet gradually be revealed to
him. And such an initiation gives a far greater value to the initiate's
very subservience than any sort of highly original "interpretation"
could ever offer. For far from weakening the indispensable spontaneity
of the actor, it confers that quality on him in the highest degree. Just
as the music permits only the purest essence of the dramatist's
personal conception to emerge, so it admits only the noblest elements
of the actor's personality.

After the Actor

As we have seen, the score has but one way of being
effective on the stage and that is by means of the actor. Without the
actor the drama is nonexistent, and without his influence over the

other elements of production, the setting will always remain a stranger to the drama itself. The actor translates what the poetic-musical text has entrusted to him into a language comprehensible to the spatial arrangement, the lighting, and the painting. He interprets the music for the inanimate setting. Any ideas which cannot be transferred to the setting will necessarily then stop at the actor. But the variable number of these ideas is the concern of the dramatist: the more he addresses himself to our understanding alone, or the more he assiduously develops a purely inner action, the less influence music will have on the visual aspect of production. For in addressing himself to our understanding, he will deprive the setting of much of the expression dictated by music, and allow the setting to supply only a minimum of intelligible meaning. And if he develops a purely inner action, he makes the actor's role purely introspective, thereby preventing his expression from extending to the inanimate objects on stage. Since, however, the dramatist should be able to arrange his text with perfect freedom and to measure the poetic-musical proportions thereof to his own taste, the setting must also be given equal flexibility: it cannot remain constant in one form while the score oscillates between both.

I have pointed out the conflict between the principle of the intelligible form and the expressive form of the production. How then can they be made to alternate compatibly without destroying the unity essential to the production?

This crucial question has no relation whatever to what one sees on our modern stages, and perhaps the reader will not readily grasp its practical significance. It will be necessary, therefore, before we enter into the technical study which follows, to determine whether the very nature of the word-tone drama may not provide the satisfactory answer to the two opposing principles. Such an investigation can probably offer us more concrete ideas as to the particular characteristics of the new stage setting.

Music by itself "never expresses the phenomenon, but only

the essence of the phenomenon." (Schopenhauer)[1] Therefore, in order to define his expression, the musician needs the poet. If a dramatic action must have music in order to be expressed, the implication is that the development of external motifs (phenomena) within this action must give way to the universal expression of their inner, purely human essence (the inner essence of the phenomenon).

The degree to which the external or fortuitous motifs are established and developed by the poem thus depends upon the intensity of the musical expression required to communicate the dramatic action. An increase in this intensity tends to nullify the external significance of the phenomenon; a decrease in intensity reduces the scope of the musical expression in order to reach our intellectual comprehension. The proportions between the musical expression and the intelligible meaning of the text are obviously of infinite variety, but from our viewpoint these proportions are peculiar, in as much as no matter what predominance intelligibility may have over the elements of expression, music never loses its ascendancy. Indeed, the text by itself can legitimately bring to the stage only the sign; anything added to this would depend on the arbitrary will of the dramatist and the director. However, as we know, music transmits itself to the stage, and by virtue of organic laws, establishes the expression. No matter how weak music's part in the drama may be for the moment, the very fact that it cannot cease to exist as music deprives the dramatist and the scenic director of any freedom of personal initiative. For the expressiveness of the production itself is infinitely superior to any mere sign; moreover, the number of purely intelligible ideas to be conveyed by such a drama in production is considerably diminished when music is employed.

Therefore, if the poetic-musical proportions may vary in the score as much at the expense of the intelligible meaning as at the expense of the expressive elements, this cannot happen so impartially on the stage. For, just as the dramatist who employs music gives up the number and the development of external motifs in order to

---

[1] ". . . da sie nie die Erscheinung, sondern allein das innere Wesen, das Ansich aller Erscheinung den Willen selbst ausspricht." *Artur Schaupenhaurs sämliche Werk: Erster Band, Die Welt als Wille und Vorstellung* (Paul Deussen, ed. Munich, 1911), p. 308. Ed.

express the inner essence of a limited number of phenomena, so must the production of his drama dispense with a large part of its intelligible meaning for the sake of its overall expression.

For example, if the staging happens to call for an artisan's room, the gallery of a Moorish palace, the edge of a pine forest—or any other kind of limited setting—one will not achieve an expressive scene corresponding to the musical expression by piling up a variety of objects relating to the artisan's particular vocation, or of Moorish designs, or the botanical characteristics of pine trees. Music does not express vocations or styles of architecture or species of vegetation. It expresses none of these things in themselves—they belong to that part of the drama directed to our understanding: they are a kind of "representative phenomena" which should be offered to us only to the extent required to make intelligible the dramatic text. A simple indication suffices to place the action in the external world, and once this is done, the setting has only to express what there is *in the place chosen* by the dramatist that corresponds to the inner essence revealed to us by the music—in other words, the eternal aspect with which all transitory forms are endowed.

Now what is it if not *light* that gives that wonderful unity to the spectacle we contemplate each day, allowing us to live through our eyes?

Lacking this unity, we should be able to distinguish only dimly the meaning of things, and never their expressiveness; for in order that things be expressive, they must have form, and form without light communicates only to our sense of touch.[1]

We have already seen how the active role of lighting tends to exclude the development and even the significance of painting on the stage, and how the hierarchy of the inanimate elements reduces painting to an inferior rank. We now arrive, by another road, to the affirmation that the sovereignty of lighting is the necessary consequence of the nature of the poetic-musical text. Thus, no matter how great the proportion of purely intelligible factors, the original and determined ascendancy of music never allows these factors to be

---

[1] By *light*, of course, I mean the activity of light, not simply "visibility."

displayed to the detriment of the expression. When at any time the sign must rule the stage alone, it will be so inconsiderable in the work of art as a whole that the reduction of expression becomes itself expressive. The alternation of the two forms will always consist in the modulation of the quantity of the expression, never in the quantity of the sign.

Later on, we shall see that lighting, the chief element of expressiveness on stage, offers a flexibility which the sign's representative, painting, cannot provide, and thus, that the natures of the technical media correspond to the roles they must assume in the poetic-musical scheme.

Now it becomes clear that a principle of production based upon any existing convention, or upon the search for scenic illusion, cannot offer a like variability without descending to absurd despotism. Only the expressive form of the production can maintain unity for the audience, because this unity consists not in the formal and intelligible meaning of the presentation, but solely in the consistency of its expression; and this, in turn, can become truly palpable only through its varying intensities.

As we shall see when we discuss the spatial arrangement, the evocation of music on stage is infallible, precisely because it is expressive. But, if we diminish the power of the material elements on stage, we also diminish the infallibility of the production—and once more, the responsibility for this falls to the dramatist. If the musician finds no possibility whatever for representational fulfillment, it is not the same for the poet.[1] The dramatist could, for example, at the moment of addressing himself more directly to our intellect, by a detail of the action or of the words, require some considerable development of the musical expression as well. If in this case the music should require that expression rather than intelligibility dominate the visual elements of production, the dramatist runs the risk either of failing to be understood, if his text takes second place to the music, or of palpably weakening the significance of the music should he fail to

---

[1] I use the divided word "word-tone poet" for clarity's sake: but this division is inaccurate. I should say "the dramatist of the understanding" and "the dramatist of sentiment and emotions."

provide it the material means for functioning as a part of the production.

Indeed, this perilous alternative concerns the integrity of the work only in its relationship to the audience—because, in the text, no such choice exists. In a state of culture less profoundly degraded and unthinking than ours, the statement I am about to make would be quite unintelligible: *living* art obeys the organic laws of life originally and effortlessly. But to us, the life of a work of art is a luxury which we place to one side of our existence. Thus, we are the ones who are attempting to discover the organic laws of a work of art and to obey them, instead of recognizing them to be the indispensable foundation of the artistic concept itself.

The dramas of Richard Wagner are instructive in this matter; they show the effect which conventional and sterile stage conditions can have on the greatest creative power that ever existed.

Here where we are endeavoring to establish the normal condition for the existence of the word-tone drama, this *significant* conflict between the poet and the musician should be classed among those obstacles opposed by our civilization to the work of living art; it cannot be blamed on the dramatic form itself. The more the dramatist will look upon the abstract record of his text simply as a makeshift device *having no value except for the duration of its production,* the more constant and certain will be the life then evoked by his work, for it is the distinction we think we must make between the text and its production which destroys the integrity of the work. A text for the word-tone drama should be regarded as a sacred mystery, the bountiful production of which will depend upon the scrupulous care of the initiates. Nor is this a paradox: the abstract inscription of this work of art *is* in the esoteric domain, whether we will or no. Money, which nowadays has replaced the social hierarchy, is also the level for intellectual and artistic manifestations, and will continue to expend its pernicious influence even farther than we might care to imagine. The first comer can buy the mysterious symbols with his money, those written signs (*i.e.,* the score) from which one can continually re-create the same life, and the abstract existence of which is cursed by their very attractiveness. With money, he can also study their mechanism, grasping their formal meaning so well that when the time arrives to evoke the living miracle, the audience attributes its effect to these symbols. Naturally, the result is that the thing which should have been secret, nonexistent, as it were, is the only thing brought to light; whereas the vital inner sesence, which cannot be bought, the only thing it truly concerned money to communicate, is ignored and unknown: it is apprehended only by the few initiates who suffer the incurable wound inflicted upon them by such profanations. Here, as elsewhere, they understand Parsifal's cry: "Deliver me, O save me from guilt-stained hands!"

In substance, then, the word-tone poet must bear in mind that it is not within his power to determine the amount of signification—only the amount of expression; and if he diminishes the representational power, he impoverishes the visual aspects, with no compensation except the intensity of the inner drama, the responsibility for which devolves upon him. In other words, since the quantity of representative indications for the setting of the word-tone drama is always minimal, the dramatist cannot make use of it to balance the *representational effect of his work.*

These considerations naturally have their place between the actor and the inanimate elements of production, for the actor always participates in the expressive element of the poetic-musical text, but does not always allow the expressive element to extend beyond himself. Therefore, the representative form established on the stage by the music is dependent upon the actor, not only from the standpoint of the quality, but also and especially on the quantity of his expression. I wished to make this fact clear before proceeding further.

The Spatial Arrangement

In our discussion of the actor, we have assumed that the other representational elements were prepared to follow him in the impetus given by the poetic-musical text. We must not forget, however, that although the actor's education can to a large extent be pursued outside of the theatre, the inanimate elements cannot be so detached from the scene of their dramatic activity. The technical development of these media is closely linked to their function; therefore it is also important to know upon what physical construction they must be established.

Nowadays our stages are built and arranged around the activity of a decorative apparatus favoring almost exclusively the illusion produced by painting. Of course, a theatre where solicitude for such illusion will not determine the arrangement of the scenery will be quite a different thing. And what essential changes will be brought about in the construction of the stage by the new system of expression?

In becoming a part of the setting, music does not appeal to our judgment: it does not say, "you must realize this or that"; therefore, the means of executing it will not be found in our imaginations. The word-tone poet who heads his act divisions, "the scene represents, etc." does so to facilitate the reading of his text; *but, if these indications are not contained within the poetic-musical text itself, they are certainly not allowable on stage.*

And this is the distinguishing factor between the setting for the word-tone drama and all other theatrical settings.

The playwright of the spoken word can place his characters in locations not necessarily indicated by his text, because he can count on the intelligible meaning of the painted scenery to communicate to the audience any ideas left out by the actors. From the very inception of his work, the word-tone poet must renounce this crutch. Thus, every word-tone drama determines its own production, so that the hierarchy of expression established by the music is the only concrete idea to be had *a priori* from the poetic-musical expression; this hierarchy in itself dictates no mode of expression other than that imposed by the importance it bestows upon the various media.

In order to give the necessary flexibility to the decorative material, the design and construction of the stage must allow each medium the development suited to it. The existing stage should be rejected to the extent that it hinders the growth of spatial arrangement and lighting. But with what other type of stage shall we replace it, since no one can foresee the demands of the word-tone poet and above all the arrangement, that is, the disposition of the material media, cannot be categorically limited by any known convention? A stage for the word-tone drama cannot be designed for one type of production only, as are the stages of our contemporary theatres: the identification between the structure and the artistic objective exists for it only ideally.

We realize how serious this problem is as we approach its practical consequences, which force us to feel that the eventual construction of such a theatre may indeed be impossible.

In our theatres, the stage and its appendages together make up an entity quite distinct from the space designed to hold the audience. United under the same external appearance of luxury and solidity, the two domains are constructed entirely differently, and the uninitiated theatregoer experiences a kind of shock when, leaving the house, he steps over the almost mathematically exact line which separates that section of the theatre from the artificial and provisional composition of the opposite domain. The proscenium opening is the only material point of contact between the two worlds. During the performance, the audience is presumed not to be aware that the same roof which shelters them also covers the actors in the strange world of the stage. The novice will always be a bit taken aback when he sees the clumsy and commonplace walls which enclose the magic world that has just captivated his imagination. And, indeed, there is a singular disproportion between the external aspect of a theatre and the abyss which separates the stage from the audience. Architects have countered this objection with an exterior arrangement which makes the construction less unwieldy and its purpose as obvious as possible. For those unacquainted with today's scenery, this arrangement is still totally unexpressive, because the box designated for the scenery, which resembles a small house atop a large one, has no relationship with the scene on the stage, and no more reason for being visible than has the basement. It is probably somewhat preferable to the ponderousness of earlier theatres, but no expressive value can be attributed to it, for it has none. What it represents is not the world apart from the auditorium, for this world is altogether fictive. The function of a railroad station or a market can be shown by its external construction; in fact, they are required to declare exactly what they are, for, alas, today we have no other style than that which is the result of a sincere confession. The purpose of these buildings corresponds materially to their form; therefore, they are expressive —and if what they express is not interesting, then that is our fault.

The appearance of the ancient theatre was just as clearly intelligible as was the ancients' whole way of life. To the Greek eye, clear and pure in vision, the complex accumulation of our modern theatre would be repugnant, devoid of all significance. The Greek theatre was either a flat circular area or an amphitheatre bounded by a horizontal line. Anything added to the circle or adjoined to the line is no longer a part of the edifice, but merely an accessory either to be concealed or to be set off from the main construction by a temporary and arbitrary character. The ancient stage was not like ours: our stage is an opening onto a small area where the result of an infinite amount of individual efforts is presented to an audience. Ancient drama was an *act,* not a spectacle; this act embodied in salutary fashion the insatiable desire of the crowd. The high rampart of the stage hid nothing; it was not a curtain, but a *boundary,* voluntarily placed between the act and the desire. There, as elsewhere, a sense of proportion served the Greeks in marvelous fashion. This sense we lack and cannot achieve; therefore, our stage is an *opening* on the unknown and the unlimited. And it is not by giving the technical mechanism of the scenery an external form, a role in the construction of the building, that we shall achieve expression in whatever imaginary space our modern soul needs to immerse itself.

As was the case in the theatre of the ancients, though, alas, for reasons having far less to do with harmony, the spatial significance of our theatre stops short at the proscenium frame. The Greek saw unity between the spectacle and its boundary: less happily, we have placed the production beyond the boundary because, not being artists, we deliberately separate ourselves from the work of art.

Thus, the drama located in the imagination (the unlimited space) has no connection with the covered amphitheatre where we crowd together, except for the proscenium frame; all the rest is fictive, changeable, provisional, having no existence except in the production.

For a production dictated by the conventions emanating as much from the dramatic form as from the audience, it is advantageous to limit the technical execution of those conventions by a stage permanently constructed; indeed, it is indispensable, for the composition of such a dramatic work is within the reach of many people and has an everyday character to which the theatre building should correspond. It follows then, that the meaningless construction of our theatres nevertheless makes perfect sense.

We have seen that the production of the word-tone drama cannot rely upon any convention whatever; moreover, this drama is exceptional and its very existence is problematic not only because of the varied faculties the dramatist must summon up for its composition, but also because of the extremely difficult and complex problems of production which do not warrant frequent performances. And the word-tone poet himself must preserve complete material freedom in his conception. At the foundation of his production is music, whose development no convention can restrain. He should not and cannot establish his work upon tastes formed prior to its existence. Each one of his dramas determines not only the *mise en scène* but even the construction of the theatre itself.[1]

Such a theatre will have no permanent feature except an auditorium, on the other side of which a fairly large area will remain empty. In this space, the *drama* will come into existence, no longer in its usual impersonal form, but in its nonessential and provisional form, where technical processes will cease to play any expressive part whatever. The existence of these technical arrangements is motivated as the audience fills the hall; as it leaves, they are rendered null and void: they have obeyed the commands of the music, assuming their proportions while sounds reverberated — with the silence of the orchestra and the actors, these proportions return to the ideal

---

[1]The second part of this study deals with the scenic conventions used by Richard Wagner in his theatrical works. Here I am not discussing the works themselves, but only the general dramatic form revealed to us by his works, adequate performances of which are still denied to us. The construction of the Festival-Theatre at Bayreuth is in no way invalidated by these considerations.

world whence they were summoned by the presence of the audience. Now they are in our eyes only temporary barracks, something to excite the interest of the mechanic, but the presence of which is not to be confused with the structure of the auditorium.

Again, I will be accused of dabbling in paradoxes: I will be told that my suggestion is unfeasible, that the expense of such buildings is out of all proportion to their purpose. Moreover, I will be reminded of the need for basements and cellars underground, of the problems of acoustics, etc., etc.

The question of expense depends only on the frequency and the solemnity of the productions. But, if a whole country flocks to exceptional ceremonies, which the performance of such works constitutes, the expenses will dissolve before the great celebration of the act. Nowadays, many popular entertainments of short duration call for building and expenditures far greater than any temporary stage.

As for technical problems, they might indeed be great if it were a question constantly of installing new mechanical devices, such as are required by today's theatres, but we shall see that the play of decorative material needed for the drama of the word-tone poet is of quite a different nature, and that its complexity does not involve such definite and troublesome consequences.

Everyone has observed that a stage setting acts simultaneously in three different ways on our eyes: (1) the ground level of the setting — that part resting on the stage floor or upon platforms which raise the floor level; (2) the middle portion, vertical; (3) and the borders or drops which limit the height and depth of the stage and mask the lights.

The bottom of the stage picture is always the most critical point in today's stage setting, because, in spite of its name it is not conceived as being set on anything. The scene painters are most ingenious in trying to solve this problem, but, as a rule, their efforts are too obvious, tending to accentuate what should be concealed. With few exceptions, settings made up of painted scenery appear to have been cut horizontally across their base, then set upon a perfectly flat surface. The leftover remnants are then stuck here and there at the bottom of the canvas drops.

As we look upwards, we receive another kind of shock: for now this painstaking yet incomplete setting suddenly takes on life, assuming as great a value as is possible — the "illusion" is at its height, and certain details, which had no significance when seen in relationship to the stage floor, now take on an importance in the overall effect. The backdrop, which before had been merely a painted canvas necessary to set boundaries for the arrangement of the scenery, now blends harmoniously with the downstage wings and extends their perspective; painted and real light meet in one lovely luminosity. The eye is fully satisfied.

But, as we look still higher, our pleasure decreases. Either the particular setting provides no reason for the use of the necessary borders, or insufficient reason for limiting the setting at the top; or again, the arrangement of the setting as a whole too obviously depends upon providing an upper line for its frame. In short, although many other combinations are possible, there are only one or two which can preserve intact the "illusion" produced by the center of the setting.

If we now glance rapidly at the whole setting, the conflicting sensations it offers us are not counterbalanced by the pleasing effect of stage center. And after some reflection, we come to regard the whole merely as a reproduction of place, subject to inevitable conventions; and the illusion it strives to give us is, after all, something that we the audience must construct in our own minds. What might be called the aesthetic activity of the spectator is deflected by this act, for we cannot participate in a work of art by substituting for its physical representation the abstraction of our thought — the production thus forces the drama into a form far inferior to its literary reality. It follows then that the whole scenic apparatus and the arrangement of the theatre itself strike us as being an infamous practical joke.

Why indeed, all this sumptuousness, all this effort, if the

illusion is impossible of realization, and especially if the search for illusion deprives the production of all artistic worth by stripping it of expression?

I naturally assume that the actor has taken his place in the setting we have just been observing. *But, unfortunately, his place is not at the center of the setting.* So it happens that the actor, the *raison d'être* of the production, and therefore the focus of our attention, is forced to move about in areas of the stage where the scenic illusion is at a minimum. The true reality of this flat or arbitrarily cut-up surface, upon which the scenery is placed, is revealed with the entrance of the actor; it is trod by living feet—and each step accentuates its significance. Obviously, from the point of view of the illusion, the better-painted the canvas, the less will the actor and his immediate surroundings be in harmony with it, since not one of the actor's moves will correspond to the place and the objects represented by the scenery. The lighting, which could give the actors some relief by means of its expressiveness, is now monopolized by the painted scenery; and the setting, almost completely subservient to the painted drops, provides the actor with nothing but the barest minimum of practical pieces allowed by the painting.

Thus is the actor explicitly subservient to the inanimate setting. The place of the action is realized in one way, the action itself in another; and the two manifestations come into contact, but are in no way related. The inanimate setting plays the role of colored engravings, and the actor merely that of their description at the bottom of the page. If for the sake of the setting, we take from the actor his independent life, we shall have a theatre of marionettes where no doubt the visual elements are more in harmony, but where they are no longer justified, and only serve to hold the attention of persons too listless to enjoy a simple reading.

The spatial arrangement of today being what it is, there is no salvation except continually to reduce the scope of the production in the interest of harmony — which would ultimately amount to denying the very existence of production at all. Popular or worthless plays are usually intended to be elaborately mounted; the genuinely literary play when written to be performed is not, on the whole.

Thus, all efforts of literary romanticism in the theatre involving settings of any consequence are inferior.[1]

Today's spatial arrangement cannot provide the actor with an area to harmonize with the scene indicated on the painted canvas, and since the entire construction of our theatres is determined by such settings, the stage of the word-tone drama could not function under these conditions, for its setting must in some way be the consequence of the ground the actor walks upon, not the reverse. Everything that is not touched by the actor is still subordinated to conditions imposed by his immediate and actual surroundings and has no way of being expressive except by means of him. Thus would the setting become one in reality, having its roots in the ground and in the drama itself, yet rising no higher than these roots could sustain it — were it not for the fact that the absolute freedom of the word-tone poet prohibits us from endowing the ground with any fixed existence whatever. The phrase "on the boards" is inaccurate when applied to music. Music is not transferred on to anything: in itself it *becomes* space. It is nonsense to say that under certain scenic conditions the act of hearing becomes impossible; anything that music prescribes is possible, for acoustical laws are a part of its nature. Thus, music reigns as *infallible* monarch over all the elements of the setting.

The flooring of our stages is laid between two virtually empty spaces. The empty space beneath the stage, the only one which could have any meaning here, is designed to make possible the appearance and disappearance of certain portions of the scenery in a direction opposite to that of the setting, *i.e.,* below. Even when the stage floor has an opening through which scenery can be moved, it still has an immobility which no amount of ingenuity has ever been able to overcome. The reason for this is perfectly clear. Our present-day conception of the scenic art requires a point of reference, a given dimension in order to establish its conventions; and this dimension is provided by delimiting the base of the scenic picture.

---

[1] I exclude from this discussion some recent attempts to replace at least a portion of the flat painting of the setting with three-dimensional constructions. These are exceptions which have no connection with the scenic principle itself, and moreover are negated by the other scenes in the same play in which such constructed scenery cannot be used.

The stage floor, in projecting beyond the proscenium arch into the auditorium, as it does in most of our theatres, sets definite boundaries for the stage picture. If it were to remain inside the proscenium arch, such a state of affairs would not exist, and these current rules and regulations, indispensable to theatrical settings run by the laws of hit or miss, would be quite impossible.

The absolute sovereignty of music begins only beyond the proscenium; its creation in space is therefore limited by one consideration only — the spectator. The arrangement of decorative materials, which we call the setting, because we set it down within a limited area on the stage floor, should have a different name and, above all, should be answerable to an altogether different conception. No longer erected upon a flat surface, it will rather *extend from a perpendicular plan;* instead of being horizontal, the section is vertical. In this sense, the stage opening becomes an absolute dimension and, *to our eyes,* the point of intersection between our independent organic life and our organic musical life. With regard to its proportions, *i.e.,* the extent of its opening, these are not limited directly by the music. Music does, however, dictate the qualities of the stage picture, and these in turn, in order to reach us integrally, themselves determine the proportions of the proscenium arch.

Let us go beyond the proscenium arch. We perceive nothing to arrest our eyes. There is a vague empty space, awaiting the word-tone poet's creation.

Today the boundaries of the setting are determined by the wings, the borders, and the floor. But, since the illusion of the painted canvas forces the scene designer to bestow upon everything outside the framework of the setting a *positive* role in the scene, so it also obliges him to give the same positive role to its material boundries. Thus, even his ingenuity is subject to highly inconvenient restrictions. If, for example, he wished to frame the depths of the stage by means of devices which happen not to relate to the subject of the painted scenery (for example, by means of draperies or a neutral frame) he would cancel out the effect of the painted scenery; thus he is faced with the alternative of dispensing with the illusion of the painting — the basis on which all modern theories of production are founded—

or of curtailing the choice of his materials and thereby simultaneously diminishing the general importance of the illusion; and it goes without saying that he stops short of this second alternative. How then could he ever serve the demands of music?

The answer is that he could not.

The production of the word-tone drama should present nothing to the spectator which does not belong to the space evoked by the poetic-musical text. Yet the boundaries of this space are determined as much by the extremely varying demands of the acoustics as by the nature of the scenic expression. The space could be very small or as large as it is possible for the eyes and ears to comprehend. However, as these boundaries are imposed upon the eye, they take on a material existence not always desired by the music. It is in this respect that the new representational concept is seen to be all powerful: for in its case, this dilemma *simply does not exist.* The new concept has no desire for the illusion, which is apt to be destroyed by an irrelevant intrusion, nor does it require the explicit, which tends to impose one single meaning upon every object, regardless of what it may be. The new concept demands *expression,* and the fact that this expression cannot be achieved except by renouncing both illusion and sign gives it an immeasurable freedom. Therefore, the mechanics of production will have in *visual terms* only the expression or the signification endowed to them by the music.

But there is still something else which contributes to this freedom, and that is the representative hierarchy which forbids the use of any of the elements of production without the actor's consent. Suppose, for example, it were necessary to *express* within the walls of a room the many-colored, limpid, and shifting atmosphere of a forest landscape. In itself this would be impractical; the intention would remain inarticulated, like a dramatic scene for orchestra alone. But — put a character in that setting, and let five minutes' worth of music suggest a mood to him, some manner of acting, it matters not what — or simply let the music flow over his physical presence like some evanescent liquid, and suddenly the atmosphere takes on life, the setting becomes *expressive;* and the walls of the room, *because they are not a part of this expression, cease to exist.* The same situation will hold true for all those parts of the setting which must of necessity be permanent: if their contribution to the expression or to the signification is obvious, or if their presence is justified by the rigidity natural to objects, they will cease to exist.

The reader will pardon me now for having established a bit prematurely the fact that the space prescribed by music never requires impossibilities. But perhaps he is shocked by the apparent paradox of this axiom: I placed it ahead of the example in order to make both more striking and to make palpably comprehensible what mere words are incapable of suggesting.

We have just projected beyond the framework of the setting. Without the evocation of music, it is impossible to fix upon a representative function or even to give the slightest example. At the conclusion of this first section, I shall go more deeply into this particular subject.

However, it still remains for us to make the connection between the purely theoretical considerations of the inanimate elements of production and the practical application of these principles. This is particularly true as regards the inanimate tools of the stage director. These may be classified under two main headings: the "terrain" fixed for the actor; and the complex apparatus of the lighting. What we term scenery, which involves a vision of dissected and painted canvas, is completely subordinated to both the terrain and lighting. Since the terrain follows the actor in the hierarchal order, I shall consider it first.

The arrangement of three-dimensional pieces is today determined by the flat surface of the stage itself, and by the surface of the painted canvas — which is also flat, but perpendicular. Thus, except for the few practical pieces which realize in three dimensions elements in the picture which the actor must use, all three-dimensional pieces are constructed at right angles to the floor. Such pieces come in all sizes and allow for a great many combinations, but because of the principle governing their use, they are none the less monotonous.

One may readily conceive the difficulties presented by the painted scenery as soon as the actor becomes involved with it, and above all we see his ability to perform completely thwarted by the bizarre apparatus surrounding him. In an outdoor setting, should he wish to sit on the ground, his position must be carefully reserved for him against the painted scenery, and the three-dimensional piece masked and covered with a scrap of painted canvas. He has no idea what he should do with his legs — to let them dangle against the perpendicular paintings on the drops is absurd — and the form of the set piece, which is designed solely for sliding between these drops, hardly provides him with a suitable spot. His hands float in air; if he wishes to place them elsewhere than on the set piece, the exact location must have been decided beforehand, and this happens to be situated on patches of the painted scenery, as big as plane-tree leaves, blackened and worn threadbare by the hands of previous interpreters of the same role. If the scene is prolonged, and if the actor's position on stage has some importance, the set piece will be placed apart from the painted drops, thus providing a thoroughly ridiculous sight,[1] or else involving the setting as a whole in a principle contrary to that implied by the scenic composition and in opposition also to the lighting of this setting.

A steep cliff in an heroic landscape creates a perfectly good "illusion" — as long as it is *painted* on the canvas, but the moment the actor has to make use of it, it is turned into one of those artificial hillocks such as are built in our public parks, cut into gentle pathways and stairs with convenient steps. The actor then may utter the most impassioned sentiments, making every attempt to relate himself as closely as possible to the nature of the ground he is supposed to be treading, but for all that, he is still floundering on his little path at a total loss; in order to understand the reason for his fit of passion, we must look at that part of the setting which has nothing to do with the actor! "Architectural" settings are easier to handle; nevertheless, for the sake of producing a sumptuous setting, with painted scenery indicating all sorts of interesting things, the actor's performance and

---

[1] The reader no doubt recalls those turfy couches, bosky sofas, and various floating chairs which make up the rustic furnishings of our stages!

the force of his expressiveness are willingly sacrificed by reducing those portions of the setting he can approach and touch. Characters in scrupulously historic costume proudly descend a wooden staircase. In their luxurious and authentic footgear they tread boards cluttered with set pieces, and appear outlined against walls and balustrades which the well-lighted painting indicates to be of marvelously sculptured marble. The costume, in contact with the set pieces and the drops, lighted by light not designed for it, is completely devoid of meaning — a museum piece, nothing more.

In another scene the painter will exhaust the resources of perspective and color in order to present a beautiful contrast of light and shade — a dark balcony with a background of luminous open sky, or perhaps a corner of a nave, its architecture standing out against the brilliant far away stained glass windows . . . a poor garret traversed by a ray of sunlight, an inn courtyard plunged in cool shade while broad daylight suffuses the upper stories of the building . . . etc. The actor, as he moves in front of these painted drops, nullifies their effect, because he is still lighted by the same artificial light to as great an extent in the supposedly dark place as in the one that is bathed in light. The first scene in the second act of *Parsifal* (Klingsor's dungeon) provides a curious example in this context. The setting cannot be too deep here, because of the scene-shift without curtain drop which follows. Consequently, the setting is reduced to a backdrop placed quite far downstage, and to a flat frame in the foreground masking the borders and wings. Such an arrangement appears to be suitable for facilitating the play of expressive lighting. What did the scene designer do? Subservient to the demands of the machinery, he sought compensation by displaying every shred of his virtuosity on the one drop placed at his disposal. Then he gave the flats in the foreground a positive role in his composition by loading them with picturesque detail. The result of all this was a most fascinating setting, because the painting was not dismembered, and was thus restored to its original value. But the actor is lost here; more than ever is his presence in opposition to the effect of the setting. Take away the actor, and we find ourselves plunged into a vast and terrifying dungeon; with the actor and the accessories of his role before us, all that is left is some very ingeniously painted canvas. The wicked sorcerer is now merely a doll between screens; his acting is rendered superfluous; the disquieting shades of his dwelling remain fictitious — and the invisible orchestra, alone in its veracity, resounds in the void.

If, as in certain modern plays, the setting is required to reproduce a place well known to the audience — a street corner, a park or place of amusement, the stage director will lavish the most minute detail upon the sumptuous realism of the accessories, the furnishings, costumes, and practicable parts of the setting. Then he will dispose of all this material between the canvases upon which the scene designer has attempted, on his part, to render his reproduction as true to life as possible by means of an amassment of *painted* detail. They are diametrically opposed in their joint efforts and their concurrence merely succeeds in conjuring up the memory of a child's toy, a doll's house, sheep cot, or Noah's Ark — in which the actor is entirely out of place. In a modern play at the *Théâtre du Gymnase* in Paris, one of the scenes depicted the entrance peristyle of that selfsame theatre through which each member of the audience had just passed, presumably still retaining a *general impression* of it. Nothing could have been easier to reproduce than this impression. Instead, the designer had erected a cardboard peristyle like something cut from a photograph, besides having obviously reduced the proportions of the model for the purpose of showing as many things as possible. As his contribution, the stage director had carried realism to the point of placing on the stage, the same three gentlemen who actually ran the theatre's box-office. The lighting, designed exclusively for the painting, therefore, had no concern with the three-dimensional elements of this reconstruction. The result was that once having recognized the setting — and not without some difficulty — the spectator was doubled up with laughter at this absurd reproduction. Now obviously, although the perpetrators of all this were not in dead earnest, still their intention was not to provoke hysterical laughter. They simply wanted to surprise their audience with a novel device, nothing more.

But it is futile to multiply these examples; everybody who has frequented our theatres on whatever rung of the dramatic ladder knows precisely what I mean: under the most varying circumstances the technical procedures are the same everywhere. But one cannot sufficiently stress the fact that *our scenic economy slights the expressive effect of the actor in favor of the illusion provided by the painted scenery,* the result being that one is as unachievable as the other.

Sacrifice, perhaps the most important principle in a work of art, is completely unknown in this area. From a strictly aesthetic viewpoint, in demanding all, we have got nothing.

The terrain of the actor in the word-tone drama is determined *above all other considerations* by the actor's presence. Here it is to be understood that by *terrain* I mean not merely that portion of the stage trod by the actor's feet, but everything in the composition of the setting relating to the material form of the character and his actions.

Since the terrain is no longer intended to produce a scenic illusion, it can be designed and constructed with the sole aim of fully expressing the attitudes which the character and his actions should evoke. However, it is only through the power of the lighting that the setting can become truly expressive, and this fact must be taken into account in its construction. Although the terrain ranks first and is dependent on the actor alone, its role cannot be isolated from that of the light. Moreover, the almost complete flexibility of light eliminates all possibility of conflict, as the terrain can comply unconditionally with the demands of the actor. In constructing the terrain, therefore, it will not be a question of knowing whether or not the lighting will make a given arrangement possible, but rather whether a given construction *with* the co-operation of the lighting will permit the actor to be sufficiently expressive — in other words, whether the actor's attitude will be given the emphasis required by the music.

There are still material demands common to every production which it will be well to separate from today's principle of stage decoration by opposing them to the arbitrary conventions of painting, in order to provide us with some guide in the development of our concept, necessarily so vague and indeterminate, of the new *mise en scène*.

When a scene painter wishes to transform a given picture into a theatrical setting, instinctively he seeks to diminish to the point of improbability all real forms in favor of fictitious ones. To him, the only essential differences between the picture in its frame and the same picture on stage is the fact that the latter is obliged to make room for those cumbersome objects, the actors; whereas the former is fortunate enough to be free of them. It is his problem to provide this indispensable place for the actor, at the same time disarranging the painting as little as possible; he will therefore divide his painting into bits and pieces in order to display it within the space facing the audience. The actor will then contrive to move about between these slices of painting, as long as he can meet the minimum requirements of his role.

Thus, the backdrop becomes the only portion of the setting which does not constitute a pitiable compromise, for it alone can show a complete painting to the audience, without doing violence to the real space — in itself the ultimate setting. But apart from the backdrop, the setting as a whole is nothing but a collection — often very ingenious, to be sure — of scraps of painted canvas overlapping each other.

Characteristic of the scenic convention in today's stage settings and indispensable to the use of painting is the fact that in order to preserve some meaning for the latter, the scene painter must display to the audience the greatest possible number of flat surfaces. This practice is contrary, however, to the basic demands — demands quite independent of the conventions of painting — of any production, and these demands may be placed under two main headings: (1) the necessity of limiting the stage picture, (2) the fictive presentation of those decorative motifs whose realization by plastic means is impossible. I shall first deal with the decorative motifs.

No matter how important the functions of the actor's terrain and the lighting may be, or how much these two principles restrict the general composition of the scene, it is obvious that the empty

· 65

space on the stage still needs to be filled with various material objects which cannot be sacrificed. Trees, rocks, buildings, walls of interiors, etc. must all be presented, even though they must conform to the proportions authorized by the active role of the lighting. Although in many cases these objects may assume a plastic form, there still will be times when this seems impossible or undesirable.

The principle of the painted drops has brought all of these motifs together in the *same* fiction. Then, the expressiveness of the actor and of the lighting give to each distinct forms which vary in relation to each other with the nature of the stage picture and the changing intensity of its expression.

Nevertheless, there is no compromise between the positive plastic realization and the painting on vertical canvas. Modern scene designers attest this by their efforts to bridge the void that exists between these two methods. But lighting can provide a most important intermediary. For this reason I must discuss lighting here, since it also plays an integral role in our new concept of production.

Light requires an object if it is to retain its expressiveness; it must light something, and encounter obstacles. Such objects cannot be fictitious, because real light has no fictitious existence. In lighting the painted canvas, the light strikes it only as *canvas,* and not as the objects that have been painted on it. But the expressive form of the production subordinates the painted canvas to the living presence of the actor. If dramatic necessity requires certain decorative elements which cannot be presented on the stage except through painted flats, the free action of the lighting will be called into question. It frequently happens that these elements are so closely related to the lighting that one can dispense with some or all of them so long as the lighting creates the effect that would have been produced by those elements. For example, the scene takes place in the depths of a forest; the uneven ground and the various set pieces call for the activity of light. The practical exigencies of the actor's role are satisfied, but the forest itself has yet to be expressed, that is, the tree trunks and the foliage. Now the alternative is either to sacrifice a part of the ground's expressiveness, as well as that of the lighting, in order to indicate the presence of trees on the disjointed canvas—or else, to express only those portions of the trees reconcilable with the practicability of the ground—and *to authorize the lighting to do the rest by means of its particular quality*. The first alternative might be adopted in a situation in which the need for representation gradually diminishes during the course of the scene: the cut-up canvas, upon which the painting is only partly visible during the time in which active light prevails, would become the bearer of signification as soon as the activity of the lighting was reduced—thus the painted flats could *signify* trunks and foliage—and the scenic expression would regain in that proper modulation the degree of intensity it had lost in permitting the expansion of painted canvas on the stage.

The second alternative permits the scenic expression to attain its greatest effectiveness: a few plastically constructed tree trunks blend into the borders, whence colored illumination, filtered and brought into play in various ways, throws onto the stage light characteristic of the forest, the quality of which leaves to the imagination of the audience the existence of obstacles they have no need to see. The minimum of cut-up canvas serves as a sign, without diminishing the activity of the light; and thus the characters as well as the three-dimensional portions of the setting are immersed in the *atmosphere* suited to them.

Thus the potentiality for change in the lighting, without the need for the setting to disclose the reason for the changes, constitutes a mediator between the plastic and the painted elements. The preceding example should suffice for the reader to comprehend the great importance of this expedient which, because of the natural flexibility of light, is one of the most productive.[1]

How, one may ask, should the surface be presented to the audience in a setting whose principle is not founded on inanimate painting, when cut-up and painted canvas is sometimes the only

---

[1] Another application of the same method: whenever, for some dramatic reason, a setting is reduced to its minimum intelligible signification, while at the same time the action requires that the character of the place be definitely shown without reducing the expression or increasing the number of signs provided by the setting and the painting (for example, the spectator must apprehend the actual existence of a window, a building or portico, a rock, the edge of a forest, ship's mast, etc.), the lighting can present these objects by means of shadows, the degree of its intensity, its varying flexibility, its colors—in fact, by all the varied modulations which it alone possesses.

possible means by which to execute certain motifs? The need to limit the scenic picture, a necessity in any production, seems to provide us with a point of reference, determining thereby the arrangement of all scenic surfaces. But such is not the case. In our theatres, the boundaries of the scenic picture are part and parcel of the painted scenery, because, as we have said, everything appearing on the stage should, in the eyes of the audience, pertain to the scenic effect. On the other hand, theatrical production regarded as a truly expressive medium precludes all that is not a part of its expression, or of that minimum of intelligible signification which it allows to the setting. In denying the priority of painting over the other elements of production, one renounces the advantage of being able, by means of it, to limit the stage picture. But what painting used to affirm to our eyes in a literal manner, the expressive form of the production as a whole does far more tellingly by *denying* the existence of objects which the painting sought to hide, and by forcing the spectator to deny them as well. This is not to say that painting can never establish boundaries for the stage picture, only that the intervention of its deception is not indispensable for this in the word-tone drama. There will be various ways of limiting the scenic picture in this drama, and one cannot depend on painting *a priori* to determine the arrangement of the drops and wings. One thing is certain: the role of painting will never be sufficiently influential to force the flat pieces to display their surfaces at the expense of elements superior to them.

Since the limits of the stage are no longer subject to the formal construction of the setting, they will be determined only through the poetic-musical text by means of the actor. How, we may ask, is the actor empowered to do this? Naturally, the laws of harmony which preside over the composition of the terrain do not prescribe the character of the stage limits. Therefore, the actor's role must contain special directions—which it is essential to define. First of all, let us not forget that the demands of sound in the word-tone drama are decisive in determining the proportions and the limits of the setting—because on stage, the actor is the musical instrument. These demands may reasonably vary during the course of the same scene and therefore require of the actor an exceptional flexibility. But there is another equally decisive reason for flexibility in the setting, which must be discovered in the nature of the word-tone drama itself.

Expression in theatrical production not only rules out visible contrivances, but also, and especially, the representation of actuality in the production as a whole. I shall explain this. Today's quest for scenic illusion requires that each setting be given specific character, the more so when this is achieved almost exclusively by painting on vertical drops and flats, and since it is deemed desirable that the painting be seen, the lighting is permitted only the most restricted variations.

When the setting of the action chosen by the author is realized by conserving for its *inanimate* aspect the greatest possible verisimilitude, there is no reason to modify the form of that setting while it is in use. The various times of day are indicated by the conventional color and intensity of the lighting, and, naturally, the better painted the setting, the less expressive these variations of light will be, because they cannot harmonize with the painting. If the action requires some supernatural transformation, the scenery will change, will be transformed in whole or in part, and the lighting will change also. However, whatever is done, except when the scene is based on expressive principles, the mobility will consist only in a succession of fixed settings, one after the other, because each must provide an adequate illusion.[1]

In the word-tone drama the variable ratio between the poetic text and the musical text, between the exclusively inner expression and that which spills over outside, between the time-durations the intensities, the sonorities—all this applied to a single unified action constitutes a bold defiance of what we call "realism." If in order to be expressive the production which results from such a text must give up the search for "illusion," good sense appears to deny it that vain search from the beginning.

It is not a question of realizing a place, *as it would be seen*

---

[1] Even the so-called *Wandeldekoration* preserves this characteristic by virtue of its unrolled canvases, all painted according to the same principle. [*Wandeldekoration* is a device for achieving quick change of setting by means of painted canvas which is unrolled from one vertical pivoted cylinder across an open space onto a second such cylinder. See Walter Unruh, *ABC Der Theatertechnik*, 2nd ed. (Halle, Germany, 1959). Ed.]

by those transported to it, but only as it is expressed by the poetic-musical text. The changes in the text determine the changes in the presentation, to the extent of their mutual dependence. If, therefore, from the theoretical point of view, change of scene is a part of the expressive form, from the audience point of view, it is merely a technical element whose establishment is not organic to the drama. *The place of action is not in itself flexible, only the way in which the dramatist wishes us to view it.* The material significance these variations have for our eyes is therefore nullified by the expressive principle of the production. In a modern setting, on the other hand, every change in the lighting or the setting always conveys the positive meaning of a natural or supernatural phenomenon: what we see in such a setting is supposed to take place in the same fashion for the characters in the play.

The *mise-en-scène* of the word-tone drama is therefore "ideal," in the sense that its material reality is subject to aesthetic considerations superior to its intelligible form, and this ideality is all-powerful because it imposes itself on the audience by perfectly concrete means, directly, without the intervention of thought.

The boundaries of the setting, which constitute a part of the spatial arrangement, no longer having to take care of illusion, can follow the changing relationships of the poetic-musical text, and particularly the intensity of the inner drama. At the same time, the acoustical demands can be taken into consideration. Now, the more interior the drama's action becomes, the more the poetic-musical text will concentrate on the actors' singing and in so doing will tend to isolate the actors from their setting. But the acoustical demands will never be in contradiction to those of the poetic-musical text, and the setting itself, as it tightens its boundaries around the characters, will accede to the demands of the poet and the musician.

The total arrangement of a scene will be a highly sensitive composition and will require great flexibility of materials; experiment will show the way to achieve this. It is probable that until such composition is attained, more or less crude methods, whose diverse designs will be established graphically, will have to be employed, to be executed in whatever material each design may demand. To these sketches will be added the notations for the lighting and the painting, and the whole will finally be joined to the score as an integral part of it.

It goes without saying that this method of procedure does not exclude any subsequent improvements which might bring to technical perfection any one of these elements—merely the proportions are noted, not their degree of intensity. It should, however, be pointed out that any technical progress should affect every part of the setting, and an improvement in the effectiveness of any one of the elements could not be adopted, if thereby the proportions of the ensemble were in any way altered.

In conclusion, we find that today's production techniques sacrifice the effectiveness of the actor in favor of that scenic illusion produced by painted flats. The hierarchy established by music does not authorize this state of affairs, for it is the actor who determines everything in the setting which is related in any way to his body and its movements. This is possible, however, only if we renounce what is called scenic illusion. Since the limits of the scenery need no longer be concerned with this illusion, they can now obey the superior injunctions of the poetic-musical text, and provide if necessary a *material* flexibility corresponding to that of the score. Within these limits, the decorative motifs which cannot or should not be plastically executed may be presented by means of painted flats whose arrangement should nevertheless be controlled by the higher principle of the scene as a means of expression. Between the three-dimensional constructions and the painted drops is the bond of lighting, which consists of producing artificially the effects evoked by certain objects when they intercept light.

I have said before that the provisional arrangement of the stage for each word-tone drama does not require the continual installation of fixed and cumbersome new mechanisms in our theatres. For those who know the mechanics of stage production, it is unnecessary to explain how much simpler the arrangement of any *mise en scène* will always be when it is conceived according to the expressive principle dictated by music, especially if the space designated for this production does not set up pre-established conventions against the dramatist, and if each scene, fixed or mobile, can be shown in all the simplicity of its own particular construction.

The Lighting

Light is to production what music is to the score: the expressive element in opposition to literal signs; and, like music, light can express only what belongs to "the inner essence of all vision." Although in the word-tone drama their functions may differ, the two elements have an analogous existence: each requires a material object if its embodying power is to be realized; it is, in the case of music, the poet, while the actor (through the spatial arrangement) provides it for the lighting. Both elements have an extraordinary flexibility which permits them to run through all modes of expression consecutively, from a simple statement of existence to the most intense overflow of emotion.

But, more than that, there is between music and light a mysterious affinity: as H. S. Chamberlain so aptly expresses it, "Apollo was not only the god of song, but also of light." (*Richard Wagner,* 1st ed., p. 196). And we feel the supreme unity of the two elements when some happy chance allows us to experience them together in the community of existence conferred upon them by Apollo. The sovereign nature of their expression appears to be an irrefutable axiom and therefore needs no justification.

However, we must consider the fact that the aesthetic sensibility of hearing is not necessarily so universal as that of sight. Some people may require a highly elaborate visual expression for music, while others may feel no need for such description at all. As I have said in discussing scenic illusion, the word-tone poet need not concern himself with the various tastes and needs of his audience;

he evokes a vision completely independent of the receptive faculties of each individual.

As far as the audience is concerned, the harmony of his work is absolute; it does not consist in an arbitrary combination of the score and its production, but rather, in the permanence of the parallel development of the poetic-musical text and the elements of production; and such consistency was already implicit in the germ fertilized by poetic fantasy—it is the manifestation of a latent force peculiar to all music.

If poetic-musical expression and visual expression, functioning separately, vary in their appeal according to the sensibility of each individual in the audience, the union of these two, organically established by the music, creates an independent *life* superior to each individual's limitations. For this organic whole is based upon "the inner essence of the phenomenon," and if on that foundation *the total expression embraces all our faculties,* then individual limitations will be transcended.

The sovereign power of light is undemonstrable to one who has not experienced it; to discuss its technical use is even more difficult. The poetic-musical text, the actor, the spatial arrangement—each is endowed with a complex and relative existence both interesting and rewarding to study. But the life of light is too simple to be analyzed. Only indirectly, by examining its misuse in our modern theatres, can we arrive more or less by induction at the normal function of light. And there are more than enough examples to validate such an approach; indeed, these very abuses and their manifold consequences have to a large extent provided the impetus for this study.

Here, I shall simply reduce the highly specialized technical aspects of lighting to basic concepts, before going on to suggest the explicit use of lighting in the theatre and its scope in relation to the other elements of production.

The general composition of the spatial arrangement operates

almost simultaneously with that of the lighting. On a stage whose ground plan and elevation have no existence, so to speak, except for that form bestowed upon them by any given drama, obviously there will be no permanent arrangement for the lighting. But no matter how impossible it may be to determine *a priori* the uses of lighting, or more important, to isolate its function from the simultaneous play of the other elements of production, a fundamental division in its uses—derived from the relationship which exists between daylight and artificial light—can be established.

Daylight floods the whole atmosphere, but nevertheless we are always aware of the direction from which it comes. But the direction of light can only be sensed by means of shadow—it is the quality of the shadows which expresses the quality of light. Shadows are formed by the same light which illuminates the atmosphere. This tremendous effect cannot be obtained artificially. The brightness of a lighted fire in a dark area will never produce sufficient light to create what we call chiaroscuro, *i.e.,* the more or less distinct shadow cast on an already lighted area. On stage this task must therefore be divided, so that part of the lighting equipment will be used for general illumination, while the rest will cast shadows by means of exactly focused beams. We shall call them "diffused light" and "living light."

In our theatres the problems of lighting are handled simultaneously in four different ways:

1. The fixed border lights, which light the painted flats, being supplemented in the wings and on the stage floor by the movable striplights.

2. The "footlights," that peculiar monstrosity of our theatres, designed to light both the scenery and the actors from in front and below.

3. Movable spotlights for focusing exact beams or various projections.

4. Lighting by transparency, *i.e.,* light intended to reveal the transparent parts of the setting by lighting from behind.

Obviously, it is very difficult for these various sources of light to work together effectively, so much so that it is impossible—as our current theatrical productions demonstrate all too well. There are too many conflicting elements for there ever to be any harmony, so completely has the function of the most powerful of all scenic media been denied and divorced from its capacity. How indeed may we reconcile a light designed to illumine vertical flats, which also lights everything else on stage, with another light which is to be used for everything except the canvas, but which illumines that too?

Reduced to such straits, how absurd to discuss the quality of shadows! Nevertheless, there is no plastic object of any kind, animate or otherwise, which can dispense with shadow. If there is no shade, there is no light; for light is not simple "visibility." For owls, night is day; only the audience is concerned with "visibility"—light is distinguished from visibility by virtue of its power to be expressive. If there is no expression, there is no light; and such is the case in our theatres—there, one can "see," but without light, and for this reason the painted setting can become expressive only in the absence of the actor, because the imitation light painted on the canvas corresponds to the equally false painted shadows. But the actor is a solid mass, which cannot be lighted by imitation light; in order to have light on the stage, one or the other must be sacrificed. If we dispense with the actor, the drama is effaced, and we fall into diorama. Therefore the painting must be sacrificed.[1]

Because the complex machinery of lighting is powerless to provide *light* on our stages, it is futile to attempt a study of its function, but the sources of light can be considered independently of the painted setting. We shall, therefore, study these sources—the experience acquired in such an unaccustomed area may prove most useful elsewhere.

Most important is to determine into which category of light (diffuse or living) each piece of lighting equipment shall be placed.

As far as it is possible to judge *a priori, diffused lighting* can best be achieved through those lights which are least mobile and easy to handle, *i.e.,* the borders, the movable striplights, and to a very

---

[1]By "painting," naturally, I do not mean "color;" we shall see later how painting will gain a new life through being sacrificed.

small degree, the footlights. Obviously, the method of their placement and use will be quite different for a setting no longer governed by a succession of painted parallel canvases—but the instruments themselves will not be very different in construction. The more mobile and easily handled lights will produce *living light,* and will demand the most careful research in perfecting their mechanism. To the relatively stable installations of diffused lighting will be added screens of varying transparencies, designed to cut down any extreme degrees of brightness thrown on the nearest objects, or on the actors as they come into these lights. Most of the mobile and flexible units will be used to vary the light and make it adaptable—an important function for the expressiveness of the whole setting. This function of light (although invisible) *belongs to the setting itself,* and will always be arranged at the same time and in harmony with the spatial arrangement of the setting, while the general electrical arrangement of the theatre can be more or less determined before its use. In discussing the spatial arrangement, we have already seen how important the partial obstruction of living light is for maintaining the expressive integrity of the scene; painting will provide still other examples of this. As far as the lighting of painted transparencies is concerned, this belongs exclusively to the painting, and has no influence upon the living light, except that it must give living light free play, since it illuminates the painting without illuminating the rest of the setting.

The interrelationship of the two kinds of lighting is a question of proportions, and the technical demarcation between them must not be absolute.

Diffused light and living light exist simultaneously only by virtue of their varying degrees of intensity. Diffused light by itself simply allows for "visibility"—or that which, in the drama of the word-tone poet, means or signifies. Living light, on the other hand, expresses night (moon or torch-light), or the supernatural. The difference in intensity between the two forms of light should be no less than the presence of shadows necessitates. Apart from this requirement, their possible combinations are of an infinite variety. However, any combination which might prevent us from perceiving the diffused light would in effect produce only living light. Such light would then be subject to the conditions imposed by the average spectator's range of vision.

To avoid the shadows would interfere with the power of living light; the whole setting, as well as the actor, must be illumined from all sides. For, by means of the diffused light, we achieve "visibility" on the stage; the shadows will be neutralized and ready now for the living light. With the exception of some rather rare instances in which one of the two light forms must operate independently, it goes without saying that we must begin with "visibility." The intensity of the diffused light will then be modified by the living light.

This fundamental difference between the two kinds of light is the only technical notion which properly belongs to lighting under the new scenic principle. Later, we shall see that color, as it becomes externalized and no longer dependent upon vertical flats, will come to be so closely related to light that the two forms will be well-nigh indistinguishable, but for the sake of clarity the discussion will take its place under the heading of "Painting," and I shall thus continue with the hierarchal order which begins with the actor.

But, you will say, is not the division between living and diffused light merely another effort toward the realism so systematically opposed by the other elements of the word-tone drama? And will not the harmony of the production be destroyed by the realistic use of light in an otherwise completely fictive setting, peopled by characters whose diction, gestures, and movement in no way correspond to the appearances of daily life?

The literal imitation of familiar forms and patterns does not produce the only life in which we know them. We can easily picture them in the most various combinations, imagine them in movement, and even changing their dimension and nature before our eyes. Music, on the other hand, is the most convincing demonstration of the ideal flexibility of time in what concerns our inner life. But, what mode of existence could we imagine for light except the opposing intensities occasioned by shadows—and how is it possible to imagine shadows but in terms of the objects causing them? There is no analogy between the pure and simple existence of light and the daily manifestations perceived by us through form and space: the first is absolute; the other but a modality beyond which our imaginations can freely soar.[1] By its very presence, light expresses the "inner essence" of all vision, because, even at the moment of perception, it exhausts any further ideas we might have of it. Form, independent of light, expresses this "inner essence" only in so far as it participates in the expression of the organic whole, either by becoming a part of the whole, or by furnishing the means of casting shadows, thus enabling the living light to function.

The ideality of the time, represented by the music in the form of the actor, then extends into space there to create a corresponding ideality. Under such circumstances, it is obvious that the ever absolute manifestations of light cannot be placed on the same level with the servile and exclusive imitation of form in only one of its modes.

The realism of the lighting, then, is not like the realism of the spatial arrangement, for the latter is based upon the imitation of a phenomenon, the former upon the existence of an idea.

This extraordinary status of lighting explains why the activity of this element, like that of an undemonstrable axiom, cannot be treated independently, but only in so far as it is applied to the specific materials provided by the other elements of production.

Painting

The more or less faithful reproduction of reality on a single plane does away with all life and all expressiveness. However, living light, when it dominates, restores that life and at the same time destroys the principles governing the use of color. The color arrangements, as well as the forms they express through their quality and variations of light and shade, lose not only their expressiveness in the presence of the living elements, but also their meaning. In order for meaning and expressiveness to be restored, both must be subject to a new principle, and because lighting has put out their spark of life, it

---

[1] Unquestionably, one of the chief attractions of high ascents is the fact that they offer us the opportunity to *participate* in proportions and combinations in space, which heretofore only our imagination could have encompassed.

is through lighting that it will be regained. In some manner painting must externalize itself and renounce its fictive life. What existence can painting achieve to make up for this sacrifice?

The painting of scenery has always been considered inferior to other forms of painting, and for good reason. Obviously, if any branch of an art is controlled by conventions foreign to it and, moreover, is denied access to its major function, it is stripped of any potential intrinsic value. Few will argue that this does not apply to the painting of scenery, for the conventions of the theatre are totally different from those which govern the art of painting as such; and the eventual purpose for which scenery is intended deprives the painter of one of his most basic subjects: the portrayal of the human body. In lending itself to the drama, from the outset, the art of painting makes considerable sacrifices for which nothing will compensate as long as painting retains the principle of its independent life.[1]

That life can be defined as follows: to set down, on a flat surface with colored materials, as much of the artist's private vision as can be expressed within the natural limitations of the process. The flat surface and the pigments are nothing in themselves but the raw materials of the painting. The essential ingredient is the artist's own vision. In order to reveal it to us, he uses the materials of his art, but deals with them only as one would with an interpreter or an intermediary, for true virtuosity will always have the negative effect of creating a wide breach between the artist's vision and his technical performance.

Standing before his canvas, the artist feels obliged, almost always unconsciously, to retain that portion of his vision which cannot be conveyed by the process he is using. This is the tacit and irrevocable pact the painter signed before starting on his path; the sacrifice is definitive in the cause of his work. Such an artist can tolerate no intermediary but his own will between the tools of his craft and the vision he must communicate. Indeed, the painter is in

---

[1] The fractional gift brought by painting to the theatre may be compared to what happens to music when it gives itself up to the opera: both become absolutely sterile in the process. For if any single element in a group of factors acting in unison becomes rooted to one spot, unable to radiate its vitality, it shrinks and grows pallid, and before long its mere presence has a deadening effect on companion elements. The activity must be co-operative in order to be effective.

sole command of every phase of his work.

When the art of painting seeks to preserve its independence on the stage, it loses the ability to comply with a personal will, since the drama becomes a barrier between the painting and the dramatist. In truth it is the dramatist who is the *artist* here, the scene painter being little more to him than an instrument. And yet the complex mechanism of the setting cannot be said to emanate directly from the dramatist's will, since, without music, the dramatic action by itself does not prescribe the form of the production.

On the other hand, everything in the word-tone poet's vision which requires discernible expression and tangible form is brought to the stage *by the music*. In music the word-tone poet finds his vision; therefore, the music must control the painting as well, if that vision is to be fully expressed. Whatever music cannot communicate visually, it will convey in other ways.

Music thus gives the dramatist the same control over the various elements of production as the painter has over the tools of his craft. The elements placed at the disposal of the word-tone poet arrange themselves in a well-defined hierarchy, starting at the proscenium opening, which corresponds to the painter's palette of colors and the flat surface awaiting his first brush stroke. Both artists, using their materials to best advantage, display *before our eyes* as much of their vision as is compatible with the media available to them. Comparisons cannot be drawn indefinitely, however, between the painter and the dramatist. For instance, the fictive and uniform nature of his art allows the painter a direct and personal control over his craft and tools. On the other hand, this particular method would spell disaster for the organic life of the dramatist's work.

When painting abandons its traditional function, it detaches itself from those material processes with which it had once formed an apparently indivisible whole. In the process of adopting an objective goal, this art responds, not to arbitrary whim, but to a deep organic need. This explains the transformation that occurs when it moves onto the stage in the word-tone drama—here, the very concept of painting takes on new dimensions.

The word-tone poet, delving into the heart of universal

rhythm, of universal proportions, has brought forth his vision: it is before us, its form inevitable to the last detail, with no trace of the arbitrary. This is when the paradox of artistic *necessity,* or the presence of a superior force, manifesting itself in a work of fortuitous origin, finds its noblest and most definitive expression.

The basic difference between the stage picture created by the poet-musician and the imaginative picture only a painter can produce is that the latter has the advantage of absolute stillness of subject matter. The painter is able to observe the object before him, to capture its appearance, and then to set it down at his leisure. The word-tone poet, on the other hand, must struggle with variations in time. A "living picture" is as ridiculous in concept as a mechanized painting would be. What a painting executed on a flat surface may lose in mobility, it makes up for in a certain technical perfection inaccessible to the stage designer, concerned as he must be with the life of the drama. Allowing him to freeze this life into a "living picture" would be tantamount to confining him to the limitations of painting, with none of its compensations. Likewise, to add motion to a painter's work through mechanization is to withdraw the artist's greatest privilege.

Color, deprived of its own life on the stage by living light, loses the benefits it once derived from immobility. If color is to perform as a valuable element in production, it must be subordinate to light. For when light ceases to be fictive in character, it destroys the relative importance of color combinations. The mobility characteristic of any stage picture requires, therefore, that the lighting assume a good many of the functions which color alone once gave to the painter. *The word-tone poet paints his picture with light.* It is no longer static colors which represent light, but light which takes from color all that opposes' its mobility.

It is obvious that a new and more detailed study must be made of the use of lighting and its effect on color in order to discover whether painting, as such, will maintain a role independent of the new *mise en scène,* outside the general concept of the stage picture.

Light may convey color in a number of ways: by means of its own intrinsic color content, or by means of the various colored glasses through which it shines. Light can also project images ranging from the most delicate gradation of hues to the sharpest effects. A shutter, placed over the source of light, can direct a beam to one part of the stage, leaving the other areas in darkness. Starting with this simple effect, we have a host of possibilities whose scope is limited only by the varieties, shapes, and combinations of transparencies used. The lighting, already made mobile by the presence of the actors, in whose activity it takes part, becomes even more so, if the light source can be moved about, if the projected images are placed in motion before a stable light source, or if the lens in front of the light source is vibrated in some manner. These colors, forms, and motions, variously combined with each other, and, in turn, with the stage picture, offer innumerable possibilities; they constitute the palette of the word-tone poet.

Both the living and the diffused light require an object on which to focus. The lighting does not change the form of these objects, but rather serves to make their presence felt, and hence to make them expressive. With the addition of color, the lighting now begins to modify the object's own chromatic scheme; moreover, a light source equipped to project a combination of colors, or an image or design, has the power to create an environment on stage, and even to create objects by means of projection. In order to be visible, projected images must strike an object as is the case for both ordinary and colored light. But, unlike simple light rays, projected images strongly affect the essential nature of these objects (for the spectator). Moreover, these objects, because of their various shapes and dimensions, respond by actively modifying the projected image. Therefore, if the interplay of colored light and painted scenery is simply a matter of chromatic dimensions, the problem of projection is in addition associated with forms. In both cases, we are concerned with the color of objects independent of the effects of lighting. This independence is, of course, relatively small when we consider the sum total of the elements making up the stage picture; yet its existence cannot be ignored any more than that of any other element of production.

Whatever color is not absorbed by the lighting remains an intrinsic ingredient of the objects (animate or inanimate) to which it belongs, and constitutes the part played in the new stage setting by *painting,* in the limited and usual sense of the word. Now since this type of painting will no longer necessarily be displayed on vertical canvases, we return to the question of spatial arrangement, and thence to the figure of the actor himself.

Let us attempt in some way to define the nature of these "inanimate" colors by relating them to stage elements with which we are already familiar.

I have stated previously that there is no connecting link between the spatial arrangement of the setting and the flat or painted elements. Light alone can furnish such a link. And yet the very activity of lighting seems to widen the breach that separates the two extremes of three-dimensional constructions and the fiction of the painted canvas. To overcome this difficulty, the spatial arrangement should depend only on its own resources and on the small amount of painted scenery permitted by the lighting. The actor sacrifices a goodly part of his independence to the visual whole of the stage picture, and no doubt plastic realization must yield to the painted canvas. But in so doing, will it not suffer distortion in the presence of the actor? Here as elsewhere, the answer lies in the rejection of scenic illusion, for if this illusion is no longer the dominant factor in dictating the plastic execution of the scenery, then we must look elsewhere for a valid principle to measure the degree of realism that can be brought to the stage through plastic media.

The extraordinary dimensions of the poetic-musical text, extending as they do into space, are not necessarily proportions we can easily relate to our everyday experience with familiar objects. Essentially, the physical form of the actor is the only point of contact between the stage setting and reality. Before attempting to develop the imitation of this reality any further, we must give close attention to the expression of the poetic-musical text: it is quite possible to imagine a scene, or even a whole series of scenes whose composition is quite independent of those accidental schemes occurring in nature. Our inner life, which is the essence of musical expression, is far removed from all such considerations as the imitation of reality—the existence of music proves this. The infinite number of details essential to nature's complex spectacle cannot justifiably be imposed upon the visual representation of a poetic-musical text. The text may employ some of these details—or it may omit them altogether, but in the final analysis, we are the masters of form, movement, light, and color. The combinations of these elements which our eyes ordinarily perceive are not definitive. This is readily understood by the man of science who, by means of his microscope or telescope, probes some universe inaccessible to the naked eye, just as the human body returns to its everyday existence after experiencing the brief pleasure of its rhythmic life. The joy we feel on beholding the physical world comes essentially not from the ever-changing, always accidental fusion of its elements, but rather from the fact that these elements are *in motion*—their activity is beautiful in itself. Now this activity touches us only when it is governed by certain rules—not arbitrary rules, but laws of a divine nature. The same elements might be assembled in a combination identical to that which had moved us before, but if they lacked the government of divine law, their mere *activity* would cast no spell, and the principle of beauty would be gone. Music finds the supreme reason for its existence in our hearts. This is why musical expression, in its true essence, is completely sacred. Thus, the spatial arrangements resulting from the dimensions of music in time are far from arbitrary in character, for they are inevitable; the activity of the elements of production therefore is beautiful in itself.

The wondrous art of sound, in revealing to us our innermost being, creates the supreme work of art by combining *artifices* borrowed from nature, whose eternal laws reside *within ourselves*. This is why in the staging of such a work of art only the actor is dependent upon the external world of reality.

We may conclude by stating that it is not the degree of realism that is important in the plastic execution of the setting, but rather whether the settings effectively express the poetic-musical intention. There are times, of course, when imitation of actuality can be useful, even beautiful, if it so happens that its forms are an integral part of the activity dictated by the music.

When the actor sacrificed his independence, namely, the arbitrary dimensions of his personal existence, in order to give expressiveness to the inanimate elements of the production, he had to renounce the *realism* of his appearance. The plastic execution of the scenic picture should do as much, in order to reconcile its activity in space with the designs of the painted canvas; it, too, must give up any slavish imitation of reality.

One last obstacle remains—and this can be overcome by the painting.

Obviously, we are not going to have the painted canvas covered with forms and colors at odds with the independence from realism expressed in the plastic elements of the setting. Nowadays the reigning decorative principle relies upon the mass and variety of objects in the painting to make up for the infinite poverty of the plastic elements; as the barrenness of spatial techniques is gradually alleviated, the *multiple* role of painting will lose importance, finally ceasing to be a makeshift device in areas of stage design where movement in space is of major importance. The painting of forms on pieces of flat canvas in conformity with lines on which the canvases are cut will be reduced to the representation on a single plane of plastic forms independent of the actors' movement. The principle of practicability will no longer be, as it is on our contemporary stages, an arrangement of surfaces meeting at right angles and masked from the audience by a vertical canvas depicting the place. Rather, the whole scenic principle will be based upon a composition constructed especially for a given setting, one whose multiform surfaces extend freely into space. This principle gives new importance to color: painting, no longer compelled to present realistic or imaginative forms on the flats, would become "color in space," and in so doing assume the harmonizing role of *simplifier*.

The color of objects, which constitutes the restricted role of painting in our new concept of production, is important for the form of the actor in general and particularly for his costume. What is the function of costume in the scenic picture, and can both the independence from verisimilitude and the limited role of painting extend to the actor himself?

Obviously, the actor's own dimensions are the only ones possible for his costume; now, in what way will the costume itself take on meaning and how much of this meaning can it convey? The question is not an easy one. We may look at it from two points of view:

1. The harmonious relationship between the actor's form and the poetic-musical proportions.
2. The harmonious balance between the actor's form and the rest of the stage picture.

Let us consider the first aspect. We attach far greater meaning to the actor's external appearance than to the inanimate elements of the stage picture. The poetic-musical text may, in certain introspective passages, tend to favor the actors: as it emphasizes them, it will have little or no concern for the other elements in the hierarchy of production, thus diminishing the scenic expressiveness by permitting the setting to have only an external, rational significance. Then, again, there are times when the significance attached to the actor may be in some ways independent of the development of the other factors. However, since the lighting, because of its great mobility, provides most of the changes in the visual expression, it is lighting which is responsible for emphasizing the partial and relative independence of the actor.

It is how the actor is lighted, therefore, that determines the relative portion of signification which his form can allow.

As we study the influence of lighting upon the actor's form, we return to its purely decorative effect, and must now discover how the actor's body can harmonize with the limited role of painting.

On our modern stages, lighting has no *vital function;* its only purpose is *to make the painted setting visible.* The actor shares this overall lighting, but, in addition, he is given footlights so that he will be lighted from all angles. Strictly speaking, the lighting designed for the painted canvas might be able to preserve a semblance of activity on behalf of the actor, were it not for the fact that the footlights nullify it completely, destroying what little expressiveness the production offered the actor through the spatial arrangement.

The paralyzing influence of the footlights extends to all plastic objects on the stage—in other words, everything that is in direct contact with the actor—and also manages to divorce him completely from the fictions of the painted flats. Nevertheless, the actor does have his own lighting, the effect of which is to make him brilliantly visible, and to allow us to follow every nuance of his facial expression. This, as we know, is the primary consideration in the staging of the spoken drama. And how is this condition fulfilled by the footlights?

The play of facial expression is a *living* thing, having value only as it harmonizes with the essential nature of the whole human face. Footlights distort the actors' faces, because they obliterate those planes essential to their character. Features, deprived of their real value, will take on an artificial one, and since it is impossible to replace the structural value of facial planes by some artifice or other, all that occurs is that the hieroglyphs of the face are exaggerated— that is, the features are separated from their essential character.

The distance at which his face must be visible in the theatre, always invoked to explain away this offensive travesty, is in fact, a very minor reason. If a mute actor were to hold his script in his hand and have the audience read his part for him, the size of the letters on the pages would not be an essential result of theatrical perspective, but merely the consequence of the actor's being mute. The situation is the same with the footlights: they destroy the normal expression of the features, which must be replaced by some abstract sign.[1] Great actors, in seeking to remedy this, devise ingenious make-

---

[1] Here there is an analogy with the absurd methods of some photographers, who light their clients' faces in such a way that not a single flaw (in their skin) could possibly escape the camera. Immediately after taking the picture, they then reconstruct the facial harmony by arbitrary retouching, all of which could have been avoided if a well-arranged lighting scheme had been used in the first place.

up to suit their particular style of acting; the result is often remarkable, but what futile efforts, when a different principle of lighting—not active from the point of view of the overall decorative picture, but *based on facial expression* (which would naturally lead to a greater expressiveness of the whole body)—could have a hundred times more effect upon nuances of facial expression, bodily positions and movement, without overburdening the actor. But the audience would then complain that they could not "see" well enough, like children who cannot "see" an object unless they squeeze it in their hands.[1]

Under this kind of lighting, the actor's costume takes on an exaggerated importance, because instead of simply placing it in light, it is so garishly illuminated that we can see its every detail. The costume designer's art thus becomes impossible, there being no important difference nowadays between a famous society tailor and the costume designer for a large theatre.

The art of costuming nowadays is governed by the peculiar demands of the opera and of the spoken drama. Costuming for opera, responding only to the blind demands of sumptuousness, has no significance. In the spoken drama, the demands are motivated by the dramatic form, which lacks any means of fusing the actor with the decorative setting—but here again, the costuming serves only to widen the gulf which separates them. A dedicated actor in the spoken drama will always consider the design and the fitting of his costume as an integral part of his role. He will spend long hours before his mirrors studying the relationship of his costume to his role—*but he does not do this on the stage itself*—for he knows that it would be utterly futile; the stage lighting serves only to make his presence "visible," without ever giving it any value. And the setting has only as much rapport with the actor as a minimum of practical pieces with which he can easily become familiar before going on stage at all. So, he ignores the stage setting just as it ignores him.

In a dramatic form in which the actor is the only intermediary between the playwright and the audience, such a situation is not abnormal. It is the claims of the stage director which then

---

[1] Similarly, the audience will complain, often most rudely, that they cannot "hear" when an actor in the spoken drama is sensitive enough to recognize the places in his part whose delicate poetic meaning comes close to being music.

become ridiculous and out of place, not the separate efforts of the actor and of the designer.

Since the elements of production should act interdependently, as is the case of the setting of the word-tone drama, the peculiar influence of the footlights, which I have just discussed, must be rejected for once and all. For not only does their use negate the very function of living light, but by destroying the scenic expressiveness, it also distorts the meaning of the production. In any case, it is a complete perversion of taste, and will never effect a balance of the poetic-musical proportions on stage. But, since the footlights are what determine the actor's general appearance these days, it follows that this appearance, to which we have grown accustomed, must undergo some vitally appreciable changes in order to enter into the new setting.

First and foremost, the artificial accentuation of features is only of secondary importance in cases where the obvious play of facial expression must yield to a more telling kind of expression and thus be subservient to the overall stage effect; usually the lighting is the decisive factor here, in accordance with the degree of representation in the poetic-musical text: the light acts not to enlarge or diminish the characteristic facial planes of the human face, but rather to throw them into relief or to fuse them with the rest of the scenic picture, depending upon whether the actor happens to be developing the dimensions of his role or withholding them.

Since the conditions of lighting for the face are the same as those for the body as a whole, they act equally upon the actor's expressions and his movements. But the costume must also be considered from the point of view of color and design.

Nowadays, theatrical costumes seem to demand the same multiple role as the painted drops, and this is quite natural, since it is the only way the costumes can establish any relationship at all with the painting. The activity of the lighting, joined with the actor's subordination in the word-tone drama, puts detail in its rightful place; and if the measure of purely intelligible meaning becomes as minimal for the costume as for the painted scenery, the requirements of expression on the other hand allow nothing in the actor's appearance which could alter its essential character. Therefore, we shall treat the color of the costumes in the same way as the decorative scenic materials—and the pictorial effect of the actors will take its place with the painted scenery. Here, the word "painted" is used according to our statement that the word-tone poet paints with light.

In any work of art, the principle of *sacrifice* depends upon the fairly narrow limitations of our senses. One might say, indeed, that the artist adapts nature for our enjoyment. But the artist himself must already possess the natural gift of reducing and concentrating the designs provided by nature, for this is the true function of artistic genius. A great painter, for example, sees far fewer objects than a mere layman, because he does not have to know each object in isolation—he grasps their mutual affinity, achieving this only by reducing the quantity of his vision in favor of its quality. Of course, the layman sees a different picture; given the same scene, their two visions would probably have little in common—but it is still simply a question of quantity and choice, the very mode of vision. In all fields of art, expressive intensity implies sacrifice. In the word-tone drama, where the sacrifice is perhaps greater than in any other art form, there is the greatest possible expressive intensity because the dramatist must renounce a whole array of things employed in the usual dramatic method as we know it. The painter, the sculptor, and the poet, on the other hand, renounces only what his particular art excludes by its essential nature. But the word-tone poet makes us participate in the origins of his sacrifice, whereas other artists merely show us the result of their work, requiring of the reader or the viewer a tacit act of reflection on its origins. Indeed, when the dramatist uses music, he must renounce everything alien to the musical expression, while music becomes the accurate and unfailing expression of the dramatist's disposition to reduce and concentrate his vision—in fact, the freedom and immeasurable power of the musical expression in the word-tone drama depends upon the *poet's* power of concentration.[1] The result is that not only do we take pleasure in his work as the complex result of an individual's exceptional aptitude, but also we *participate* in the artist's genius, without having to think about it. Music, through an act of incomparable generosity, *transforms us*

[1] See Wagner, *Gesammelte Schriften*, IV, 174.

into "mediums," much like the dramatist himself. In order to express "the inner essence of a phenomenon," the word-tone poet rejects the extraneous elements of that phenomenon; what he puts before us is the ultimate reason for his sacrifice — namely, music; and in this way he will realize for his audience the reduction imposed upon him by music — or, the simplification of nature in favor of the intensity of his expression.

The Auditorium

It may seem strange that a form of drama so indeterminate in its proportions should be forced to adapt itself to the fixed and permanent construction of the auditorium. As long as some temporary constructions must be set up for the production itself, then why not go further, and build an auditorium especially designed to meet the varying visual and acoustical demands of each successive presentation? Although the question seems natural, it implies a most serious aesthetic inconsistency.

The *expression,* as such, has no absolute existence except in the soul of the one experiencing it, and the methods for communicating to the soul are themselves of only relative value.

The Greek performer took his position before his audience, and asked only that they have attentive eyes and ears. As a true "medium," the actor's whole being put up as little resistance as possible to the expression. The word-tone poet employs more complex methods; his whole organism appears to burst forth, multiplying itself and thereby displacing the centers of resistance. But the truth is that any resistance to the expression must be conquered first in the poet's soul: the vision he discovered in music, if it is to be revealed, must overthrow all obstacles set up against it by a limited and nonessential personality. The life of the poetic-musical text depends upon the successful solution of this problem.

Once this has been achieved, the dramatist stands invisibly between the stage and the audience. With one masterful hand, he calls forth the score — the product of his genius; with the other, he respectfully lifts the curtain and invites us to watch with him the real drama — *which is the product of music.*[1]

The interior action, *directly* communicated by the word-tone poet to our ears, is *at the same time* revealed to our eyes. As spectators, we have come to see and to hear — and the seats we occupy need only fulfill the general visual and acoustical conditions required by the drama. The production is then presented through the means at its disposal and in a manner appropriate to the range of our senses. It would be detrimental to the music to rearrange the auditorium for each new production. Music does not require our assistance: as it addresses itself to the whole human personality — through the medium of the drama — music asks only for our undivided attention, in sum, a receptive spirit served by healthy senses. Music has the power to fill all other requirements.

The word-tone poet himself carefully determines the acoustical conditions of the auditorium, but he is also aware of music's inexhaustible dramatic resources, and therefore allows it to act freely. All that he can do is to prepare a favorably disposed audience opposite that ideal space where the music will come to life.

Our present-day theatres can be as little concerned with the problems of acoustics as they are with visual problems. Evidently, their arrangement was determined by a preoccupation with far more vital matters, since no provision has been made in them either for hearing the orchestra and the singers clearly, or for seeing the stage. It is obvious that for the drama born of music, conditions based on acoustical laws will be all important in determining the construction of the auditorium, and by their very nature, these conditions, as we all know, cannot be contravened, no matter what visual demands there may be.

I would place the orchestra in front of the stage as it is in the Festival Theatre at Bayreuth (thus far no better place has been discovered for it), for the orchestra belongs in the auditorium. Its evocative role requires a location outside the stage. If the orchestra were placed on the stage, so that it became a visible part of the setting through its combinations of sounds in space, it would destroy

---

[1] According to Wagner, "In the drama, the activity of music becomes visible."

the hierarchy of production by endowing the scenic picture with an arbitrary value. The setting would then cease to be a means of expression, and the auditorium, in turn, would be forced to obey its injunctions.

The orchestra, however, evokes the scenic picture through the medium of the actor; therefore, the stage setting must convey to the audience the changing volume contained in the actor's singing role. The proscenium opening allows the voice to reach the auditorium, but once the sound passes this opening, the auditorium itself must meet the acoustic needs of the audience. On the stage, all responsibility lies with the temporary construction of the stage setting, which is determined by the actor, who, in turn, is subservient to the demands of the poetic-musical text. Acoustically speaking, therefore, the auditorium has only to take into account the orchestra and the carrying quality of the actors' voices from beyond the proscenium arch.

However, on the stage there is one element of expression whose legitimate employment seems irreconcilable with the hierarchy of production. This element is any vocal or instrumental music which is not supplied directly by the actors (neither by the soloists nor by the chorus) and whose presence is not motivated by the purely intellectual meaning of the text. So far as I know, until now, this kind of music has never been used except in *melodrama*.[1]

Although much maligned, melodrama is still the purest manifestation of the instinctive longing for music in the drama. In itself, it has no relationship to opera — its end is always *dramatic*. In a less praiseworthy sense, the music serves to tickle the nerves of the audience by infusing a certain excitement into the play or by expressing to the spectator a dramatic conflict or hidden purpose too subtle for the scenic presentation. In its best sense, melodrama, as it passes through many variations of the lyric mode, may succeed in revealing the Idea hidden beneath the external layers of action and words. When music sounds within the shadowy labyrinth of our

---

[1] There are no examples of this in Wagner's dramas. This is a characteristic explained by the Master's position with regard to production, as we shall see in Part II of this study.

emotional life, as the dramatist has revealed it to us, we feel that we have passed from the troubling state of doubt into pure truth. For music always tells truth, as Richard Wagner assures us. Without resolving our problems, it delivers us even from the desire for their solution, and for a fleeting moment transforms us into "pure instruments of perception."[1]

The basic defect of melodrama is the impossibility of reconciling the spoken text with independent musical sounds; this disparity, however, is its main strength. Instead of hiding hypocritically behind beautiful clothes, as does the opera, melodrama publicly avows its superficiality, and the result is that we experience quite keenly the original essence of each element of the production as it is placed before us.

And the *mise en scène* itself affects the melodrama because of the place assigned to the instruments (or to the singer) performing the music.

According to its nature, a work will require either a full orchestra or perhaps only a few instruments. Usually, the orchestra is situated in the pit in front of the stage, just as it is in the opera. This arrangement is obviously bad since it distorts the relation between the stage and the auditorium and between the music and dramatic action. However, if the instruments can be placed on the stage behind the scenery, the music and the words of the play will be fused into a unit, thus giving melodrama a more normal existence; for in this case, the music is neither the source of the drama nor its active commentary, but simply the *presence* of an element of expression superior to the spoken word.

Melodramas based, like Schumann's on Byron's *Manfred,* or Bizet's on Daudet's *l'Arlésienne,* are extremely crude products, notwithstanding the talents that went into their making. The sinister tremolo marking the villain's entrance in any run-of-the-mill popular play possesses a far more genuine aesthetic quality than the bizarre combinations of these two over-brilliant works.

What dramatic significance can music have, when it ex-

---

[1] So Schopenhauer defines the essential nature of genius.

presses the positive action on stage, and also comments on it, and, far from controlling the drama, simply lumps together in one basket overture, interludes, melodrama, choruses, songs, etc.? One wonders at this point why the audience too does not join in the singing, in order to climax such an embarrassment of riches!

Here, as in the opera, music is treated as a deluxe accessory with which, alas, it is presumed we could never become surfeited. Thus, the composer sees his purest intentions collapsing in the confusion of his own aesthetic barbarism. If the opera had not poisoned us to the very marrow of our bones, the existence of such works would not be possible.

In discussing melodrama, of course, I do not mean this kind of score, but rather those extremely unpretentious musical effects, sometimes quasi-improvised, in whose unexpected charm all theatre lovers have delighted at some time or other.[1]

Such incidental music must be absolutely independent of the *intelligible* meaning of the action (a chorus of peasants in the wings, the echoes of distant ballroom music, a serenade, etc. do not belong to melodrama), for it is such independence which has characterized melodrama and distinguished it from its beginnings from opera. Moreover, the music in melodrama should not develop outside the production (in overtures, entr'actes, etc.). Any sensitive artist will understand that the two conditions imply a great technical reduction in musical composition, and also that the use of any part

---

[1] The final scene of a production of Zola's *l'Assommoir*, which I saw at the Chatelet in Paris, proved to me the extent to which a scenic director's unconscious improvisation can go. The scene showed a busy street, covered with snow. The facade of a public dance hall, lighted by colored lanterns, contrasted vividly with the mournful carriages and deserted benches concealed in the darkness. On the sidewalk, the main character of the play, a poor woman, was begging timidly and unsuccessfully, while the hurly-burly of the nocturnal festivities of the dance hall attracted the passers-by into its furnace-like glow. Exhausted, the beggar woman finally sank into the snow, there to succumb to misery and starvation. This scene would have come perilously close to failure, such realism being incompatible with current ideas of production, had not melodrama come to the rescue. What was decided upon (undoubtedly by sheer luck), to fray the audience's already distraught emotions, was this: as the curtain went up on the stage, a handful of stringed instruments, placed in the pit before the stage, played Schumann's "Träumerei," delicate pianissimo, for several reprises. What better way to throw into relief the triumph of vice than to couple it with this sensitive display of peaceful dilettantism! Such an intent is obviously too refined to be attributed to any modern director—we can only say that here was sublime unconsciousness at work.

of the auditorium should be proscribed either for instruments or for voices.

Thus defined, can the principle of melodrama be applied to the word-tone drama — and, if so, how can it be reconciled with the role of the orchestra in this kind of drama, and with the relationship of the auditorium and the stage?

The orchestra, which evokes the production through the medium of the extrinsic form of the actor, cannot go beyond the point which ideally separates its duration in time from its proportions in space. The purely technical laws governing the *mise en scène* are no longer the orchestra's concern: it has surrendered its creation to them. Now, if for any reason, the word-tone poet wishes to bathe the scene before us anew in the purifying atmosphere of music, he is free to do so; only he must remember that the transformation *has already taken place* — that the music of the drama is already incarnate upon the stage. Therefore, the backstage music assumes responsibility only for a development in the production that is *already fundamental to it*. The orchestra, on the other hand, has no other end than the drama: thus, the dramatic expression evokes the scenic picture; and whatever musical sounds are used on the stage will be distinguished from the orchestra and the singing by the absence of *dramatic* expression. Consequently, backstage music will never be used unless its expression is justified by the scenic picture, of which it remains independent.[1]

As we see, the principle of melodrama remains the same for the word-tone drama as for the spoken drama: neither form will tolerate confusion between the action proper and its lyric development. Therefore, the admission of backstage music is in no way prejudicial to the hierarchy of production; indeed, it provides the word-tone poet with an inexhaustible source of expression.

---

[1] It goes without saying that the backstage music may begin as the curtain goes up—even beforehand—since the restrictive conditions surrounding it are not in time, but in space only.

When the acoustics of the hall are established on a fully reasonable foundation, we shall pass on to a consideration of the visual conditions — and here we are faced with a new difficulty. The arrangement of seats for the audience depends upon the dimensions of the scenic picture, and more precisely upon the proscenium frame. If these dimensions happen to be indeterminate, how can we establish the place to be occupied by the audience?

I have pointed out that in the new theatrical system, the proscenium opening will become an absolute dimension, in the sense that *for our eyes* it is the point which separates our independent organic life from our organic musical life. I also suggested that the size of this opening is not directly limited by the music, but that music does prescribe the qualities of the setting, and that these qualities or elements, in order to reach us harmoniously, in turn prescribe the proportions of this frame from the stage itself. And herein lies the solution of the problem. Indeed, if the expressive power of the setting is to be preserved, the auditorium must quite definitely be built according to the most universal visual and acoustical laws, and this is because the innate nature of the expression is to expect nothing more from us than the integrity of our physical faculties. The two conventions essential to every artistic manifestation as we know it are diametrically opposed: either because we are warped by a corrupt state of culture, we think we should impose upon the work of art the same conditions that civilization imposes upon us; or else the limitations of human nature in themselves force us to sacrifice one element for the harmonious realization of another element. The essential conventions for an art founded upon expression will be affected only by this second reason; and, what is particularly remarkable, the expression never fails to compensate us for our sacrifices to it, for it determines its proportions in accordance with those of our receptive faculties — and does this *without our help*. We have called the expression to life by our very disinterestedness — and gratefully, the expression *reaches out to us*. Therefore, if the relationship existing between the place of the spectator and the frame of the stage does not demand conventional limits for the frame, it is not we who arbitrarily impose this condition, but the expression, whose absolute power on stage has only *ourselves as object.*

The partition-wall of the auditorium, behind which the drama unfolds in its provisional technical form, must be broken by as large an opening as possible and seats must be arranged so that the spectator can see the stage whether the opening for a particular setting be large or small. The concern for reconciling these dimensions within the particular bounds of each production is a matter for the stage itself, and presents no problems if the stage is governed by the principles of expression.

It goes without saying that no one location in the auditorium should distort the expressive meaning of the production, so that the sight lines in all sections of the house will preserve the expressive content of what is happening on the stage. This, as I have said before, is the only consideration, apart from the music, which directly influences the composition of the scenic picture because, just as the spectator must be seated where he will have an adequate view of the stage, so all stage effects must be planned to be seen. This appears especially in the lighting — where "diffused light" establishes the first condition for the overall production, which is to enable us to distinguish objects on stage.

Conclusion

> "Believe me, our deepest wisdom here
> is oft to us in dreams made clear."
>
> Hans Sachs, in Wagner's *Die Meistersinger*

That precious document, the dream, teaches us more about the basic needs of our personality than the most scholarly investigation. A mysterious thread is stretched across our whole life in sleep, creating the unity comparable to the relationship of cause and effect in our waking hours.

How inexhaustible are the possibilities of dreams — so declares the respectful observer with admiration, and often with fear and regret. Indeed, the life of the intellect will never be able so clearly to display the inner resources of our being, nor to allow such free play of our latent powers, nor, above all, to realize so fully and beguilingly our most secret longings.

For the *artist* particularly, the life of dreams is an incomparable source of joy; although essentially it does not initiate him into a new world, the dream life confers upon him limitless power. With Hafiz, the artist cries

> Yea, if you would know my meaning clear,
> Then enter my kingdom, O jubilant one! . . .

The imaginative life of his soul celebrates in dreams the intimate reality of the artist's true existence: this fictive life no longer has to be brought forth by dint of the laborious effort to communicate to others — and this always imperfectly, as is unhappily the case with most artists — instead, it is the result of the association of certain harmonious elements obedient to the will of the artist who recognizes their eternal value. This association is a spontaneous phenomenon, the issue of one individual desire. The extraordinary joy it imparts rests in the fact that the creator has no longer to struggle against the inertia natural to objects and to people: now the cerebral function comes alive of its own accord.

The inexpressible nature of such a creation leaves a profound impression in the soul of the artist. If the mystic yearns for heaven, the artist yearns for the dream, and his whole productivity bears its influence.

In hours of vibrant hallucination, the poet feels, although he may not always wish to confess it, how inflexible and powerless words are, even as the vaguest of symbols, to communicate the imperious vision of his soul. So it happens that the better part of the vision, the very essence of it, remains untouched, unexpressed — and, it would seem — inexpressible. When the poet, after long considering his completed work, returns to the source of his inspiration, endeavoring to relive the intoxicating hour which impelled him to extend himself so inevitably for others, he is forced to admit that the one element he was powerless to communicate was *mobility*. His efforts had been chiefly directed at establishing within us the perpetual motion of his vision by a kind of definitive synthesis. However, although he may not understand the nature of this mobility, no one knows its value better than the artist. Therefore, he seeks to suggest his vision to the reader, and thereby perverts the means he employs. If only he could evoke at will his soul's invention as in a dream! How recalcitrant are the elements of our conscious life — yet, when we sleep, quite spontaneously they realize our most secret desires!

There does exist, however, an incomparable source of revelation, which, like our dreams, *obeys the desire to create a conclusive reality.* May the poet come to possess it, his unsatisfied fantasies showing him the way; may his incurable yearning be transformed into a burning, a palpable need: for the conscious life *can* create the dream; the poet knows this, feels it. By concentrating his vital forces, the artist can bring about this miracle, which will henceforth seem to him to be the only true purpose of his work.

The source of his revelation is music. And along with its power to evoke his vision, music also *expresses* the profound desire which is its origin and reveals to the word-tone poet himself the essential nature of that mobility he believed beyond his power to express. Now he understands that it is this constant juxtaposition of the eternal element with the non-essential, of the idea with the phenomenon, which endows his vision with an infinite and *moving* schematic variety, those everchanging patterns which cannot be expressed in words. By allowing the artist to contemplate what heretofore he had simply experienced as a passive agent, music now makes him actively capable of communicating to others: in full consciousness, the poet-turned-musician, or rather, the poet in whom the "musician" is now revealed, will bring to all of us his secret, unconscious experience of the dream-life.

In order to further this purpose, he must carefully investigate the laws governing the elements subservient to music and arrange them so they are as flexible as possible. Out of the dramatist's deep desire, comes a kind of inner concentration; this the music abstracts, diffusing its expression in luminous and everchanging waves.

When he writes his score, the dramatist makes use implicitly of the medium of the actor as the painter uses his brush; and ultimately the actor radiates over the stage the light with which he has been imbued, there to create the reality so ardently desired by the artist.

The hierarchy of production, which from the technical point of view seemed to be the result only of certain limitations necessary to the communal life of the various media of expression, must in fact be regarded as having a function equivalent to the dream — as a kind of spontaneous objectification of the aesthetic desire. Its value carries the stamp of humanity to the highest point, and if we agree with this, we merely authenticate the perfect concordance of our faculties.

The reader who has come this far with me will now understand the gravity with which I have treated certain questions that did not at first perhaps seem germane to the discussion. There is attached to all such technical procedures as bridge building, electrical machinery, and similar material combinations an importance implicitly contained in the language of the trade, although the technical terminology can only imperfectly demonstrate the importance of what it is applied to.

In matters of art, the principle of beauty is evoked in addition, and since this principle is higher than any other, it is impossible to demonstrate. What distinguishes the craftsman from the amateur is not only his technical knowledge of his methods, but also his constant identification with his lofty aims. A conversation between painters, for example, is dull only to those for whom the terminology remains only a jargon, failing to evoke the ever inexpressible vision of form and color.

But the vision contained within the theoretical demonstration which makes up this first chapter cannot be invoked integrally except by a text based on these principles. How, indeed, is it possible to give an example of hierarchy of production, for instance, when we lack the poetic-musical text which is the source of this hierarchy? If necessary, one could probably invent dramatic situations and surround them with sufficiently detailed explanations, as an artificial substitute for an actual text, and upon these imaginary foundations gradually construct the scenic picture. As a matter of fact, I attempted to do just that. But, after many efforts, I was convinced that any such example, far from properly illustrating the theory, would only distort its significance completely, especially since the readers would quite rightly expect to find there the application of principles whose existence and beauty are quite inseparable from music.

Music and music alone can arrange the elements of production in a harmony of proportions superior to anything that could ever be conjured up by our imagination. Without music, this harmony *does not exist,* and therefore cannot be experienced. There the reader will agree with me that to attempt to replace music with words would be just as delusive as to explain color to one who was born blind.

The dramas of Richard Wagner have revealed to us a new dramatic form, and their marvelous beauty has persuaded us of the vast possibilities of this form. We now know what the purpose of music is and how it can be manifested. But these dramas, in revealing to us the omnipotence of musical expression, have introduced us to the specific relationships existing between the musical duration addressed to our hearing and the scenic space where the drama unfolds before our eyes. Unfortunately, in the presentation of these dramas we have felt a painful uneasiness, resulting from the lack of harmony between the duration and the space. The reason for this impression is to be found in our contemporary theatrical conventions, which are altogether incompatible with the use of music in drama. This fact has led us to the study of how the use of music can influence production, whence comes the discovery of the hierarchal principle governing the various elements of drama, a principle involving a complete revolution in theatrical techniques as we know them today. Now, Richard Wagner, nevertheless, himself produced his dramas on today's stage and that is still the only way we can see them performed.

The present conditions of the word-tone drama, therefore, are not the normal ones for this work of art; and if we wish to experience Wagner's dramas in the form revealed to us by them, it is essential to discover to what degree the Master's vision was in accord with the methods of staging available to him, as well as any influence that such methods might have had upon his original creation.

As to the future of the word-tone drama, a future implied

102 ·

by the preceding theoretical considerations, many will question not only its value, but chiefly, the practicability for any such future. I believe, however, that such doubt rests on a misunderstanding. The union of the poetic-musical text and the other elements of production in itself is indispensable. When Wagner showed us the purpose behind this very real union, he was simply formulating an imperious need of human nature, and if the exact quality of his work is inimitable (as are all works of genius), this still does not imply that the *purpose* of his drama and the *means* necessary to implement it are forever beyond our power. We can study this purpose by absorbing ourselves in the Master's works; the study of the expressive media, on the other hand, requires a vast independence with regard to untried or revolutionary kinds of drama. Today, our corrupt civilization makes any such freedom exceedingly difficult. However, the sublime expression of the eternal elements of humanity must ever be born anew from the soul of music — and in return, music asks from us only an unreserved trust. We must, in order to answer the call of music, become conscious of our natural resistance to it and attempt to conquer it.

I have undertaken this study in the service of music — and the reader I think will agree that with such a master no efforts are too great.

PART II

RICHARD WAGNER AND THE *MISE EN SCÈNE*

"The German builds from within."

—Richard Wagner

In discussing the dramatic works of Richard Wagner, it seems to me that nothing can so clearly define the situation as these words of the Master himself. We shall see that they are in fact the key to a complex problem, and that only through them can we understand the *practical* reality of the word-tone drama, and from this point of view understand the Wagnerian phenomenon and determine the character of subsequent works designed to assure the survival of this art form.

H. S. Chamberlain, in his book *Richard Wagner,* has shown how the highest aspirations of the German dramatists and musicians have always been more or less consciously directed to the creation of a work of dramatic art uniting music and poetry in such a way that each has an equally important role, thus filling in the too obvious gaps we find both in music and drama when they exist as separate art forms. Chamberlain shows beyond question that "a century of striving on the part of poets and musicians reached its peak — *am Ziel* — in Wagnerian drama," and that the Master of Bayreuth fulfilled the burning aspirations of his predecessors, and the revelation for which he was responsible can be considered both the ultimate achievement of an ascendent movement toward expression and the beginning of new efforts and developments in the theatre.

From the first point of view, Wagner's dramatic work, as it evinced the aspiration of German poets and the invincible endeavor of German musicians, derives from the characteristic nature of all German art.

The nature of this creativity is clearly expressed by the

104 ·

manner in which Wagner achieved fully conscious artistry. We know, indeed, that it was impossible for him to effect a true union of music and poetry as long as he sought to find the solution of his problem in a special technique; but he transformed the nature of his dramatic work for once and all when he became conscious of the *purpose* which demanded this union.

For this reason, the efforts of Wagner's predecessors should not be thought of as a search for the ultimate form of integrated expression — that is, a technical method by which language and music could be organically united — but simply as the desire to distill from a too limited poetic imagination or from an inordinately unfettered musical expression what is common to them both, and to express this in a demonstrable form.

In every truly German work of art, concerns of form are subordinated to those of expression, which is to say that the German artist's vision belongs to a world in which technical methods are in themselves of secondary importance. "The German builds from within." He employs whatever means are at his disposal for the sole purpose of expressing something which exists only in his own soul. If the resultant expression is beautiful it is because the ideal is so lofty that it can be expressed only in this particular form. Wagner has proved this. He was able to achieve a form of consummate grandeur for his dramas because of the greatness and pure beauty of that which it revealed to us.

In considering a fundamentally national artistic production, and especially in a treatise concerned with form as is this one, it is important to establish that for the German artist form is not an aim but a *result* of creation.

Now music, since its form exists only within the composer's soul, must of necessity develop with greater freedom than any other art. The word-tone drama, which is deeply rooted in music, grows from within in a similar manner; it thus bears witness to hidden sources, and its form is inevitably a result, and hence it is the German work of art *par excellence*.

In this drama, the poetic-musical text is governed by the absolute will of the dramatist; but the visual production of the word-tone drama which results is not governed by the will of the dramatist and consequently it requires experience quite different from that acquired through composing words and tones. Here, indeed, the cultivation of the visual sense, of the feeling for external form, is a necessary and determining factor if the music is to be effectively communicated in production. The magic which the dramatist creates for the ear must now be evoked also for the eye, and this particular procedure bears only indirectly upon the intimate longing for expression which gave birth to the drama.

What, then, can a sense of external form mean to an artist for whom form is simply the result of a more profound expressive power? Obviously, nothing more than an *expedient*. Cultivation of his physical vision will have only a relative value. To the German it does not matter whether this or that form is in itself beautiful, whether a production is harmonious in itself, but rather whether there is a *harmonious relationship* between the expression which issues from his soul and the space in which he bodies forth that expression.

Thus, if the artist is to be capable of judging the harmony of this relationship, a balance must be achieved between his desire for expression and the form of that expression. The scores of Wagner's work indicate his extraordinary desire for an artistic expression, but unfortunately the form in which these scores have been presented shows that complex circumstances have not permitted his intentions to be adequately expressed. Therefore, if we are to understand the significance of production in Wagner's work, that is, to understand the relationship between his desire for expression and his feeling for form, we must first determine which of his intentions (as he has revealed them to us by his writing and by his actual production methods) he was able to fulfill. Only then can we evaluate, through the principles of the hierarchy created by the music, his conception of production, and judge what influence this conception has exerted upon the construction of his dramas. Only on the basis of such knowledge can we approach his work with an awareness of its meaning.

When Wagner attempted to produce his dramatic works in the conventional opera houses, he encountered those obstacles which are inherent in the typically German nature of his art, namely, the score and its basic dramatic demands. When he attained full maturity as an artist, he abandoned the traditional opera stage and wished to build one designed for the presentation of his own work.

The important question is, did Wagner make this change because he found the form of presentation on these old stages no longer suitable? The answer is no. Then, as before, social conditions thwarted all his efforts, conditions involving the complete corruption of what we call art, and particularly the art of the theatre, which carried in its wake not only incompetent audiences, but incompetent performers as well. If the evil against which Wagner was fighting had been merely one of technique, he would certainly have overcome it because of his boundless energy. Wagner, however, was fundamentally a German genius; for him form must be the result of a state of feeling, and could not be established artificially for its own sake.

At Bayreuth, where the Master made the supreme effort at least symbolically to create conditions far beyond his power to achieve, it was not the formal conventions of production which seemed to him to weaken the value of the end results, but rather the fact that no audience could be found to appreciate this symbol.[1]

A study of Wagner's life through his writing is most enlightening in this regard, for it proves that the greatest obstacle to the fulfillment of his ideal was never the *formal* theatrical conventions already in existence, but only the state of society in which his works had to live. For example, whenever a favorable atmosphere could be created artificially, from a purely dramatic viewpoint, for one evening's performance in a given theatre, as at the first performance of *Tristan and Isolde* in Munich, he did not complain of the means of production at his disposal. On the contrary, he was so completely pleased with that performance of *Tristan* that we may call it, as Chamberlain does, the "first German Festival."

The Master obviously felt that a clear and faithful production of his dramas was perfectly possible under the existing methods

---

[1] Just as the material obstacles which opposed those first productions seemed to grow more out of the uncertain state of the heterogeneous elements which had to be united than out of the nature of those elements.

of staging; and when he finally built the Festival Theatre at Bayreuth, he arranged everything relating to the *stage itself* in accordance with these methods.[1]

He saw nothing in the new conditions imposed by music upon the action of the drama except the purely dramatic results, and the reforms he introduced in production methods were limited to these alone. As to the formal conditions which, as we know, are the result of the musical time element, he took no interest in them, and seems even to have ignored them completely.

Despite its many and serious imperfections, the stage at Bayreuth is the only convincing demonstration of the Master's reforms. Yet this very stage is evidence that the distinction we have made between external conditions and purely dramatic effect is not an empty theory, but often a tangible and grievous reality. Everything that springs *directly* from the deep longing for expression in the German soul finds its most perfect expression in Bayreuth. But the disparity between the score and its realization on the stage, which did not spring directly from Wagner's artistic intention, gives to the visual production an artistic value so inferior to that of the score that the drama loses its integrity in performance.

We know that Wagner built his Festival Theatre especially *for the production of the* Ring. Thus from a technical viewpoint, the existence of this stage, designed for this specific music drama, leaves no doubt as to the Master's ideas about staging. But it is still possible that even there, where his will seemed to be law, the Master was obliged to make many significant compromises. It is therefore important to know what his theories were at a time when, at the height of his artistic maturity, he nonetheless found himself, because of particular conditions, furthest removed from any practical realization of his work whatsoever; and obviously it was also a time when his dedication as an artist had to be utterly free from the paralyzing influences of material reality.

Two of Wagner's most significant essays, "The Art-Work

1I exclude the arrangements peculiar to the auditorium and the orchestra in the Festival Theatre, for these are only indirectly related to the form of the production on stage.

of the Future" and "Opera and Drama,"[1] were written in this period. They are definitive and so closely related to his conception of the *Ring* that they are virtually part of it. These essays are too comprehensive to be considered here in full, but both are made more valuable by the existence of the drama with which they are so closely linked and for this reason are useful in clarifying the Master's aims. Through them we can supplement in theory the ideas to be observed in practice on the Bayreuth stage and can test their validity. Here, of course, I refer only to those portions of the works in which the exclusively *technical* application remains independent of those ideas of the future which are characteristic of Wagner's thinking.

In his "Art-Work of the Future," Wagner argues that the normal existence of the new drama can be imagined as the perfect flowering of a culture no longer tolerant of the portrayal of the human body in painting and sculpture. "If man does homage to the principle of beauty in his own full life, develops his own living body in beauty, and rejoices in the beauty that he thus reveals, surely the living, perfect, active body itself is the subject of and the artistic medium for the expression of this beauty and man's joy in it: His true work of art is the drama, and the redemption of plastic art is like the magic transformation of stone into the flesh and blood of man, of immobility into mobility, of the monumental into the temporal." (Collected Works, Vol. III, p. 106, 1st ed.) "The art of painting the human body cannot thrive where, without brush and canvas, the beauty of man presents itself in perfect form within the most alive of artistic settings." (III, p. 175) And the Master adds: "But landscape painting, the consummate and most perfectly definitive of all the fine arts, will become the real life-giving soul of architecture. It will thus teach us to construct the stage for the dramatic art-work of the future, in which this art itself, imbued with life, will picture the warm, living background of nature for the living man and not for his imitation." (III, p. 175) Still later in this essay, Wagner stresses the

---

[1] We know that the final conception of the *Ring* came after these two essays. Therefore, I do not intend to offer here a demonstration based on a kind of simultaneousness which would only be gainsaid by definite dates: I merely offer a proof of the intimate relationship that exists in the artist between the rational consciousness of his art and the execution of his work.

great advantage which the landscape artist will enjoy in his new relationship with the supreme work of art. "What the landscape painter, in his urge to communicate what he saw and conceived, has heretofore crowded into the narrow limits of the framed picture. . . . He will now use to fill the broader frame of the tragic stage, shaping the whole scenic space as evidence of his power to re-create nature. The illusions, which he could merely suggest with his brush and the most delicate mixture of colors, he will now bring to perfection through the artistic use of all available optical means and the artistic employment of light. The seeming crudity of his artistic tools and the apparent grotesqueness of his method of scene-painting will not offend him, for he will realize that even the finest brush is only a humble instrument in relation to the final work of art, and the artist can not feel proud until he is free; that is, until his work is complete and alive, and he and his instruments have become one with it. The work of art which he sees completed on the stage will give him infinitely greater satisfaction, in this frame and before the crowded audience, than his previous work, created with finer instruments. He will certainly not regret the use of the scenic space for his work instead of the plain piece of canvas. For at the worst, the artist's work remains the same in whatever frame it is seen, as long as it makes its subject intelligible; at any rate, in this new setting it will become more alive and universally comprehensible than it was in the framed painting of a landscape." (III, p. 182)

To consider painting and sculpture of the human body as fundamentally the same art is not an error in theory, but it is a serious technical error. The essence of painting is far more complex than Wagner understood it to be and, what is more important, far more subject to limitations than that of sculpture. The stage scene is not the equivalent of the particular life of painting as such, and is still less a redeeming transfiguration of it. The human body, *living in space,* has no normal relationship to color distributed on just any surface, and the mere presence of the body, independent of its environment, has nothing in common with the *object* of painting.[1]

---

[1] In the previous chapter, I have already gone into this subject, and for a more comprehensive treatment, I refer the reader to page 61.

When Wagner speaks of landscape painting as a "warm, living *background* for living man and not for his imitation," he seems to be assuming the impossibility of the union of man and background, and although his further conclusions may not be consistent with this attitude they are wholly logical in their particular application. Yet several times the Master suggests the possibility of such a union. For example: "In so far as it is within the mime's power, he will have to express visually man's inner life, his emotions and his longings. To capture man's stature and motions in three dimensions, the stage in all its breadth and depth belongs to him." (III, 184-185) Or again, "the landscape painter fills the stage with artistic truth: his design and color, his warm and vivid use of light compel nature to serve the highest artistic intention." (III, 181) In another place we find the two concepts of background and fusion combined: "If architecture and particularly scene painting can place the dramatic performer in a natural milieu and give him, from the inexhaustible well of natural appearance, a background that is always rich and meaningful, so the orchestra, this vital body of an infinitely diversified harmony, gives the individual performer as a foundation the inexhaustible source of nature's element, as it were, that is both human and artistic."

Here the idea of the modern orchestra appears: "The orchestra, in a sense, dissolves the rigidity and immobility of the stage setting into a kind of flowing and elastic impressionable ethereal surface." (III, 187) Yet Wagner apparently does not mean by this that there is a positive equivalence between the suppleness of the orchestra and that of the stage; he is only comparing the role of the orchestra with the incurable rigidity of the scenic material.

In "Opera and Drama," where the haunting atmosphere of the *Ring* is most poignantly felt, any concrete ideas about staging are virtually non-existent. Rather, his concern is with a recapitulation of historic questions related to opera, and with a minutely detailed development of theories regarding the new dramatic form, but only from the point of view of its direct relationship with the conception and composition of the musical-poetic text—scenic principles are simply ignored. The score, and particularly the actor's sung declamation, is naturally so involved with the presence of the performers on

· 111

stage that Wagner does frequently discuss this aspect of production, but still without bringing in any of the other elements. It seems as though Wagner felt that he lacked a scenic principle corresponding to his poetic-musical thesis, and that he gave those problems related to the scenic aspects of production as little stress as possible. The above quotations from the "Art-Work of the Future" reveal a far too characteristic lack of understanding of technical conditions to permit us to assert that the Master was aware of the disparity between his dramatic creation and his ideas for its presentation on the stage. This same deficiency may be observed when we consider the lack of balance between his external vision of *form* and his expressive power, a deficiency which we are compelled to ascribe to that peculiarly Germanic inadequacy in appreciating the visual aspects of art. The vast importance conferred by the Master upon the actor, and upon the actor *exclusively,* is a direct result of this imbalance; for it should be noted that such prominence does not belong to the hierarchic order. Wagner did not hold the actor to be the first and only equation between the scene and the inanimate elements of the setting; but when he had realized his conception by means of poetic-musical methods, and given the actor his role, instead of establishing the mutual relationships of the other elements of production by means of the *actor's role,* he simply returned to the intelligible content of the text in order to dictate the place of the action from it, without necessarily even considering the actor. Thus does he digress from the organic necessity of his work; and probably the arbitrary nature of the way in which his works were staged prevented him from making note of the methods used, or at least from publishing any ideas he may have had concerning them.

This disparity causes an inevitable conflict, for Wagner's creative power sometimes impelled him to express the oneness of his characters and their environment. Then the word-tone poet is torn between the all-powerful intensity of his genius and the inadequacy of his means of representation. What are customarily called Wagner's unreasonable demands regarding production of his works, the *tours de force* he demands of the designer, the technician, and even the actor, are merely the result of an expressive intensity out of proportion in principle and in fact to the means of scenic representation—a conflict inherent in *his basic conception of the drama*. Since the expression is much more intense than the means of visualizing that expression on the stage, the first always predominates, placing difficulties in the way of a unified production, which the existing methods of staging are incapable of overcoming.

We have established the fact that Wagner's theory and practice of production are fundamentally the same as those of our theatres. But since the incompatibility between the score and the production will of necessity influence the basic intention of the drama itself, the question remains to what extent the dramatist's sense of form will affect his power of expression. We cannot discuss Wagner's work until we see this problem more clearly.

Is a sense of form a contributing part of that governing intention which the word-tone poet seeks to realize in his score? By this we do not mean that picture of the action of his work which must occur to every dramatist, but rather a definitive materialization of this picture in space, in a space capable of furnishing an atmosphere appropriate to the action. There is no doubt that the dramatist who writes his play *for production, and for production* alone, will instinctively place it in a definite setting.[1] If the dramatist employs music, the demands of the time pattern, as well as of the dramatic action itself, subject him to an even more precise vision of scenic space than if he were to make use of the spoken word alone. Therefore, if he accepts a setting dictated by a convention alien to his work, he proves that he does not consider the music capable of prescribing the form of production. This amounts to his not knowing that music actually does just this. What are the consequences for the word-tone poet

---

[1] The inferiority of so many modern plays in which the author has sought perfect harmony of production within his creation itself may be imputed to the rudimentary craftsman has the ability to cut his vision to fit known methods of staging; the and conventional state of staging in our theatres. In such cases, the commonplace sensitive artist, on the other hand, prefers to detach his drama from this Procrustean procedure as far as possible, and thus becomes a "closet dramatist," not a man of the theatre—and the genius, alas, renounces both of these alternatives.

when such is his state of mind? First, he is compelled to make his score dependent, no matter how slightly, upon whatever scenic space is imposed upon him; second, when he is in the act of creation and therefore at the peak of his expressive powers, he will tend to forget that his idea is to be realized on a stage. As a result, he will waver between those pictures which his *relatively sensitive* imagination creates and those which are the result of his poetic-musical expression, pictures which move so swiftly that he cannot see them clearly.

It is this conflict that explains Wagner's attitude toward production. There is no doubt that he considered the conventional forms of staging satisfactory—in need of reform in practice only, not in principle. The fact that he set the *Ring* in the conventional manner at Bayreuth proves this. Obviously his sense of visual form was not appreciably developed beyond this convention, which did not offend his own vision. A highly developed sense of form dictates not only a choice of media, but mainly their proper use. In accepting the traditional means of staging and setting for his dramas, Wagner displayed a defect which explains why he failed to recognize the limitations of the decorative methods of our stage.

Indeed, the imagination of so great a genius lost its way on the road of scenic realism and demanded certain patterns in production which no art can accomplish without great sacrifices: painting and sculpture sacrifice movement; poetry appeals to the mind alone; scenic art is subject to the materially limited laws of expression and signification. It is evident that these patterns, impressed as they were in all their realism upon Wagner's vision, engendered great poetic-musical intensity. But the transposition of this intensity onto the stage must be invested either with a musical *expressiveness* having no correspondence with the realistic poetic intention which originally influenced the musician, or simply with the *signification* which is at variance with the musical life. Thus, either the poet suffers from being unable to evoke the incidental part of his vision; or, worse yet, the musician must sacrifice all visual expression in order to approximate the signification demanded by the poetry.[1] If, on the other hand,

---

[1] I have already mentioned this subject in Part I, page 23.

the conventional method of staging did not preclude the possibility of the music's being conveyed to the stage by means of the hierarchal principle, the work of art would be enhanced by allowing the rushing tide of musical expression, the true element of the word-tone dramatist, to sweep aside all regard for the stage setting. Since Wagner was unacquainted with the laws of the scenic hierarchy, he was tempted to overlook the demands of the stage whenever his drama became the expression of a deep inner emotion. Therefore, he was continually sacrificing the scenic life of those very passages which he considered the most important of his dramas. The alternate use of realistic motifs appropriate (in principle at least) to the modern stage and motifs of pure expression, not adaptable to that stage, seriously impairs the spectacle presented to our eyes and requires of the audience an act of reconstruction contrary to the aims of word-tone drama.

This is the most critical point in the staging of Wagner's dramas.[1] We see here how the disparity between a sense of form and the power of expression, in affecting the intention itself, can disturb the harmony of the poetic-musical factors and, through the visual representation on the stage, extend its discordant influence to the audience itself.

If it is to have unity, a work of art must be produced in a favorable social milieu. Indeed, its very existence depends upon such a milieu. As the painting of the Italian Renaissance clearly demonstrates, this dependence always implies a concession, more or less considerable, and more or less unconscious, to prevailing standards of taste.[2] The price of harmony is this incontestable decadence. We know that the Wagnerian drama owes its existence to the Master's increasingly uncompromising attitude toward contemporary culture.

[1] This dilemma is of no concern in today's theatres: incapable of opposing sign with expression, because scenic conventions destroy the nature of both signification and expression, today's stagecraft is satisfied to reduce all production motifs to one arbitrary level, thereby coming off quite cheaply by reason of failing to satisfy any one of the dramatist's demands.

[2] And in quite another sphere, certain specialized theatres in Paris.

His work had to be prodigiously intense; for it was not a sublime interpretation of contemporary thought, such as Raphael presented to his epoch, but rather a violent revolution, a revolution similar to those instigated by the speeches of a social or political reformer. There had to be a price, as there always is, for such great power; and the price Wagner paid for the triumphant reverberation of his magic throughout the world was harmony—harmony without which a less powerful creation could never have survived.

A harmonious work of art in our time must be the product of the artist's ego. Only the *intense personal desire* of the artist can overcome the deeply rooted hostility of our culture toward any artistic activity. This desire must be present if the artist is to realize his aims and if he is to have any positive influence on his audience. Had Richard Wagner's desire to overcome his society's hostile attitude to new kinds of art been equal to his unlimited poetic and musical powers, he might have discovered a form of production that adequately expressed his aims. But such was not the case. His work, even before he was fully conscious of his purpose, was a work of silent self-sacrifice; the crushing responsibility of his peculiar genius drove him day after day along a path which could mean only sorrow and destruction for himself as an artist. His wonderful, optimistic dreams sustained him for a long time. Elated by the mere *possibility* of their fulfillment, he found the strength to create those colossal works at which we now marvel. But he drew his materials from reality—that very reality which entails a thousand and one compromises for all who venture into it. Bayreuth is the symbol of this majestic dilemma, and if the idealism of such a symbol is of inestimable value to us, its material result permits us to feel deeply the great tragedy of the vision of such an artist as Richard Wagner.

So the poetic-musical expression of Wagner's dramas not only fails to correspond with current methods of production, but what seems far more important, it fails to meet his own formal requirements. The harmonious relationship between his sense of scenic form and his power of expression is consequently open to question. Is it not exceedingly audacious to make such a statement about one of the greatest geniuses who ever lived; and moreover, should we not have more respectful and complete confidence in the lofty wisdom of the dramatist?

Once such a significant error has been established in theory, it is very important that the error be adequately proved before going on with the discussion. Furthermore, such substantiation should not be arrived at in general or biographical terms, but must come from a consideration of the dramas themselves. This I am going to attempt to do.

The most impressive feature of the Wagnerian drama is its *idealism*. By this I mean that the visual elements of the production have the same relationship to the musical expression (and to the drama) as that which "allegory has in relationship to its literal content."[1] This does not mean that the music exists in one sphere and the drama in another, but rather, as Wagner himself explained it, "Where other arts say 'This means,' music says 'This is.' " The music, as it accompanies the phenomenon expresses, nevertheless, only the "inner essence." It is of an eternal nature, in contrast to the purely incidental character of any dramatic action. Thus, by its use of music the word-tone drama becomes a *necessarily idealistic* creation and the balance between the poetic-musical intensity and the intensity of the visual representation is not a question of absolute value but, as we have seen, one of expediency. The quality of the visual representation is not dependent upon any analogous quality in the poetic-musical text, but the text does dictate, according to the superior laws of the musical hierarchy, the nature of the production allowed by those laws. It should not be supposed that the idealism of the text implies that its realization on the stage is a random matter; nor does it imply that the mounting of the drama is based upon principles at variance with the text. Leaving aside the obligations of the hierarchic order with which we are already acquainted, in order wholly to apprehend this idealism, everything of a nonessential nature *with respect to the*

---

[1] H. S. Chamberlain, in *The Drama of Richard Wagner*, mentions this relationship; and I have already discussed this question from another point of view in Part I.

poetic-musical text must be eliminated from the staging from the very start, because the only nonessential idea to be preserved in producing the word-tone drama is the dramatic action itself. In this way we should at once be able to sense the eternal nature of this action as it is revealed by the music. Our aesthetic pleasure consists of being able to range between the two extremes of external appearance and inner reality. If the visual aspects of the production divert our attention, as so often happens when useless and alien elements are combined to achieve an effect not dictated by the text, our field of aesthetic activity is unfavorably enlarged, and we find it difficult to follow the central dramatic action, which is, after all, the most important consideration. Since the drama exists in time, the unfortunate result is that the eyes are trying to perceive the meaning of the action through the technical effects, while the music, the true means by which the action is revealed, is vainly resounding in our ears. We hear the music, we even listen to it, but because our attention has been diverted by the visual elements of the production, we think of the music only as something that supplements and enhances the production and are thus disturbed by the great disparity between the intensity of the music and that of the rest of the production.

The visual aspects are therefore of great importance in the word-tone drama, for the idealism which is the very soul of this kind of drama appears consistently only when it is in harmony with the production.

That Wagner was aware of the value of the visual elements (both scenic and mimetic) is evident in the arrangement of the Festival Theatre at Bayreuth. But strangely enough this otherwise purely idealistic genius did not have an idealistic visual sense. He unconsciously violated the principles of unity which governed his work. For example, he considered sight to be nothing more than a realistic function which the dramatist should approach only in natural terms, terms completely unrelated to the *ideal* expression of the music and the unique intensity which such expression implies.

It is quite possible that psychologically the intensity which Wagner has put into his scores could not have existed without a counter-balancing tendency towards realism in production. His deficiency in the creation of an outward form may thus be regarded as the antithesis of his prodigious inner power.

The fact remains that the transcendent idealism of Wagnerian drama, instead of suggesting to its creator an appropriate form of production, moved him towards a mode of production alien to the musical revelation, and one to which the contemporary principle of staging therefore presented no serious obstacles. If on the one hand, the Master had not given his blessing to existing scenic principles at the time when he built the Festival Theatre at Bayreuth; and, on the other hand, if he had not given proof in his writings, and probably in speeches, that methods of staging appropriate to his works were still in their infancy, we should have no justification for drawing these conclusions. Without such evidence we should have to confine ourselves to a consideration of the works themselves and run the risk of submitting them to inappropriate or arbitrary critical standards. Fortunately, the Master himself spared us this danger.

The situation, however, is so complex that it would be hopeless to attempt to present Wagner's dramas properly if we had not formulated a principle independent of the poet-musician.[1] But is this principle actually independent? Is the law of the hierarchy infallible and can we apply it in every case regardless of the dramatist's own ideas about production?

A priori, this seems to be so and in the first part of the essay we have adopted it without scruple. But now we are considering a work of art which actually exists and if our conclusions are to have any validity they must be applicable here as well. However, in order not to complicate our task and confuse our judgment with biographical considerations, we shall discuss only the dramas of Wagner's second period.

Every true artist will understand how difficult a scrutiny of this sort is, and the risk that is taken of casting an almost sacrilegious slur upon the work of art least adaptable to rational analysis. I should like to inspire sufficient confidence in the reader to have him follow me without aversion in this dangerous undertaking. Perhaps

---

[1]See page 26 of Part I.

the conclusions reached will exonerate me.

Tristan, Parsifal, the *Ring,* and *Die Meistersinger* are so utterly different from one another that it is possible, even before considering each one separately, to grasp the individual character of each.

In *Tristan* we find ourselves from the outset on the threshold of a totally subjective world; the first act is comparable to a last glimpse of the material and tangible world. In the second act the threshold is crossed and the door is closed. The mysterious atmosphere of this interior world can be conveyed to us only by the music, and Wagner himself says that here "only the music truly speaks." At the end of this act and during the following, however, the voice of the music is interrupted by the cold voice of rational reality. It is as if the world of the mortal and the arbitrary had intruded through invisible openings into this created realm of eternal and unique desire.

In *Parsifal* the action on the stage is composed of a succession of diverse situations which serve the sole purpose of dramatizing a miracle which is taking place within the soul of the pure and innocent hero. Through this miracle Parsifal achieves a knowledge of himself; his purity enables him to enlarge his knowledge of all life, and in this way the supreme brotherhood of the universe is revealed to him.

In the *Ring* the central action is not only more complex, but because it takes place within the soul of a god, it emanates from him and is multiplied in all his creatures. The episodes of the drama thus acquire great significance and require an extensive dramatic action for their realization.

In *Die Meistersinger* the imaginary world is only a pretext and does not actually constitute the drama. Here Wagner's aim was to portray the complete and lasting triumph of a noble personality over the seemingly fatal power of selfishness. His treatment of this theme is remarkable; he allows the seething world of petty personal interests to claim our attention and then imbues this world with a musical expression of incomparable intensity and brilliance without, however, transfiguring its external appearances. Finally, he justifies the paradox by transforming his hero, Hans Sachs, into a thinker and a poet, so that through a succession of infinitely skillful touches the intensity of the musical expression is attuned to the particular character of this poet. From the first to the last note of this drama, the conflict and the victory are stated simultaneously—the conflict by the material action in contrast to the pulsating power of the music which the action engenders, and the victory by the sole fact of this power. Naturally, I do not mean to imply that this contrast was entirely deliberate on Wagner's part. It is impossible to estimate how much conscious artistry went into the composition of a work of such genius, and we only wish to confirm what the work itself attests without considering the personality of the artist.

From this we may conclude that of these four dramas there are two, *Tristan* and *Die Meistersinger,* whose general visual form grows necessarily out of Wagner's dramatic intention, and in which only the detail may present some contradiction of that intention. Indeed, in *Die Meistersinger* the sequence of realistic events could not be interrupted without destroying the drama's essential harmony, and in *Tristan* it is only by reducing to a minimum all scenic activity in favor of the free expression of the inner drama that Wagner's basic intention can be fully expressed. On the other hand, Wagner's production ideas for the *Ring* and *Parsifal* offer a vast field for invention.

In the spoken drama the nature and sequence of the episodes have to occur in a rational world. The invention of the playwright is therefore subject to the realistic laws of cause and effect. The action of a drama inspired by music on the other hand is dictated by a time pattern which is not essentially controlled by the laws of causality and therefore requires a totally different approach to the problems of production, because the word-tone dramatist gains complete control of time, and is hence left to his own devices unless a definite form of presentation is implied in the dramatic conception itself (as was the case in *Tristan* and *Die Meistersinger*). If the word-tone dramatist fails to recognize from the very beginning that he controls the visual elements of production, he inevitably will come to depend on the already existing conventions. As a result he finds himself deprived of a powerful means of expression which nothing can replace, since the existing conventions, far from enriching his vision, actually tend to destroy it. Wagner found himself in such a predicament with *Parsifal* and the *Ring,* so that the influence of the contemporary principles of staging is more apparent in these two works than in *Tristan* and *Die Meistersinger.*

In *Parsifal* and the *Ring* the episodes of the plot do not correspond to the essential inner action, but whereas in *Die Meistersinger* the contrast between the external events and the inner meaning is central to Wagner's intention, in the *Ring* it is the complete development of this external life in itself which must be the cause of the conflict in the hero's soul, and converge with the inner life to form the denouement and the conclusion; hence the colossal dimensions of this drama.[1]

Parsifal did not require such a complex plot structure, for the transformation within the hero's soul is not brought about by a series of causes and effects, but results from the hero's vivid realization of universal suffering. The events which bring about the suffering are of only secondary importance to the inner action. Thus, the production problem in *Parsifal* differs from that in the *Ring* in that the duration and sequence of events are determined by the duration and sequence of the psychological development of the hero and not by the events themselves. Therefore, the ideality of the musical time pattern is far more independent in *Parsifal* than in the *Ring,* because the inner action, the object of the drama, is entirely within the domain of the music: its duration is by its nature limitless. Furthermore, the visual expression which must be evoked by this inner action is abso-

---

[1] If need be, one might imagine that if the complete development of the characters in *Die Meistersinger* had been central to the action of this drama, Wagner would have had to prolong its presentation over a period of several days; and, conversely, that if the conflict in Wotan's soul had come about merely through the contrast between the god's presence and the external life of the other characters, then the *Ring* would have been reduced to lesser proportions.

lutely indeterminate: Only through suffering can the hero's compassion be revealed, but there are innumerable kinds of suffering. Consequently the fable in *Parsifal* assumes a particularly arbitrary character. To avoid too great a disparity between the episodes of the plot and the high significance of the musical expression, it was necessary to set the production in an ideal atmosphere where the episodes could acquire a kind of universal significance and would be in harmony with the inner world which was revealed. This Wagner did, and it is well known with what artistry he seized upon a traditional form of suffering and by means of the music identified it with the suffering of his characters. Nevertheless, this defers but does not solve the problem of staging this drama.

The time patterns of the music in the *Ring* are extremely complex. The human life which determines the drama's general form and the sequence of its episodes is continually being disturbed by the mythological anthropomorphism of certain of the characters. The epic poem can easily encompass this kind of complexity; so can the spoken drama, although it is necessary to reduce its scope considerably. But the extreme facility with which the music can express it creates a problem for the word-tone dramatist which presently we shall see is entirely one of production.

The evolution taking place within the soul of Wotan is *expressed* by the episodes of the play as well as in the passages devoted especially to him. Wotan's personal existence and everything else in the drama are but two aspects of a single phenomenon. From a purely naturalistic point of view, the incidents are responsible for Wotan's developing awareness, but from the standpoint of the poetic intention of the drama the incidents themselves must be considered to be that development. Because he is a god, Wotan has the painful privilege of at the same time revealing and contemplating his own soul. How can the two aspects of this conflict be presented consecutively *with clarity?* How can the musical pattern be flexible enough to find a mean between complete and poetic independence and relative subordination to the realistic order of facts?

Thanks to Wagner's special genius, the episodes of the *Ring* are remarkably intense and well-defined. However, there are passages where the music is strictly subordinated to the realism of the plot, which deprives them of the free expression with which other passages can be invested. Is their intensity solely due to the power of genius or is it part of the dramatic action? A drama which is in a sense the objectification of the soul of a god obviously cannot be too rich, for his magnitude is revealed through his creations. On the other hand, the indispensable space dedicated to Wotan's personal existence remains completely undetermined. Nothing can dictate its dimensions nor its order; it is the domain of pure musical expression, and the more obvious this is, the clearer will be the realistic opposition and the ideal identity of the two faces of the drama.

Before these apparently contradictory conditions, Wagner found himself captured by the principle of the inflexible setting based on an impotent realistic convention. As we have seen, Wagner's vision could adjust to the realism of sequence and form; only the inflexibility of the setting was opposed to his conception. And yet he sought mobility through extreme realism. The notion that an *expressive* setting could achieve the mobility he was seeking seems never to have occurred to him.[1] For Wagner, everything that happened on the stage had a real existence.

All the scenes of the *Ring* are laid outdoors and nature in all its aspects is used throughout the play. Thus, the role Wagner assigned to the landscape painter in "The Art-Work of the Future" would theoretically have its richest opportunity for practical application in this drama. But Wagner was too much the artist to use a work of art merely to illustrate his theories. He would have been more likely to use his theories to explain the artist's irresistible but still little understood impulse to create. Although at different times he says that the painted drop is a background which the landscape artist provides for the actor, nevertheless, when it comes to the specific dramatic conception, only man and nature at grips with each other, the actor plunged *into* the scenic picture, can satisfy him. But natural phenomena are highly mobile and the human being in the

---

[1] *Parsifal* shows a definite tendency toward such idealism, but this is due more to the general nature of the story he chose than to a new conception of production on the part of the Master.

midst of natural phenomena partakes of this mobility. Then a harmonious relation is established between them. We know that in order to be united, actor and setting must sacrifice; the actor must yield some of his personal independence and the setting must dispense with a considerable portion of signification (multiplicity of specific detail). The setting will thus acquire an expressive character which will influence the dramatist's intention, for as soon as the word-tone poet can depend on the setting as a means of expression, he can permit his intention to develop freely. The opposition between expression and signification remains the only law restricting and guiding the creation of the score. A drama in which nature plays so large a part as in the *Ring* is therefore incompatible with the principle of production adopted by Wagner. But if the creative impulse is strong enough it will transgress all conventions, break through all barriers. This occurs in the *Ring*: Wagner ceased to adhere to those very conventions which he had endorsed; he wished to present on a traditional stage the phenomena of nature with an impracticable realism. In short, he believed he had achieved freedom in visual expression, but he was unaware of the secret of that freedom. This contradiction is inherent in the score of the drama and must be acknowledged if it is ever to be properly produced.

Only the above-mentioned intensity of the episodes, since it depends upon a sequence of realistic events, is affected by this contradiction; for it was only with respect to this intensity that Wagner failed to appreciate his inability to achieve complete freedom. The pure musical expression, on the other hand, exists in and dominates a boundless sphere which is the natural element for a creative power such as Richard Wagner's, and neither its conception nor composition could be affected by any extraneous consideration. Except in the purely episodic passages, the purely musical expression attains a power in the *Ring* which has never before been equalled in the history of the arts.[1] But since this sheer musical expression is

[1] By the *episodes* I mean the passages in which Wotan's creatures seem to act of their own volition, and by the *pure musical expression* those passages in which they are only the agents of a significance imposed upon them by the independent life of the god. Wotan, himself, touches the episode only lightly and his appearance almost always establishes the element of pure musical expression.

by nature alien to the intense realism which controls the intention of the rest of the drama, it disregards any possible scenic movement, and constitutes a series of rests within the form of the production as a whole. A *mise en scène* created on the expressive principle can permit all relationships; more, it can realize them progressively with perfect timeliness. When I speak of "rests" in the form of the production, I refer to a type of poetic-musical combination perfectly legitimate in itself, but to which the scenic principle utilized by Wagner cannot be adapted, which he did not realize, and which incontestably constitutes a violation of the integrity of the production.

Thus, we find in the *Ring* both realistic episodes which are almost impossible to present adequately on the stage and a completely independent poetic-musical expression which is in conflict with the form of production adopted for both.[1]

What is true of the score of the *Ring* applies to a certain extent to that of *Parsifal,* although in the latter the scenic requirements are far simpler. The music controls the whole poetic conception of *Parsifal,* so that the realistic elements in the plot must be kept to a minimum, in order that the divergence between the realistic elements and the great significance of the musical expression shall not become so great as to destroy their mutual relation. To avoid this Wagner has employed every device at his command. There is hardly a moment in the drama when the realism of the plot is not in some way tempered or idealized. As he makes Gurnemanz say, "Here, time becomes space." This eliminates the idea of a specific locale. And when the object of this paradox becomes some other locale, Wagner again evokes his characteristic magic to confuse time and space. The interrelationships of the characters are of an ideal nature, without material analogy to those set up by real life. Some of the characters are ageless, personifying in a vague and disturbing way the idea of the transmigration of souls. In much the same way, such elemental ideas as death, sleep, and physical pain assume straight off a transcendental significance. As in ancient drama, the law of cause

---

[1] If one wished on this basis to penetrate much further into Wagner's conception, one would infallibly lose one's footing. It is as artist, conscious of the strength of one's artistic convictions, that one must hence forth grapple with the technical problem.

and effect is almost entirely eliminated as a motivation for the action, with the obvious purpose of emphasizing the evolution within Parsifal's soul which is the direct effect of the action. As for the setting itself, Wagner has succeeded remarkably well in uniting it with his poetic idea. The setting unfolds and is several times transformed before our eyes; even the daylight seems to be subject to a divine or a diabolical principle which transcends physical law. But this almost ideal mobility remains, nevertheless, deeply realistic, in the sense that the characters take part in it consciously; they even cause these transformations, under the influence of ecstasy or of some supernatural inspiration.

Thus, the *Ring* and *Parsifal* are similar in scenic conception for, contrary to all appearances, their production is realistically conceived. They differ only in that in the *Ring* the scenic requirements are impossible of fulfillment, while in *Parsifal* they are achieved through the idealization of the setting, which here almost achieves an expressive form, without violating the intent of the artist. Indeed, the characters in *Parsifal* are, to some extent, an element of expression; and it is as such that they are presented. To achieve this effect, the poet has relieved them of all responsibility to reality, and as a result their participation in the drama is itself drawn into the realm of pure expression.

In this respect, as in all others, *Parsifal* may rightly be called a *Bühnenweihfestspiel* (holy festival of the theatre), for it consecrates the stage upon which it appears. Indeed, Wagner accomplished a miracle in his last work. He overcame the obstacle and problems of visual realization with weapons more powerful than any technical principle.

The four dramas we have discussed thus present four very distinct combinations. *Tristan* requires the absolute minimum of specific visual realization. The treatment of the **poetic-musical text** is in perfect accord with Wagner's idealistic dramatic intent, and the stage directions at the beginning of each act serve more to orient the reader of the poem than to set the stage. In this drama Wagner's scenic conception is powerless to interfere with the free development of the poetic-musical intent, and the production can be visually expressive without positively violating that intent. Thus harmony is established in the very origin of the drama, and oddly enough, independently of the author.

Nor could the conventional principles of production directly influence the conception of *Die Meistersinger,* since in this drama the essential action lies in the powerful opposition between the musical expression and the logical meaning of the episodes represented. Consequently, the realism of the characters is carried over into the setting without limiting the expressiveness of the locale chosen by the poet. Here, as in *Tristan,* although for other reasons, the poetic-musical intention is completely independent of any principle of production, and as a result it can achieve some degree of unity on the stage.

We have seen that the production of *Parsifal* constitutes the victory of an idea over the resistance of the technical method, so that if we were to make the *mise en scène* a true medium of expression, we should but complete the work already begun by Wagner himself.

Does this mean that these three dramas can serve as examples of the theoretical principles developed in the first part of this work? In a certain sense they can, for each in its own way is evidence of the strength of the musical urge from which the drama is born. They prove that this urge, fertilized by the poet's imagination, grows outward from within, into a form which is necessarily organic. But this proof is *negative,* for it merely indicates that when the dramatist's conception of the setting is incompatible with the character of the poetic-musical means which he uses, he can still be impelled by the force of the poetic-musical means, *but only in certain cases,* to free his score from the paralyzing influence of an inappropriate principle of production.

Wagner, however, never came under the highly *suggestive* influence which the full awareness of liberty in production would have provided. If he was able momentarily to break through the hard shell of scenic convention, it was due to the force of his genius and the nature of his poetic-musical means of expression. The *Ring* is sufficient proof of the instability of a freedom that is the result of a *technical* reform.

The score of the *Ring* has something in common with each of the other three dramas. The passages of pure music are, of course, similar to those in *Tristan*. *Götterdammerung,* in principle, is akin to *Die Meistersinger,* and throughout the *Ring* there are glimmers of an idealism that reminds one of *Parsifal*. Now, in so far as each one of these combinations can constitute by itself a harmonious whole, their successive presentation by means of a scenic convention incompatible with any one of them, which prevents the producer from treating each one individually, is unfavorable to a unified production. Furthermore, as we have seen, the main obstacle is the kind of realism which Wagner believed he could make independent of the scenic principle which he had adopted.

Thus, in the last analysis, the imperfections of the *Ring* are the result of a technical error in Wagner's conception of its production. This is the only one of the dramas of the second period which cannot be realized on the stage without resort to compromise. Although the marvelous brilliance of the score is lessened by a form of production that tends to reveal rather than conceal this error, at the same time this brilliance re-establishes in relation to the audience by its potent magic a harmony of which we could not conceive if we did not know its cause.

In the Appendix to this study, I shall present the general ideas on which the *mise en scène* of the *Ring* should be based. And a sketch of a project for the *mise en scène* of *Tristan* will demonstrate how the expressive principle can be applied to Wagner's concept.

Let us review briefly the ideas considered in this chapter. Wagner's scores are essentially and distinctively German creations; that is, they spring from a desire which does not have form as its object. But as dramas they must be presented on the stage. The artist will be able to conceive of the appropriate form of production only if his sense of visual form is in harmonious relation with that inner urge of which the score gives evidence. Wagner's attitude toward the staging of his dramas, the design of the stage at Bayreuth for the production of the *Ring,* and the theories expressed in those writings which are closely linked with this production, lead us to conclude that in Wagner such a relation was defective. Indeed, the resources of today's stage are incompatible with the use of music, and Wagner in adopting them was necessarily influenced by them. On the basis of the theories established in Part I, we have been able to investigate the complicated nature of this influence and its effect upon Wagner's last four dramas.

It now remains to be seen how the German artist can acquire that sense of form which Wagner lacked, how he can give to his work a form of presentation worthy of it, and in thus achieving the radiance of that marvelous treasure to which Richard Wagner's work bore witness, authoritatively extend his influence.

PART III

THE WORD-TONE DRAMA WITHOUT RICHARD WAGNER

The Ephemeral Existence of the Work of Art Based on Music

Music is essentially a *living* art. It is not a thing to be preserved in the dry annals of literature like plants in a herbarium, nor is it an abstract form of thought; rather, it is a living expression of the soul. Its irrefutable immortality, like that of all living organisms, consists in an ever renewed growth. By dying in its temporal form, it perpetuates itself. The dramas of Richard Wagner cannot escape the law of death and renewed life. Their existence, which is based on music, is ephemeral and their abstract transmission impossible. How can we assure their posterity—for, without a tradition, mere isolated productions of the word-tone drama could hardly satisfy us; and how can we prove ourselves worthy of having been contemporaries of such masterpieces?

We must first acknowledge the undeniable fact that the present existence of these dramas is the only existence they will ever have. Their fate may change for better or for worse, but cannot be radically altered. These dramas will not live: *they are alive now*. And the reason for these conditions must be sought in the works themselves.

A great work of literature can, in the course of time, assume various kinds of existence, for it lives subjectively in the mind of man. As time passes it may take on a kind of historical interest, but the truth it portrays transcends time and its documentary value is at best incidental.

On the other hand, a work of art born of a longing for musical expression has a relatively limited existence, for music is so inextricably linked with the period of its creation that it lives

· 131

only in that period. We have observed that the essential elements of form used in Wagner's drama are organically united, and that their presentation as a unified whole on the stage is subject to a mathematical necessity emanating from the origin of the work itself. If such a unified presentation is possible, if it finds in the years allotted to it favorable conditions, this will be proof that it is no internal defect that has prevented it from shining; the work as it develops normally will be able to perpetuate itself in a direct line. But if our time is incapable of such an *integral* production, indeed, if it is alien to it, and if this situation persists over many years, then we must also acknowledge some flaw in the work itself. I repeat, a work of art based on music cannot hope to achieve immortality and can rely for its existence solely upon its transient qualities. It is imperative, therefore, to find out what that flaw is, to determine something about the imperfection of the relationship between that work and its environment, and through this knowledge, to attempt to establish normal relationships which will assure, *this time by an indirect line,* a genesis for the work of art.

We have already shown that the Wagnerian drama was not developed in accordance with those principles of word-tone drama which we established at the beginning of this study. Then Wagner's attitude toward the realization of his works on the stage and certain passages from his theoretical writings on the theatre support the conclusions of the preceding chapter: that there were qualities within the dramas themselves which made a unified production of them impossible; and that on the other hand his drama had no relationship whatever to the dominant attitudes and beliefs of his time. If we are to establish what conditions are necessary for subsequent works of this kind to flourish, we must discover the cause of that lack of relationship and learn to what extent this failure resides in the structure of the dramas themselves. Then we shall know why the works of Wagner cannot perpetuate themselves in a direct line, and we can determine what the essential difference should be between his work and all subsequent word-tone drama.

Until now, we have not discussed this problematic future of the word-tone drama, because, in examining the Master's dramas,

132 ·

we were concerned only with the technical flaw which marred them; and Part I of this study, being of a completely speculative nature, did not take into consideration the possibilities for the continuing existence of the work itself. We shall deal with these in the present chapter.

The Modern Intensity of Musical Expression

In one of his essays Wagner writes that the unusual development of modern music indicates one of the basic needs of his time: the long-felt desire for greater expressiveness, as it approached the drama through Beethoven, became a need for revelation. Thus, the intensity of musical expression as well as the *object* of that expression had become a matter of great importance by the time Wagner began composing.

Wagner's dramatic work proves the all-powerful expressiveness of music in revealing to us the *object* of the expression; this is the mission of his drama, and we know how triumphantly he fulfilled it because of his ability to drive his already prodigious powers to the point where they could overcome all obstacles.

But the important question is whether this immeasurable longing for expression which modern music seeks to satisfy and the extraordinary intensity of expression which it had to acquire to convince us of its object are the result of an innate disposition in this means of expression, or, are they, as seems more likely, evidences of a thoroughly decadent culture? When so much must be expended to satisfy us, is it not because our palates are so burned by alcohol that we can taste only the most highly spiced foods? There is no doubt that Wagner has stirred our sated souls. He has forced us to hear and to understand his voice. But at what price? . . .

Like all messiahs he has come bringing "not peace but a sword"; for every revelation is in itself a judgment on the condition which has made it necessary. Wagner is an implacable judge. In his creations we atone for the mean lies of our expediency. "Here is what was needed to convince you," the Master seems to say. "What are you to do now that an all-consuming desire is infused in your veins?"

What, in truth, are we to do? This is why I entitled this last chapter: "The Word-Tone Drama *Without* Richard Wagner."

Relationship Between Wagner's Dramatic Works and His Environment

Volumes would be required to explain even briefly the source of this longing for expression which modern music is attempting to satisfy and the obstacles set up against its fulfillment, which have evoked the mighty power of a Richard Wagner. Such a book has never been written, but implicit in the writings of Wagner, Nietzsche, H. S. Chamberlain, and others is, I think, the idea that the intensity of modern musical expression, and particularly Wagnerian intensity, is not a fundamental necessity to this medium of expression. Our corrupt civilization has made it indispensable; Wagner used it as a formidable weapon and with it he was able to achieve his aims, but to continue to wield it would be like striking at empty air, or like repeating familiar words, as children do, with no regard for their meaning.

Just as Wagner's drama is the culmination of century-long attempts to develop the arts of music and poetry, so the music, from which is was created and whose increased expressiveness made this drama possible, is the culmination of a century of development in expression.

The future of music, *of music as Wagner shaped it to his own purpose,* is indeed a delusion. It has reached its peak; its development has ended.

This would not be so if Wagner's creations represented only one step in a glorious ascent, but his genius urged him up all the steps which had separated Beethoven from the dimly seen heights. Wagner's accomplishment is the sum of an unbelievable number of experiments. He was strong enough and his life long enough for the fulfillment of his mission only because he never deviated from his purpose. He must therefore be regarded not only as the one artist who reached the summit, but also as the one in whom all the creative energy of the century was concentrated. In this sense he is a Nietzschean *Kulturgewalt* who achieved his end by using every means within his power to the limit of its effectiveness, and in that way caused a revolution which laid the foundation for a new order of effort and development. Such strength knows none of the hesitancy of those who follow the beaten path; its one concern is to find a weapon strong enough for the victory. Wagner found such a weapon in modern music and used it unflinchingly. In so doing he armed himself with all that his day could provide toward any evolution. For music and what it expresses is the supreme defiance hurled against the forces of materialism and utilitarianism in our century, but to push it to its furthest limits is to exhaust with one stroke our present-day resources. All whose spirits have been moved by the Master recognize in him an incomparable dynamism. The more stifling the environment the stronger the inner power. Wagner chose his weapons well; or rather, he himself was the most effective weapon to resist the enemy and conquer it.

One can conceive what a strange figure the man cuts who unnecessarily attempts to raise the same weapon: he mistakes the means for the end, the sword for the victory.

To be sure, his mistake is completely understandable, for after all, Wagner's weapon happens to be a work of art, and, as such, a constant source of delight to the observer and an inspiration to the creator. In addition to his dramas, Wagner has also written several provocative theoretical essays. It is no wonder then, since the fire of his genius prevented him from ever clearly evaluating the situation that brought about his dramatic work, that he necessarily had to believe in the possibility of a survival of his methods, and that he confused the all-consuming intensity of his evocative power with the work of art "in which there will always be something to invent." (Wagner)

In one sense he was not mistaken: these methods will remain essentially the same. Wagner discovered them, but no one will ever again use them as he did. Although it is not inconceivable that at some time another genius of his stature might appear, the impetus provided by the adverse conditions of his particular environment will never again exist.

As a result, there is a real contradiction between the quality of Wagner's works as art, and the nature of their permanent revelation. Every work of genius implies such a conflict to some degree; in Wagner it emerged so sharply because the form which he adopted forces the music to carry the whole burden. The great intensity of the music corresponding to our present needs could not fail to convince us. Without the intensity of music, we would have remained deaf, but with it the work of art is marred.

Thus there was a close relationship between Wagner's dramatic works and the time of their creation. It is evident from a sociological point of view that we are at fault, but from an exclusively artistic point of view, the fault lies in the drama itself. This is why a unified production of Wagner's works is impossible. The life of these works is a militant one, but if the time should ever come when conditions are more favorable for the production of word-tone drama, the years of Wagner's dramas will be over.

A work of art which is most controversial when it first appears can gradually shake off its revolutionary aspects; if it still has sufficient value to survive its own times, its existence is transformed, refined, and sometimes we marvel how superior this condition is to the preceding one, even though the work's intrinsic worth had been there from the start, and how it was ignored by its contemporaries. But, as we have already pointed out, this prolonged existence, which remains *subjective* for the signs drawn from the intellect, cannot be so for the work of living art. As Wagner's dramas become further and further removed from their own time, they will eventually cease to exist. To prevent this loss we must strive to refine them, to give them new life by reconciling them with their environment. Thus will we approach the harmony which must govern this form of drama, and any revolutionary changes will have fruitful consequences, whose influence it is as yet impossible to measure.

How To Release Musical Expression From Modern Intensity

It may be objected that our appetite for musical intensity has not been appeased by Wagner's work, but, on the contrary, has been increased. Why then renounce his work in favor of a work of art seemingly founded on the same principle? First, if there is indeed a renunciation, *for us* it is quite a relative thing, since Wagner's music will be a powerful influence for many years to come; and as for those who are now surfeited with it, the inevitable period of imitation will in a short time give them ample food.

Nevertheless, the objection is not inconsequential. Can the word-tone drama really be effective without the Wagnerian intensity? On the other hand, how can we dispense with this intensity since modern culture gives no indication of tempering our desire for expression? These two questions resolve themselves into one, which to answer is to lay the foundations for the "Word-Tone Drama Without Richard Wagner," and this I shall strive to do.

The realistic way in which Wagner conceived of the visual aspects of production — a result of his lack of a sense of form — was not incompatible with contemporary principles of production, but his poetic-musical intention and achievement were irreconcilable with these principles. The result of this conflict was an intensity and complexity in the musical expression which paralyzes the effect of the visual elements of production and *makes their harmonious interplay impossible.* The visual aspects of production which are also a powerful source of expression can be effective only when they are in accord with the music. They cannot function fully in the production of a Wagnerian drama; in that drama they do not constitute, in the strict sense of the term, a means of expression. We must also remember that not only is the expressiveness of the production diminished by the intensity of the music, but the music runs the same risk if the production lacks unity. There must be reciprocity, each in its own realm, and each with its peculiar requirements.

The synthesis required of the spectator if he is to enjoy the production as a whole becomes extremely difficult, if not impossible, in Wagnerian drama. The state of mind necessary for the enjoyment and comprehension of the poetic-musical text is incompatible with the realism of the staging. If the discrepancy between the two sensations is too great, the conflict too positive, the eye will always be the

· 137

first to surrender; it will simply *record* the spectacle in order that the spirit may be released to enjoy the absorbing and overwhelming elements of the score. Undeniably this is what usually happens; in the case of spectators of sensitive and cultivated taste it has become such a common occurrence that it is known as "Wagnerian hypnosis," or, when other influences enter in, "Bayreuth hypnosis," doubtless an inaccurate term, but not without analogy to the spiritual state it is intended to designate.

However, the soul, thus released from the visual demands of production, still has a need for expression which can be satisfied by nothing less than the full resources of a Richard Wagner. Wherever the dramatist must rely on the staging to supplement the vibration created by the score, he encounters the spectator's visual inertia, a state for which he himself is responsible. In these passages where the dramatist fails to make such use of the staging, the music loses much of its effectiveness because it needs the active co-operation of the eye, and the spectator is not prepared for this. A painful sense of insufficiency ensues, and the listener longingly waits for the music to envelop him anew. This awakened and sustained desire eventually becomes an aesthetic perversion with which we are all more or less familiar.[1]

Far from allaying the modern appetite, the Wagnerian dramas, so far as form is concerned, strain and confuse our already wavering powers of concentration. Such an assertion may seem arbitrary to anyone who can enter into the action of those dramas (I use *action* in the Wagnerian sense), and for whom that action is naturally inseparable from the poetic-musical means which reveal it. What do score and production mean to him who is filled with such inexpressible joy that (as Chamberlain says) it seems at times as though the Master himself must materialize before him? Such a state of exaltation temporarily destroys all our critical powers; it forever enriches him who is privileged to experience it.

Without lingering on the objection, however legitimate, that there are very few individuals capable of reaching and maintaining

---

[1] Naturally, the dilettantes rather than the artist bear sad witness to this when they render Wagner on the piano.

such a heightened state of awareness, it should be noted that we are not here questioning the depth and beauty of Wagner's works. To discuss them would be vain, to challenge them a sign of madness. Wagner's great revelation lay precisely in what I call the "action" of his dramas, not in the means he employed to communicate it to us. That action is the generative principle of his work, which will perpetuate itself and whose continued life is assured. To perceive it fully is to know Wagner's genius not only in the letter, but in the spirit; beside it the means of representation are secondary. We have accepted the existence of this inner life in Wagnerian drama as an incontestable fact. We are now concerned only with finding a way of evolution which will assure its continued existence.

However, if the inner action of the Wagnerian drama is unquestionably related to the methods used by the Master to reveal it, it is no less certain that these methods cannot be handed down and employed again. We must, therefore, either admit the impossibility of the word-tone drama's survival or consider the Wagnerian method as one which may be modified without destroying that inner action which is both its content and its aim. But how can the permanence of such a revelation as Wagner's be doubted? Music alone provides the answer; any attempt to transfer the Wagnerian idea into a work which is not based on music is a contradiction of that very idea. There is, then, no alternative: we must succeed in finding a visible form for the inner life which can be given a unified existence in time, the only existence possible to music.

However that may be, we regard the Wagnerian intensity as the *sine qua non* of the inner *action* of his dramas — that is, of the word-tone drama — and it is difficult to conceive this inner action as existing under any other poetic-musical conditions.

Since Wagner was deprived of truly expressive means of production, both for the audience and for his own art, he was forced to strengthen the intensity of what means he did possess. Furthermore, since Wagner could conceive of production only in realistic terms he was constantly threatened with seeing these tokens of realism reduced to nothingness by the dramatic intensity of the inner action. As a result, he was obliged at times to use all known natural phenomena, and sometimes even to combine them in a supernatural guise, not only to compensate for the poverty of the production, but to make it even partially expressive of his poetic intention. Nevertheless, he was always handicapped by the fact that the visual element of production in his dramas had the *same* reality for the actor as for the spectator: it was *essentially* realistic. As a result, the actor, the interpreter of the poetic text and the principal means whereby the inner action is embodied, could never attain for himself that independence which characterizes the inner action.

Wagner knew that he could make his intent clear only by the total domination of the spectator. But since he could find no way for the visual aspects of production to have this effect on the eyes of the audience, since he did not even realize that such an effect was possible, he relied solely upon the power of his music to control the spectator. Thus the inner *action* was not affected, since it was born of the music, but the manner in which this action was presented bore the marks of the violence resulting from the use of realistic principles of staging. Hidden in the poetic-musical text, the inner action is subject to commentary and diverse interpretations; for although we feel definitely that Wagner has uttered all his thoughts, holding back nothing proper to the work of art, we are nevertheless aware how enigmatic is his language and what *an exaggerated role the intensity of the music has played in our enthusiasm.*

For the Master, such considerations did not exist. He has said that the true artist stands before his finished work as before a mystery, but he refers only to the mystery of the unconscious beauty of a work created in perfect consciousness and the artist's unawareness of the effect of his work upon others. If Wagner ever had the slightest doubt about the effectiveness of his method, it could only have been the result of a vague awareness of the inherent disproportion of his work; and in his case, this seems highly unlikely.

Since the *inner drama* can be communicated only through the score, it appeals only to those who can understand its language; *but without the assistance of the other elements of production this language becomes more and more difficult to comprehend.*

Almost everyone is instinctively moved by the emotional

power of the poetic text and the realism of the production, but few can really enjoy a Wagnerian work as a unified whole. And the highly developed sense of form possessed by this minority demands a kind of unity that Wagner was unable to achieve. They are not always able to bear the temporary dislocation of their receptive system, and as a result, despite great efforts, they find little pleasure in the production as a whole. We must conclude, therefore, that the essential part of the *action* which Wagner sought to dramatize is not totally dependent upon the intensity of his music. To consider the two as inseparable is only to confuse, without surrendering, the accidental form of the drama in production with its psychological and aesthetic reality.

It now remains for us to discover how to dispense with the Wagnerian intensity. First of all, a clear distinction must be made between the simple desire for expression for its own sake and the desire to satisfy the demands of modern musical taste — out of which Wagner fashioned his most powerful weapon.

As we have said, music with Beethoven, in drawing near to drama, clarified our desire; no longer were we concerned only with the expression, but with its object as well. In possession of the object, our desires have necessarily evolved, and although expression remains our sole safeguard against being overrun by the representational principle, henceforth it must always be applied to a known object. This powerful craving became with and through Wagner a conscious need. Critical analysis of Wagner's dramas from this point of view (and this alone), is indispensable, for only through such analysis will we be able to separate the drama's inner action from its outer form, to possess it independently. Thus we acquire the right to order freely the form in keeping with our needs, the form best adapted to the brief period of its existence. Expression, become the subject of rational analysis and, consequently, its value no longer absolute, will submit to the requirements of balance, which will no longer allow it excess.

More avid for expression than ever, our ardor has been tempered — I might say almost Hellenized — and *harmony of expression* will evermore be our goal.

This desire for harmony is noticeable in all contemporary

art and accounts for the laborious and groping quality of all modern works. The lyric poet, in the way he chooses and combines words, seeks to suggest music; the playwright refines the action and the settings of his play in such a way as to give an impression of vagueness with the same purpose; the painter, in an attempt to achieve an expressive quality similar to that of music, makes use of all the virtuosity his brush will yield to strip his work of all that is not essential to the expression of his idea; contrary to the painter, the sculptor, unfortunately less well received than the painter in our cultural climate, attempts with all the special resources of his art to draw from it the complex of planes and perspective characteristic of modern polyphony.

Those who are opposed to this aim of musical expressiveness move violently to the other extreme, producing works of a purely realistic nature. This reaction, however, is eloquent testimony to the fact that the desire for greater expressiveness is an undeniable influence in our time. It is impossible to remain neutral; *we either desire music or we do not*. Whichever stand we take, a *unified* work of art is our goal. One side attempts to achieve it by sacrificing every effect which cannot be integrated with a feeling akin to music, and the other by excluding music entirely and depending with a childlike faith on the conventions of realism.

And the musicians? No doubt most of them stand in the midst of the battle. Despite their understandable ardor, their existence as individual artists hangs by a thread, for the weapon they carry is highly dangerous and few of them know how to use it. A single false move and it will turn against them. Some proceed cautiously, and in so doing sacrifice that spontaneity without which any artistic conception is stillborn. These are the modern mathematicians of music, who, however, do not have Bach's reason for composing marvelous counterpoint. Others strike out frantically to the right and left, only to fall bathed in blood and honor, with no ground gained. The wiser withdraw into their own souls, where they build and fittingly adorn magnificent palaces. Obviously theirs is the best course, since it is in the culture of the individual spirit and not in the pool of an already shared heritage that ideas germinate and grow.

But this last kind of artist eventually allows his longing for greater expressiveness to become a debilitating vice, the cravings of which he satisfies by a means which, being incompatible with the life of the community, can never produce a work of art. For music can no more be made light of than can the holy blood of life. And today less than ever can the struggle for greater expressiveness be renounced with impunity for a return to a primitive instinct.

There is still another kind of musician who is keenly aware of the true *aim* of music but cannot formulate a feasible abstract idea which can be divorced from the Wagnerian intensity. Thus he wavers in distress between the impossibility of achieving the Wagnerian intensity by mere technical means and his urgent need for expression which, under such conditions, cannot but elude him. Poets despair of their lack of musical power, for like musicians, they believe that the object of their yearning is inseparable from the Wagnerian method. If the impossible is achieved and the poet and musician collaborate, they are denied the most elementary conditions for materializing their idea on the stage. For without knowing it, their mutual need for harmony has drawn them to each other. While they work together, nothing intervenes to spoil their feeling of satisfaction, but when their work is produced on the stage, the harmony suddenly becomes a chimera.

The position of the word-tone dramatist, or more accurately, the musical dramatist, for today this is what he has become, is no better. If his taste is highly developed and he is sincere in his purpose, his primary concern will be to temper the fire of his longing for musical expression in harmony with his more moderate poetic intention. He knows that if his music is to be accepted he must in some way reproduce the Wagnerian method, and he feels that this method is the only one which will satisfy him. Technically he can emulate the Master, but he has no illusions about the true value of his work. He knows only too well that the force underlying and justifying the Wagnerian storm of intensity is not his. He racks his imagination for a likely theme; out of his tormented longing he invents pictures which only increase his despair, and in the end he is forced to admit that, like all writers of drama — although on a higher level — he is

· 143

simply seeking a pretext to compose music. How heavy the score of *Die Meistersinger* must lie upon his heart! Weary of the struggle, he abandons drama and turns to the unhindered creation of music, with or without a text. The only solace for the emptiness in his own soul is that he finds evidence in the work of the painters that they are as distraught as he.

Ours is a period in the world's history in which we find the strange spectacle of musicians wanting to be painters, and painters consumed with the desire to write music. Each shows less and less interest in the art form whose technique he has mastered, without, however, quite daring to renounce it. There are many artists whose conversation and bearing indicate a high degree of culture, but who are nevertheless obviously ill at ease looking at a finely painted picture or listening to a piece of modern music of great beauty. Literature becomes more and more a desirable palliative; it at least neither burns nor wounds. It permits our craving for music to be realized in an enchanting vision, without troubling it with impossible embodiment in space, and leaves the mind's eye completely free to evoke "musical" marvels.

But what will happen to the theatre in the hands of such eccentric artists? At first it will go on, through the sheer force of inertia, to follow the beaten path it has known for so long, but beside that stagnant existence, another life will be awakened, restless, seeking, infinitely complex, in which the two extremes will express themselves less clearly than in the other arts.

Realism, the principle which excludes music as a means of expression in the theatre, collides head on with the scenic realization, that is, with the *mise en scène* in the broadest meaning of that term. The opposite principle of idealism, which requires a suggestive character in the *mise en scène* to express visibly the inner action, fares no better than the realistic one, for the contemporary method of staging and design is a hybrid, incapable of serving either style adequately. Jealous of their own integrity, both the realistic and the idealistic strive to avoid all contact with the visual aspects of production, considering them only as a necessary evil. Under the guise of psychological truth, the realistic playwright selects his themes and characters and places them against a more or less random background; or else he limits the visual aspects of production to the few patterns within the range of realistic scenic illusion and blends the actors with this environment. Idealism, product of the desire for music, does not include in its design the *mise en scène* and considers the visual aspects of production as decidedly inferior, or else it is forced, in spite of everything, to give them a semblance of expression, bolstering them with such factitious devices as melodramatic music, living pictures, pantomime, etc.; all attempts at absolute realism or at absolute idealism are bound to fail in so far as they are made by means whose union rests upon an arbitrary convention.

Once the nature of this arbitrary convention is discovered by analysis and vanquished, we shall see whether the pretensions of realism are compatible with the idea of any theatrical production whatever. We may well doubt such a possibility.

As for the idealistic method, it will have to undergo an apprenticeship, for the freedom it will gain by a revolution in staging and the revelation of its limitless powers will necessitate the strictest of disciplines. Such a discipline will have to be based on some principle. What standard can we find for the fluctuating proportions of the various elements of production?

A Governing Principle for the Dramatic Conception

Awareness of the *need for harmony* should be the sole arbitrator in this important but difficult matter, and since we are concerned here only with questions of proportion, a governing principle can be established on the basis of harmony. This principle must apply not only to the *mise en scène* as it does in the hierarchy of production, but to the dramatic intention as well. The recognition of the need for harmony, impossible before the creation of Wagner's dramas, and first revealed by them, has also forced us to recognize the fact that this need cannot be fully satisfied by Wagner's marvelous master works. We found the reason for this failure in the intensity of the musical expression necessary to induce our belief. This is, in fact, an admission that we ourselves are directly responsible for the lack of harmony in the Wagnerian drama; and no doubt that is why we have been able to detect it.

Because such intensity makes harmony between the elements of production and the poetic-musical text impossible, that intensity must be sacrificed to the degree in which harmony is to be achieved. In Part I we have already spoken of the *production notation* — of the need to add to the score, by means of conventional signs, specifications for the entire physical production, and particularly for the acting. If it is impossible to establish a true harmony without the use of such notation, obviously the adoption of this system will impose limits on the musical expression. It might then be feared that since music is the soul of the drama any limitation of its intensity would tend to limit its range and depth. Would not the work as a whole in consequence be, if not actually destroyed, at best appreciably weakened?

Such a concern indicates a misconception of the artistic center of gravity, which is not in the work of art, *but in us*. Were it not so, Wagner's work could never have been created, for it was we who had to furnish the necessary counterbalance which his work was forced to disregard.

Our problem, then, is to incorporate this counterbalance into the drama itself, and the very existence of this problem confirms our conclusion that the artistic center of gravity is in our soul, since only we can determine what the proper degree of equilibrium should be.

Visual expression will not offer a simple compensation for the sacrifice of musical intensity, but it will replace it positively by giving to the poetic-musical text a *new* resonance. Yet, it is a mistake to speak of compensation at all, for the relationship of all the elements in the word-tone drama is of such an organic nature that one element of production can never compensate for the sacrifice of another. Theirs is *one* life which flows through the whole organism. Thus, to increase the expressiveness of one weak element so that it is in harmony with the others is to enhance the vitality of the work as a whole.

It remains to determine the influence which the *mise en scène*

146 ·

as means of expression will have on the other elements, and thus to regulate their mutual interplay. The hard-won freedom from restricting conventions will still be subject to the conditions imposed by the environment given to the fleeting existence of the work of living art; and the question of proper environment — which for the German is synonymous with visual art — by becoming cosmopolitan will extend its scope to the relation of the work of art to the precise period of its existence in time.

This brings us again to the question of nationality (or, if one prefers, of race)[1] which has so much bearing on the future of the word-tone drama that it is important to clarify it as much as possible before going any further. The so-called *Latin* and *Germanic* cultures stand in such sharp contrast to each other that we may limit our observations to these two; furthermore, because of their strong influence in the theatre, we shall consider the French, and especially the *Parisian,* as typical embodiments of those characteristics fundamental to Latin culture. For the sake of clarity we must omit a consideration of anything that is not typical of the two cultures, and so doing, draw a line of demarcation between them which does not actually exist.

Latins and Germans

H. S. Chamberlain was the first to apply the term "German drama" to the dramatic form originated by Wagner. If one wishes to apply the term only to the dramas of the Master, "German drama" becomes "Wagnerian drama," for with Wagner a century of development reached its goal. In this sense, historically, Wagnerian drama will constitute more an *epoch* than a work of art, for all future experiments in this form will evolve from his ideas. The result will be a new stage in German cultural growth, a stage that will be marked by the normal development of a sense of exterior form, the visual art, and this new sense of form must take a quite different way from that of a Latin race.

Latin culture is derived from a sense of form. It is by means

---

[1] It goes without saying that I attach not the slightest political notion to the word "nationality."

of external form that the Latin artist discovers the inner driving power of his work; and it is only through form that the Wagnerian drama was made intelligible to him. However, since Wagner's form was extremely defective as a harmonious whole, according to Latin standards, the Latin was compelled to delve deeper into the source of that irresistible allure which Wagnerian drama nevertheless had for him. In this roundabout way he succeeded in grasping the Wagnerian idea. Possession of that idea in itself constituted a very important evolution in Latin culture. The comprehension of the idea, stripped of the nonessential processes of its manifestation, acts as a far more powerful stimulus than when the processes themselves exert their overpowering influence, as they do for the Germans.

The close bond in which Wagner has linked language and music not only makes any translation of his drama impossible but also has created a music that is *German,* in the fullest sense of the word. Wagner says, "The indispensable basis of perfect artistic expression is speech . . ." and ". . . the vital point of dramatic action is the verse-melody of the performer." Since the discovery of this principle enabled him to master the poetical-musical element, Wagner had to make his music conform to patterns suitable to the German language. Music had hitherto been considered a universal art, independent of language or nationality. In divesting it of this uniqueness, and thereby making it serve a higher aim, Wagner imposed on it the restrictions of the particular language of the word-tone dramatist. This fact, disturbing to the artist, is still not generally understood, and will no doubt be one of the last of the Wagnerian principles to be recognized.

The close union between poetry and music in the Wagnerian dramas we understand, but despite this, the general scope of the musical expression seems to imply a completely independent source. In *Tristan,* for instance, we understand that what Wagner calls the "verse-melody of the performer" determines the motifs of the musical-dramatic pattern; and yet caught in the atavism of our musical sensations, we are unable to separate the general significance of those motifs (in terms of musical sounds) from their accidental form determined by the author's language. Obviously the whole musical composition, since it is made up of these individual motifs, is dependent upon the language which has engendered them.

This statement should not be taken literally, since we all know that there are numerous motifs and developments in a Wagnerian score which are not prescribed by the written text. But since the almost miraculous unity of speech rhythm and musical pattern stems from the fact that Wagner's words and music flowed from the same source, and since music, by its nature, is indefinite, the musical conception is suffused with the peculiarly dynamic quality of the German language.

Consequently, Wagner's methods have only a relative value for the dramatist who does not know the German language. To apply them, as is done today, to no matter what language, proves to what extent our aggravated desire for music can blunt our sense of the most elementary appropriateness.

No matter what his theories or experiments may be, it is clear that the Latin artist can never use the Wagnerian method as a means of realizing the Wagnerian idea. But it is equally clear that this idea will be assimilated gradually to that concern for form so characteristic of Latin culture. Thus, in its own way and without violence, it will gradually form a tribunal by which virtuosity will have to be judged. Its influence will be felt first in those arts in which language plays no essential part; thence it will spread irresistibly into the language itself bringing about unforeseeable transformations.

This is true cosmopolitanism — a cosmopolitanism which is not communicated by a telegram and which cannot be restrained by the uniform lies of the press.

But what is to become of music while this slow evolution of the Latin sense of language and the German sense of form is taking place? This situation is incontestably highly critical and since it depends strictly on what happens to it in the realm of the German drama, we shall for the moment consider only German music.

The artist who speaks the tongue of Richard Wagner is indeed fortunate. If he is a musician, he can develop his own thoughts almost unconsciously through the Master's method, without violating his own integrity. In this way, although he will not be original, he is certain to achieve harmony. He speaks in the "Wagnerian" tongue and unconsciously begins to think in the same way — that is, to give to his thinking an intensity of *form* which is not its own. This is extremely dangerous, for he must have an almost excessive respect for others as well as for himself not to replace his own thinking with the technical development of the Wagnerian thinking. Such imitations are neither stimulating nor productive. The chief value of any idea is that it contains within it the germ of other ideas. To store these embryonic ideas like the wheat of the Egyptians in a pyramid, no matter how impressive, is to deprive them of their fertility. The German *composer* for a long time to come is condemned to this role, very attractive to him and to his audience, but a little ridiculous.

Since the word-tone dramatist, whether Latin or German, will not find his inspiration in Wagner's technique, he must seek it elsewhere. What the Latin has gained through the invaluable acquisition of the idea in the German drama, he returns to the German in another form. No doubt, there must be a free interchange between the two races, but it must always be remembered that it is a mutual exchange and one race must not be permitted unduly to influence the other.

For a long time German culture has been stifled by the oppressive effects of French genius. Even today, this oppression is a serious obstacle to the realization of a national culture. The laborious beginnings of Bayreuth prove this.

The ground on which the two cultures will be able to exchange their gifts of necessity ought to be a national one, where the dominant idea of each race will be expressed most purely; that is, wherever the unharmonious juxtaposition of the two races will not have exercised its deleterious influence.

With Wagner, Germany has taken the necessary first step, for what Latin culture can give to the German must be refined by the latter before it can be accepted. The creation of Bayreuth gave the German the rare opportunity of expressing the dominant idea of his culture in a purity which seemed hardly possible in our contemporary civilization. At Bayreuth, he was able to share with the Latin the priceless treasure of the Wagnerian *idea*. Here, on this eminently national ground, he will be able to accept what the Latin has to offer, for Bayreuth will act as the filter which will guarantee the purity of the foreign element and thus make it possible for the German to assimilate it.

In devoting a chapter to Bayreuth, I shall describe only the conditions of *exchange* between the two races; this is the only point of view from which I wish to discuss Bayreuth.

Bayreuth

"Bayreuth is like the morning prayer on the day of battle."

Nietzsche — *Richard Wagner at Bayreuth*
Part III, 2nd edition, p. 137.

With these words Nietzsche captures the full significance of Bayreuth. From his great vantage point he is able to view the distant horizon and with one glance ascertain the relative heights and grandeur of the peaks. "We see," he continues, "in the picture of that tragic work of art at Bayreuth the very battle of one with everything that opposed him — with seemingly unconquerable forces of necessity under the banner of might, law, custom, convention, and the order of the universe."

From the more limited and essentially practical approach of this study, Bayreuth — although the many problems it raises are not the kind which make for peace — is no longer a symbol of battle but a place for the exchange and blending of cultures. In inviting us to its festivals, the spirit of German genius demonstrates great candor and purity of motive. In presenting itself with no thought of retreat, no hint of guile, it displays that intense pride and complete lack of vanity which always characterize genius.

Because our judgments are constantly disturbed by the innumerable compromises of everyday life, and the constant dissimulation necessary to reconcile them with each other, we have tended to assume that there must be a hidden motive behind every daring undertaking. We seek the motive for such rashness. Usually our suspicions are justified; the motive is there, hidden, and in most cases ignoble. Satisfied, we turn now to the undertaking itself; we are pleased to be able to treat it with the detachment it deserves, and so avoid being duped once more. Furthermore, if the achievement has not been hallowed by time, our admiration is usually colored by unfavorable and contemptuous reservations.

Time has not yet hallowed Bayreuth; to the dismay of some, opinion on Bayreuth remains, for many reasons, a matter of personal feeling. And so we stand before this rare phenomenon, armed with our modern skepticism, ready to season our enthusiasm and aesthetic pleasure with disdain and disparagement. We look about us and are amazed to discover no sentinels, no barred doors. All is open to the full light of day.

The irritation awakened by such impudence is gradually replaced by a rare kind of peace; the prying mind abandons the search that leads nowhere. Enervated by the deception and compromise of daily life, we had cautiously withdrawn into ourselves before coming to Bayreuth; now the soul slowly unfolds, and the whole being is flooded with the awesome, meditative peace which such ingenuity demands of the spectator. We realize indubitably that the German genius, far from betraying itself by a childlike self-confidence, has given evidence of its noble origin and has fulfilled its mission. The future will continue to bring further proof.

Because this *truly* national manifestation leaves unchanged the fundamental differences existing between races and cultures, it offers each of us the only opportunity we will ever have to sense clearly to which culture we belong and to understand the essential characteristics of our own race. Because of its novelty, this kind of perception will long remain intuitive, but frequent repetition does not impair it. On the contrary, simple intuition gradually deepens into understanding. The majesty of Bayreuth increases until the day when the foreigner, fully aware of the benefit bestowed, and grateful for the revelation of the German genius, knows how deeply he is obligated to that genius.

But it is not only the foreigner who undergoes this spiritual evolution: the German must be the first to feel its salutary effect. By providing him with the proof of the unconquerable vitality of his race and the original purity of his blood, Bayreuth permits the German to understand how much this purity has been weakened by the ill-advised introduction of certain foreign elements. At first he feels vaguely uneasy; a painful disquiet stirs within his soul. Finally his conscience seems to point to all those corruptive elements and to demand their rejection; and Bayreuth, insistently and unceasingly eloquent, makes their sacrifice inevitable. But his feelings are complex; he wonders why these foreign elements cannot be assimilated. Why have they, since they are good in themselves, become destructive? *It is because the benefits are not mutual.* For in all areas, this is a state of sterility and a symptom of sickness and perversion.

Bayreuth offers the German the entirely unhoped for opportunity to recover his health and his strength. From now on the German genius can give itself freely and fully, and receive in return what such a gift alone merits.

If the foreigner feels eternally obligated to a race whose genius has bared its very soul to him, the German, by the same token, must feel the responsibility for the consequences of that revelation. The fundamental purity, without which he could not have revealed himself, is his assurance that no foreign element can influence him without vitalizing and enriching him. The German's responsibility is twofold: he is bound, through the example of Bayreuth, to guard carefully the treasure of his race; and he is forbidden to let the treasure lie unproductive in lonely splendor like that legendary gold in the depths of a cavern.

Only through exchange can wealth be created and increased. This is a necessity for Bayreuth, all the more because such an exchange complements the ingenuous pride characteristic of this manifestation of genius. But we must agree upon the nature and conditions of exchange. Here, we must be particularly cautious, for if Bayreuth offers Wagner's artistic heirs a safeguard against the corruptive influence of alien principles, it is not necessarily a pledge of the purity of foreign intentions. How can we be sure of this purity? By what touchstone can it be tested?

Obviously this must be the chief concern of all those to whose hands the festivals are entrusted.

Here again the burden rests upon Bayreuth. Since the German genius has moved ahead of all the others, it must assume the responsibilities of leadership. *"Noblesse oblige!"* Not only must it maintain this position of pre-eminence, it must prove by the elevation of character and the resulting behavior that it is worthy of such a privileged position.

The attitude of the beneficiary—and we are all beneficiaries of the Wagnerian creation—can be judged only in the light of that benefactor. Therefore, it is Bayreuth itself which must provide Germans and foreigners alike with the means of expressing clearly by their attitude the aims which inspire them. Thus if Bayreuth from a certain point of view is a touchstone for the foreigner, the foreigner is also a touchstone for Bayreuth. The reciprocity here is absolute.

Those who possess and realize the Wagnerian idea at Bayreuth are in an extremely privileged position, since the existence of this idea has conferred upon them a power and a prestige to which they lent their good will but which they did not themselves create. In return they assume a grave responsibility, for they must enhance the value of their heritage by making Bayreuth a place favorable to cultural exchange.

Any foreign influence, to be fruitfully assimilated by the German genius, must have originated in the revelation of that genius in the soul of another race. The generative act is simultaneous on both sides.

The manifestation of the "German drama" conforms admirably to this condition. The inner essence of that form of art, in order to be revealed, demands that the foreigner sacrifice the particular desires of his race; it is the human soul, stripped as completely as possible of its non-essential characteristics which will best respond to the appeal of the German genius. But such self-sacrifice can not last long. After the revelation, nature reasserts itself, and a curious struggle takes place in his soul. Deeply moved by what has been revealed, and henceforth unable to do without it, he nevertheless cannot yet reconcile it with his own ordinary mode of life. This highly productive state of mind forces the soul to renewed activity and is the precise moment when exchange between the two races becomes possible, an exchange which thenceforth they can make *openly* by a reciprocal gift which enriches them both.

The principles foreign to "German drama" have been momentarily silenced; their deference, testifying to the poverty of their intentions, has in a way purified them. They emerge from this trial more clearly defined and consequently more conscious of their value. Through contact with a truly national expression they can reassert those values peculiar to their own nationality, and just as the German genius could give itself only in a completely original form they have acquired the means and the right to do as much for the German.

During Wagner's lifetime, Bayreuth was in a constant state of conflict, and the Master's sole concern was to have it survive at any price. This struggle makes his two short essays dedicated to the Festivals of 1876 and 1882 (the *Ring* and *Parsifal*) among the most moving of his works. When one considers what it must have meant to see his lifelong dream come to life under such unsatisfactory and precarious conditions, and yet the sense of solemn pride he must have felt when he saw the fruits of his unprecedented labors finally realized, it is impossible not to have a profound respect for the manner with which the great genius speaks of his work. Nothing defines Richard Wagner's heroic stature more clearly than those simple essays. We sense in them not only the artist's complete objectivity towards his creation, which is now and forever delivered from his soul to the "desolate light of day," but also a passionate desire for the acceptance of his work and through it of himself, thus to unite the two through one beautiful magic spell.

And so speaks the magician himself. There was not a stone in the theatre which he himself did not put into place, and even though he is full of praise for the work of others, it is he who had to bear the crushing weight of responsibility for Bayreuth. The initiative and the energy were his alone. Only the sheer intensity of his genius moved aside the great mass of opposition; only the independence of his spirit conceived and executed such brilliant work in the face of the discouraging obstacles of everyday life. Surrounded by deep affection, he nevertheless stood alone. He *alone* could measure the distance between the fire burning in his soul and the flickering flame he kindled on the hill of Bayreuth. With childlike, unconscious generosity he viewed the result of his own labors as enthusiastically as any ordinary spectator.

The numerous defects of production were nonexistent for him as long as he could ascertain the slightest understanding of his aims on the part of his staff. His ideal of a "utopian" community, with which he has been unjustly reproached, was actually realized at Bayreuth. The inexhaustible patience of genius has nowhere been more magnificently demonstrated than at the Bayreuth Festivals held during Wagner's lifetime.

In the two aforementioned essays, Wagner never confused the technical aspects of production with the "dedication which creatively supports the attainment of a carefully cultivated consciousness of correctness." Despite the faults we have pointed out in his ideas concerning production, no one saw more clearly than he how much experience was still needed before perfection in the visual aspects of production could even be approached. Wagner himself substituted for perfection in staging, both for the craftsmen and the audience (in this case he made no sharp distinction between them), the "spell" and the "dedication," which he managed to sustain by the sheer force of his personality. Outside of his controlling influence, there are now only the works themselves, and their production will necessarily result hereafter only from experiment, from experience.

In this sense, and in the others too, Bayreuth is in itself a stirring drama, and nothing less than the highest and most steadfast faithfulness on the part of the spectator from year to year is needed to sustain in our indolent spirit the living memory of the forever departed "magic spell."

Wagner's creation at Bayreuth (by which I mean the Festival Theatre as well as the dramas themselves) is so powerful that it will retain its vitality for a long time to come, and thus will compensate for the many defects of technique inherent in such an enterprise. Nevertheless, Wagner's ideas become more and more separated from their original manifestation; they travel and take root everywhere in men's souls. It is therefore necessary that the former try to follow them, for it is no longer possible to unite them and merge them in the same fervor. It is natural that for certain persons only the idea exists, and consequently its manifestation stubbornly maintains the same unfailing prestige; they see with their souls, and they identify that inner vision with what goes on on the stage. The production merely substantiates their inner vision and exists only through that vision.

Such individuals are the artist's natural allies, for they help to spread and preserve his ideas, but they can do little or nothing to help improve the standards of production. Nevertheless, they generate a tremendous amount of energy, and if we are to profit by a similar kind of energy, the same freedom must be granted to the production as is now granted to the principles underlying it. For if only Wagner's poetic ideas are allowed to thrive, Bayreuth will become a purely abstract world, and will cause the continuance of the Festivals to be, if not wholly superfluous, at least so inadequate to the constant realization of the idea that they will become for the cultivated but unprepared audience a source of irritation and of corrosive criticism.

If we wish to preserve an *organic* existence for Bayreuth, that is, to maintain direct contact with those who have kept the idea of Bayreuth alive in their hearts, we can accomplish this only by stripping it of that vague character of subjective symbolism with which the first productions were of necessity invested for lack of more concrete methods. The existence of Bayreuth, so positive in its effects until now, is bound eventually to degenerate into a *popular* rite, whose outward form the initiated will still respect but not sanction.

If Bayreuth separates its artistic life from the free expansion of the idea, the opportunity for cultural exchange will be impossible; and if Bayreuth is denied this, an essential part of its great mission will be negated.

To be sure, Wagner's works would not be directly affected if this happened; they are too deeply rooted in the souls of too many people for that. Bayreuth *as an ideal* is immortal, but Wagner's faith in its actual survival would have proved illusory. Once conditions favorable to cultural exchange ceased to exist and a new battle began, it would be impossible to estimate how long the salutary effects of such reciprocity would be delayed.

If then, without Wagner, the production of his works can grow only out of experience, this experience can be obtained only through *exchange*. German genius has done its part; it has given the whole of itself. To ask more of it would be to fail to recognize the nature of its contribution. If it is to survive such great generosity, the German genius must accept those foreign elements, whose assimilation it has made possible.

Henceforth, *Exchange* and *Experience* are one and the same for Bayreuth. To attempt to achieve one without the other is to negate the very dignity of Wagner's work.

As soon as we speak of exchange, we leave the field of theoretical speculation. The obligation to provide a fruitful ground for exchange is a general notion which can be reduced to concrete terms. Since exceptional conditions have linked Bayreuth with a few outstanding personalities, its existence necessarily implies personal obligations and responsibilities. Not only the existence, but also the *fruitfulness* of the exchange, depends on these few privileged people.

The innate worth and continuing power of the treasure entrusted to them depends upon the attitude with which they carry on the management of Bayreuth. In a way, this treasure also belongs to all who can make it their own, thereby enriching their lives forever. They, too, have a right and an obligation to protect and manage this common property: their voices must be heard and, as I have already pointed out, the major responsibility of Wagner's artistic heirs is to hear them above the cries of the masses. Our times seem propitious for this. It is far easier today to discern the intentions and sincerity of those who raise their voices than when Bayreuth was in the process of being created. Later, out of respect and devotion to Wagner, thoughtfully we might turn away from the place he dedicated for the shared activity of all the faithful and seek an alternative elsewhere. The result of such a justifiable desertion would very likely be the deathblow to German genius. Deprived of the security which Bayreuth could offer the German genius with regard to foreign culture, yet obliged to accept the elements offered by this culture in exchange for its revelation, the German would be plunged into a new period of struggle and defeat. For if Bayreuth closes its doors to cultural exchange, it will withhold from the foreigner a sanction which he must have.

Obsessed for centuries with the idea of Form, the Latin has sought salvation in the purely subjective power revealed by the Wagnerian idea. If the Latin is rejected, he will descend into the sad confusion of our degraded institutions, and withdraw once more into his old life. Stimulated by a new idea, but incapable of enduring the sacrifice necessary for its realization, the Latin will pervert the holy flame, making it appear so enticing that the German, unable to resist, will again fall under the influence of that very culture which it was his duty to enrich. Perhaps the Wagnerian idea was destined to pass through such a painful stage of development, and its subsequent growth may be even more complex than we had supposed.

The death of an original genius such as Wagner always evokes the anguished cry: "What is to become of me?" Here the unfathomable mystery of personality appears in all its tragic grandeur. The work of art, left in the hands of those who neither conceived nor created it, suddenly loses that harmony which only its creator could sustain. It collapses and disintegrates; it is restricted by being forced into a thousand new combinations. The work of art needs unlimited vitality to survive so many transformations.

Wagner was fully aware of this, and according to Nietzsche, he had anxiously sought a home for the child of his flesh and blood. Since he could find one nowhere on this earth, he proudly built one himself. His illusions found peace in Bayreuth, but as Chamberlain adds, ". . . only in the grave."

Wagner could have had no illusions: the home of his child was in himself, and Bayreuth was but a symbol. He hoped that the Festival Theatre would be a visible manifestation, intelligible to all, of that inner life which he took with him. This was the meaning of the Mausoleum: all of his personality that could be transferred was given to us before he died; whatever was transferable of the particular nature of his art has been perpetuated by Bayreuth in an artificial life. The battle for the continued existence of Wagner's creation at Bayreuth is therefore inseparable from the faith we owe to genius.

Except as an idea, today Bayreuth exists only in the *Festivals*. If the Festivals are denied that exchange which could bring them new life, they will gradually petrify, become a veritable mausoleum for the drama, and a complete denial of all the Master's intentions. If this happens, Wagner's Bayreuth will be exiled to the abstract realm of the imagination, and exist only in the minds of the few.

But things have not yet come to such a state. Bayreuth is more firmly entrenched than ever. Financial conditions are improving, audiences are growing larger, and the productions, because of the work of a highly intelligent staff, are securely established. Everything is ready for a productive exchange. Even the discrepancy, still manifest today, between the growth of the Wagnerian idea and the extremely slow progress of production methods, is eminently suitable to the initiation of new ideas.

Let us assume that these new ideas will be welcomed as they deserve to be, so that we can determine how the exchange will be most beneficial to the two nations who will be its beneficiaries. In this way we shall be able to determine the conditions necessary for the existence of a work of art based upon music but controlled by the need for harmony aroused by Wagner's dramas. Our task will be made easier by the fact that the future of modern music resides in the realm of German drama, and is therefore bound to be closely connected with Bayreuth.

The opportunity which for the German lies in visual art, and results from experience not yet possessed by the Germanic peoples— it will be taught him by the Latin. On his part, the Latin, in trying to reconcile his desire for form with the profundity of the German drama, will gain a new sense of form, which will free him from the arbitrary desire of his race. He will come to understand that form must be subordinated to the *Harmony of the whole,* and since he already has a mastery of form, he will be that much more adept in discovering what elements of form must be sacrificed in order to abide by the higher principle. His goal cannot be the "German drama" any more than harmony can be anything but a result for the German. Each must preserve the essential and instinctive originality of his own culture, but each will be enriched by the contribution of the other.

Although Bayreuth must be the magical meeting ground of the two cultures, I shall now conclude this chapter, dedicated especially to Bayreuth. My whole essay is based upon the artistic revelation, for which we are indebted to Wagner's Festival Theatre, and if I felt obligated to write about it at greater length and in more detail, it is because Bayreuth is the only factor in this study whose future development ought to lie in the hands and depend on the good will of perfectly honorable men.

Germans and Latins

I have pointed out that the idea of German drama became accessible to the Latin *through form,* and although to the Latin, it was an imperfect form, it still provoked him to discover the reason for its irresistible power.

If one can by theoretical demonstration bring the German close to any artistic goal whatever, it is because by cultivating honor in himself, he succeeds in shining abroad, and because that is the German's sole means of producing an original work, obviously for the Latin the same demonstration will remain obstinately limited by his own logical system of thought and will not move him a step in the direction of the work of art.

The German controls the form with deliberate forethought; the Latin has no need for such deliberation unless the form he has created does not fully satisfy him, and even then he will make use of it only after having exhausted all the possibilities the form can provide his artistic observation.

How the German Genius is Revealed to the Latin Genius

Consequently, the Latin set out to observe the Wagnerian drama. In addition to his disadvantageous position, were the damage done to Wagner's dramas by the operatic stage, the sickly orgies of the concert halls, the monstrous translations of Wilder[1] and company; the whole pitiful procession of mediocrities. But Wagner's music triumphed in spite of everything; it was unquestionably overwhelming, and awakened in the soul new and disturbing emotions. Little by little it became evident that the text on which this music was based was no ordinary opera libretto, and that the key to the unique power of the music lay in the text. The Latin then turned to the German language for the sole purpose of understanding Wagner's poetry, and he discovered after a careful study of the poetry's form and technique an inseparable union of language and music. Having grasped the meaning of the work as a whole from the score, the Latin now journeyed to the Festival Theatre at Bayreuth, and returned from this decisive experience with the conviction that Wagner's dramas are marvelous works of art and his "theatre" the creation of a genius. Still, he was dissatisfied with the production. His strict sense of logic had been continually violated, his ears had grown weary, and his eyes . . . ah, his eyes had been subjected to a very crude ordeal.

He now returns to the score, and in the end is forced to admit that he derives more pleasure from it than from its performance on the stage.

Up until this point the Latin has been enslaved by form alone. Now the divine nature of the music touches the depths of his soul, although he still considers the intensity of Wagner's work simply a matter of technique. He soon finds, however, that this so-called technique defies critical analysis. *He discovers that it is possible to be caught up by the beauty of the work without entering the sanctuary.*

He realizes this very well. It troubles him, and he compares the effect which the works of his own culture have upon him with that of the Wagnerian drama. This comparison is the beginning of understanding. For the first time the Latin perceives that the Wagnerian form is, in fact, *no form at all* and that it can be neither analyzed nor criticized. It must, then, spring from a mysterious source. If he discovers this source, will he still not be in possession of the

---

[1]Victor von Wilder (1835-1892) a Belgian who translated several of Wagner's dramas into French. Ed.

work of art? Was not Wagner's aim to create beautiful music for beautiful verse? All the Latin's artistic desires were satisfied if he could attain such a goal. Is it possible that there is something else to the German conception than this?

Yes, the German guards an incomparable treasure in his soul. When it shines forth, this treasure is transformed into beautiful music and beautiful verse, vitally united. That is the whole secret.

The Latin begins to understand. The divine score penetrates more and more deeply into his soul and plants there mysterious seeds. A new life begins to pulsate; its pulsation arouses in the artist, accustomed to the century-old superficiality, an emotion he never before experienced. The score . . . Bayreuth . . . Richard Wagner . . . all these, already deeply respected by him, shine now in a new and more brilliant light. This radiance is like a temple which no longer excites enthusiastic observation or criticism as architecture, but has become a place of contemplation.

In this way the German genius is revealed to the Latin. But this moment of unforgettable rapture is followed by a sobering reflection. The treasure in the temple is not his own; the Latin must approach it from without. In spite of everything, he admits sadly, the temple is identical with the treasure it has disclosed; its beauty is but the reflected radiance of an inner light.

"It is in the nature of the German spirit to build from within: Eternal God truly dwells in him before he builds a temple in His honor." (Richard Wagner)

This truth explains quite naturally the dissatisfaction, the disquiet, and the disappointment which a Wagnerian production at Bayreuth created in the Latin, and also the great pleasure he derived from reading the score. Indeed, the poetic-musical elements are the only ones the German has mastered. Only through them can he express the deep longing of his soul, only through them can he display the treasure entrusted to his race. So long as the Latin, supported by the memory of orchestral music, confines himself to reading the score, he experiences the purest product of the German genius, a product whose beauty stems from the viable secret in the poet's soul, a creation whose form as such is not the artist's aim. On the contrary, the transference of the score to the stage demanded of the German an ability he did not possess; although by nature he was not opposed to such activity, it was an experience as yet absolutely unknown to him. The Latin has long had such experience, and the productions at Bayreuth not only disappointed him, they made him doubt his own judgments concerning the score as well. For with the realization that the productions failed to satisfy his need for meaningful form, he was also aware that his concept of form was not applicable to the score which he knew so thoroughly.

This dilemma I have pointed out as the eminently fruitful moment in which an exchange between the two cultures is effectuated and in which the prolonged and sincere efforts of the Latin can culminate. The knowledge that their respective failings spring from diametrically opposed sources will prepare the necessary groundwork for such an exchange between the two cultures. The process of assimilation will be a long and complex one for both, *but must certainly produce tangible results.*

The task will be far simpler for the German than for the Latin. The German, whose culture gave birth to the Wagnerian drama, will have no difficulty in recognizing the inner meaning of the new drama. His only concern will be how to make the production expressive of this meaning. Although he lacks a technical control of form, he nevertheless can appreciate its importance as a force. In seeking a form of production worthy of the masterly poetic-musical text, he becomes conscious of his own deficiencies in this area, and at the same time he feels within himself a cord the Latin drama has been unable to pluck. Confident of the divine beauty of the German drama, he can safely invite the Latin to share it with him, for the two cultures are attracted out of mutual respect for Wagner's genius. Their mutual communication will be precisely what each culture requires in order to return enriched to its own sphere. The Latin has willingly sacrificed his need for form in order to understand the inner meaning of the German drama. Once he has achieved this understanding he can use his sense of form and technical ability to conceive of a production that is fully expressive of the poetic-musical text. And this is all the German requires; in return for this contribution, the

Latin receives whatever of the German spirit is compatible with his own culture. The treasure he has glimpsed is not his, but it will influence and change his whole approach to the problems of form. Henceforth, only the *total expression* of existence, the vibration of all the cords, will satisfy his newly awakened longing.[1] But what will he substitute for the organic radiance and energy of the German drama?

We know that from now on the harmony of expression he has learned from the flaws inherent in the German genius will become the Latin's supreme law. His great experience of form enables him to foresee the sacrifices necessary for the achievement of such harmony, and it is this principle of sacrifice that must govern the creation of the work of art, which is now within his reach.

The question of exchanges between races brings us to the heart of the problem. The future of the word-tone drama, which seemed so doubtful when we analyzed it in theoretical terms, now becomes a fascinating possibility. Our faith in its future wavered before the overwhelming brilliance of Wagner's work. With the firm conviction that any work of art can find its center of gravity only within ourselves, we now feel a greater hope in the ability to perpetuate the work of art whose *existence* the Master has revealed to us.

I say "existence," for this art, more than any other, must exist *in us;* its fleeting life is dependent upon our own. By bringing the work of art into accord with our own natures, we create a relationship that will benefit even the most insular aspects of our culture.

The Desire for Harmony

When we use a concrete example to illustrate a theoretical truth, we inevitably diminish the significance of that truth. Any example entails all sorts of contingencies which cloud the issue, and

---

[1] "For the torch of life can only be kindled and burn by using the whole organism of thoughts and emotions."—Johann Gottfried Herder.

what is gained in amplification is lost in harmony. Compared with the theory, the laws which govern the technical aspects of theatrical production seem poor expedients, indeed, and are subject to countless contradictory considerations. And when we apply the theory to the production of Wagner's work alone, we must limit it even more, for it is difficult to study his work without taking into account certain biographical and personal considerations. When we turn from his works to a consideration of ourselves, the question of national culture becomes crucial. Since we are anxious to find those conditions that will be conducive to the development of the word-tone drama in our society, we cannot disregard this all-important question.

Quite to the contrary, we have reached the point where theory is only of relative value. Just as an artist, familiar with the rules of his art, ignores them, because he knows that the new idea he wishes to embody can never be realized by a slavish obedience to rules but must come from the identification of his will with the materials of his particular medium, henceforth we can mingle our desire for harmony with the doctrine of the word-tone drama, requiring no other rule except this desire, for its identity has now been established for us.

The efforts of two such different cultures as those I have taken here as types will obviously produce totally different results. Since, however, the work of art which will satisfy them both is derived from music, we must begin our inquiry with a consideration of the race whose very soul is music, the Germanic race.

The Future of Wagnerian Methods for the German

The century-old aspirations of the German race found in Richard Wagner their supreme representative and liberator. Today, the German, having been stimulated to the utmost by Wagner's *musical* power, has the alternative of either producing a genius capable of bringing *new* impetus to music, or else following in Wagner's footsteps.

When we consider the origin of Wagnerian music, it is

obvious that music cannot be given additional impetus through technique alone. Only a creator, in the fullest sense of the word, could do this, and such creative power is not yet within our reach. We can no more conceive of it than we could have imagined the existence of a score such as *Tristan and Isolde* at the beginning of the nineteenth century. Therefore, only the second choice remains. But is the continuation of the Wagnerian method a sufficient challenge to the German composer?

It is useless to discuss works whose only aim is to reproduce artificially the passionate vibration characteristic of Wagner's creations. Everyone will understand the pathological side of that tendency and at the same time how natural it is. It has no value except as a kind of safety valve for some and as a technical initiation for others—a very superficial initiation doubtless, but necessary for the understanding of works whose exterior method is the same, but whose origin and aim are totally different. The musician, here, will find himself at a dead end. He may still lull himself into a state of intoxication by the most fascinating polyphonies for a long time, but in the end he *must* perish, because his virtuosity, great as it is, is not an expression of the innermost feelings of his culture.

The truly German musician can be concerned only with the *basic intention* of his art; he will try to develop a creativity *of which music will be only the expression.* Wagner has bequeathed to him a priceless instrument for that expression, and as he uses it the musician obeys a compelling necessity; he knows that in our time it is the only medium he has for conveying his vision to us. To master this instrument is, for the German, to break the resistance of matter so that his soul may sing unrestrained. The ultimate value of such an improvisation depends therefore upon the inner resources of the improviser. *Only by means of his inner resources can the musician develop the Wagnerian methods.*

Among the less educated it is common to call piano lessons "music"; to be a "musician" means to be able to play that instrument. This is a gross mistake, but we are equally extravagant when we term one who has mastered the technique of his art and can amuse us with it a musician. And since the time of Wagner, mastering the orchestra and the human voice is no more "music" than playing the piano. This is simply a skill in handling the tools of music, but does not prove that one has any spiritual impulse to use them. The musician, of course, must be a master of his instrument, but he is entitled to be called "musician" only if an irresistible inner force has driven him to that mastery. *Music,* in the usual sense of the word, *is not the object of his desire,* but the means of expressing it, and this is why the so-called "musician" requires the instruments that we know.

The study of music will become more and more a *subjective* experience. The sharp distinction that exists today between those who have a full command of the medium and those who have not will gradually break down, and those too feeble to acquire mastery of music will find in other kinds of activity the means of influencing "musicians" properly so-called, those who study *music* and are able to acquire the necessary skill.

Such a study occupies a lifetime and implies not an advance in technique, but rather the continuous development and maintenance of a spiritual capacity. In distinguishing between the object of musical expression and the technique of this expression, the German tacitly supports one of Wagner's most inspired principles: "In the art work of the future there will always be something new to invent." This must seem paradoxical to those who consider the *craft* of first importance.

Under such conditions the musician — one who studies "music" — is a poet, and the means of expression he employs will soon give rise to others, and before long it will be possible for him to realize his poetic-musical intentions in production. The poet-musician thus becomes a dramatist and his only remaining task is to establish a harmonious relationship between the elements which he controls directly and those whose materialization merely derives from the former: between his score and its production.

At Bayreuth (we are assuming here that the exchange has actually occurred) the Latin has taught the German that his drama, by the very nature and origin of its *action,* does not permit any visual effects—any realism in production. Therefore, if the concept of such a drama is to remain constantly *faithful* to its origins, and, moreover, if it is submitted to the reduction regulated by the notation system of production, its staging will be effected according to the hierarchic principle, which excludes all other vexatious alternatives, and knows no technical impossibilities. Faith in this principle will enable the German dramatist to perfect his visual sense of form and thereby acquire that feeling for proportion which he now lacks.

Soon he will come to realize that great sacrifices will be required before he is able to develop fully and freely those means of expression that are characteristic of his culture. Scenic realism, however false it may be, exercises a great influence over a people whose sense of form is only slightly developed. The German more than any other artist is attracted to realism; thus when he renounces it, he will not even have the satisfaction of having understood its artistic hollowness.

The other sacrifice will prove even more critical; he must discard everything in the poetic-musical text that in any way seemed to him to be directly related to the use of realistic production techniques, for only gradually will he be able to replace the imperfect proportions, of which he was unaware, with a new harmony which will be fully expressive of the dramatic idea itself.

Furthermore, he must simplify his dramatic idea so that it can be expressed by those elements under his control; if he fails to do this, he will make the same mistakes in production that Wagner did, without possessing Wagner's tremendous creative powers to balance the consequences of his mistakes.

The production will provide the means whereby the German dramatist can develop his dramatic idea to its fullest extent, and reveal to him a new source of invention at a time when it seemed that every source was dry. Certain changes in the Wagnerian method, contrary to my earlier statement,[1] will gain for the German artist the right to follow Wagner in order to blaze a *new trail* for himself.

---

[1] See above, page 143.

Parisian Art

The Latin *artist* enjoys the same popularity among his own people as the German *musician* does among his; the difference lies merely in the result. The Latin artist knows that all the intricacies of his creation are appreciated and that each of his innovations will be received with enthusiasm—at first for their novelty, and later, if their value surpasses that of a mere vogue, as original creations. Between him and his audience there is a tacit understanding: a "surface" understanding, in the broadest sense of the word. This results in a mutual need for variety, which in the final analysis is nothing but a clever and dazzling *status quo*.

The Latin would never analyze the relationship in this way. The public *exists* as the consumer, the artist, as the producer; and the insatiable appetite of the one is stimulated by the virtuosity of the other, who kills himself trying to satisfy his clients. The Parisian wastes away his day between aroused and satisfied desires, an imposing caricature of the weakness of the Latin race.

The performance itself is already highly enjoyable; to tread the boards oneself is even more so, and to achieve this end, any methods are acceptable as long as they are used with unquestionable virtuosity. It was the same in the ancient drama; the chorus took part in the action and hastened or retarded it by its commentary. The actors, supported by the chorus, gave all in their power—even at times exceeded themselves—in order to keep the chorus in a state of constant ecstasy. The work pleases them all, and yet they do not believe in it; they play in it because playing and seeing others play is their life. It is as simple as that.

This, of course, is an extreme example; yet an attentive and unprejudiced observer finds expressed therein with great candor the genius of the race. It is possible for him to recognize beneath the dazzling masquerade of the Parisian theatre all of the essential traits of the Latin race.

One of these traits is particularly pertinent to our subject and should be discussed more fully. Among Latins there is a greater reciprocity between artist and public than there is among Germans. They are not far from sharing their activity. Thus, compared to the situation in Germany, the Latin work of art is in a far better position. The Latin *audience* makes a marked distinction between the various kinds of artistic activity. For example, in Paris, every type of dramatic production has its own special theatre, which generates the same atmosphere for the audience as the play being presented there. Similarly, the special characteristics of every art form among the Latins find a ground especially prepared for them, and a public trained and disposed to enjoy them. Thus every work of art is presented "in a favorable light."

Such classification in the arts is determined primarily by a sense of form, and it cannot be denied that this is a most outstanding aesthetic virtue. If like any virtue it has its shortcomings, it still remains a sign of a superior culture and is perhaps the one substantial contribution that the Latin can make.

However, this sense of artistic form, which the Latin has inherited and which is central to all of his art, cannot continue to exist in our contemporary society without becoming trite and popular. In order to protect it from the kind of popularity incompatible with the dignity of art, the artist is forced to limit the appeal of his work, refining it in such a way that it becomes a luxury to be enjoyed only by the aristocracy. When we debate whether or not a work is "artistic," we have in mind this kind of refinement. To be sure, usage may change the practical application of the expression, but its essential meaning will remain the same.

In a culture such as this, *living art* always has an extremely aristocratic tendency, for if it becomes popular it will cease to be art; and since its life is an ephemeral one, it will remain subjected to the despotic influence of fashion. Such art cannot endure, and lovers of art will turn to works in other fields, such as literature and the plastic arts, whose performance is based not on current tastes, but on more fundamental values.

This system is difficult to apply to music, since music originates and develops in the human soul, a realm beyond the jurisdiction of fashion. Therefore, French music has become either an exploitation of form for its own sake, or a more or less skillful imitation of German forms.

The Conflict Between Latin and German Art:
Its Solution at Bayreuth

Yet a Beethoven symphony or a Bach cantata are greatly appreciated in Paris, where more care is lavished on their presentation than in their native land. With no apparent hesitation, the Parisian can turn from a subtly lighted exhibit of water colors, giving evidence of the highest skill and most delicate taste, to the concert hall, where he listens with rapt attention to the mighty voice of German genius. He then returns immediately to the enticements of those artists whose creations have been shaped by his own sensuality. This indicates that he is sensitive to the beauty of a form which is but the outward radiance of an inner light, and the reverence of his approach confirms the awe this form inspires in him.

German music touches the religious nature of the Latin. If one observes the facial expression of the staunchest skeptic listening to such music, he will see in it something of the untutored devoutness of a peasant attending Mass. The divine character with which the Latin has always invested his ever-renewed enjoyment of form is suddenly revealed to him much more deeply, embodied in such sublime magic that he cannot fail to recognize the presence of the unknown, and he worships it from afar.

However, these worldly Parisians can dismiss religious sentiment almost as soon as they leave the church, and when they return to their normal nomadic life they experience a feeling of mingled relief and remorse. The Parisian would like to reconcile his joy in revelation with his worldly pleasure, but he does not know how to begin.

Unsuspectingly he goes to Bayreuth[1] to learn. The religious act of German genius, expressed in an intelligible and meaningful ceremony, makes contact with the Latin, becomes for him to some degree measurable. The disturbing contrast between the water color exhibit and the Beethoven symphony having found embodiment, the artist of form can now *understand* it. He feels that the delicate vision of colors and forms must be guided by some principle other than

[1] Remember that I am supposing that the exchange between the two cultures has been openly achieved with all its consequences.

172 ·

caprice, and that the elusive unknown must limit itself in a more tangible expression, in order to unite with that vision.

Just as the ecstasy of the ascetic could be expressed to people of artistic sensibilities only through magnificent frescoes, so the unknown divinity of German music can be communicated to the Latin only through a symbol which he can apply to the richness of his own life. It is impossible for the Latin to deny his heritage. Form and form alone can satisfy him. If he is to reconcile his two aesthetic pleasures he must create a new form which mediates between the two and so is supremely comforting.

In harmoniously combining the two purposes of art, he fulfills the highest aim of his culture. Why should the inevitable compromises of our sad modern life trouble him, now that an integrated and completely satisfying form resides in his soul? He is sure of its existence and can deduce it from all other manifestations of art.

Musical Desire in Latin Culture

Latin art, based as we have said on highly aristocratic principles, has been strongly influenced by the *longing* for music, and there is even some evidence that the Latin artist is attempting to create an integrated work of art. It is hardly necessary to add that such attempts are of a distinctly "artistic" nature and have a public conscientiously seeking to understand and accept them.

Since the so-called "lyric" theatres are inadequate for any kind of experiment, private enterprises have taken the initiative. Unfortunately, the element of speculation has had a paralyzing effect on some of them, and only by retaining their completely private character, could they escape the standardizing influence of fashion. Whatever the Parisian may wish to think, a feeling of classification is inseparable from conservatism. It is so agreeable for the artist to be able to depend on an audience that he fails to find strong enough motives for neglecting the conditions necessary to its existence. Inertia, more characteristic of the victims of fashion than of any others, easily accepts ready-made forms whose production can be achieved without effort in accord with public demand. Those private productions, far from simply importing popular entertainment into the salon, have come into being because of the inadequacy of the generally accepted models, and are motivated by a desire to avoid such forms. The Parisian, however, rightly considers such pre-established sympathy between the audience and a work of art an essential condition for aesthetic enjoyment.[1] He clings to this, the only solid ground in the sea of his desire. All his efforts are colored by this necessity. He is always seeking form, and upon self-examination he finds within himself only the desire for form, never a governing motive for creating it. That is why at times his loyalty to existing forms seems to be a matter of moral necessity, and as such seems to be regarded as a virtue.

Therefore, private initiative is thought of as rashness, even heresy, with the result that in most cases, either through lack of courage, pertinacity, or talent, such initiative has no influence.

The already highly developed culture of the Latin must go a step further in order to understand that the *combination* of certain technical media is in itself a form, that this form is no longer the controlling principle, but quite simply, the *mutual* relationship of the various media.

Because of his habit of breaking a production down into its component parts, the Parisian has grown accustomed tacitly to provide the inner impulse quite independently. He feels obliged to add a part of himself to each work, and since this produces in him an awareness of his high state of culture, it gives him boundless pleasure. Artists take advantage of the fact that the Parisian cannot forego this habit. The "artistic" method becomes one of pure suggestion, often bordering on obscurity, if not meaninglessness. If the Parisian is ever going to be persuaded to give up this seductive activity, he must be provided with a *new one;* so far no one has attempted to do so.

The passivity demanded by German drama of its audience is fully justified. The poet-musician addresses the soul of the spectator

---

[1] Usually the Parisian is much less impressed than the German by the community of interest which makes an audience at Bayreuth so interesting. He is used to this in Paris, although to a less striking degree.

in a language perfectly comprehensible to it, one which responds to its inmost desires. If the German is to attain these heights of contemplation, his soul must be in a state of complete repose *before* witnessing the performance.

But the artist of form has no soul to which one can communicate so surely. His soul must be captured through harmony, and since that harmony is both the aim and the result of his art, the receptive faculties of the observer must be in a state of perfect balance, but not in repose. The audience must always feel this harmony and affirm it anew. This active participation on the part of the audience establishes a totally different relationship between the creator and the audience from that which exists in Germany. The German *musician* speaks to his listeners in their own language; the Latin *artist* expects his audience to participate technically in his work. The German is successful in purely human terms, while the success of the Latin is more exclusively artistic.

Hence, it seems possible to capture the attention of the Latin audience by other means than pure suggestion, and to replace the subjective element which suggestion stimulates with the perhaps superior pleasure provided by a harmony established independently of the spectator; that is, a harmony which he does not have to co-create for himself as he observes. This arrangement would certainly be *new* and what it demands of the spectator would constitute the indispensable harmony between the audience and the production. And this is precisely what will assure the Parisian of the existence of a "form."

Fashion

There remains the destructive influence of fashion, always most perceptible at the high point of the artistic hierarchy created by the Latin.

The individual details of a work of art are especially subject to its influence. The structure of any art form is always limited; it is therefore within this limited structure that the need for change must express itself. Thus, if the artist is to meet the insatiable need of fashion for variety, he will have to use every means at his disposal to combine the fundamentally limited number of technical devices into as many variations as possible. Such is the demand of fashion for virtuosity. In every field fashion resembles a chemical process—a continual quantitative analysis of an already known quantity. "The creation of a fashion," says Wagner, "is a mechanical process." And again, "Its activity is arbitrary alteration, unnecessary change, and striving toward its very opposite, that is toward absolute uniformity." Yet again, "Fashion orders and rules where really everything ought only to obey and be subordinated."[1] But fashion can "order and rule" only in those situations where the desire it seeks to satisfy is stronger than all others. If a form can be developed with a stronger motivating force than the desire for change, with an organic unity that can resist fashion's influence, its power will no longer prevail.

The form which the German drama has suggested to the Latin fulfills these conditions. It feeds the ardent desire for harmony through the countless possibilities it offers, and since it too is based upon change, it serves to overcome the influence of fashion.

The "Musical Play"

The essential difference between the German drama and its Latin counterpart—which we shall call the *musical play*—is its relationship to the hierarchic principle. From its very beginnings, German drama has been completely controlled by this principle, which sees the actor as the sole intermediary between the poetic-musical text and the inanimate elements of the production. The musical play adheres to the principle far less stringently. As a result, the *mise en scène* of the German drama is within the grasp of all, while that of the musical play follows an aristocratic bent, and appeals only to those chosen few who are capable of enjoying it. The musical play corresponds to the major developments in Latin

---

[1] I refer the reader to Wagner's thorough discussion of fashion in *The Artwork of the Future*, Vol. III, pp. 45-49.

art and also to the taste of the Latin public.

Yet, the expression "the musical play" is extremely vague. Unlike the German drama, the source of its score and text is not so deeply rooted in the soul of the poet, so that the one standard heretofore automatically established by the poetic-musical text must now be relinquished to the caprice of the individual poet. This means that the nature and degree of culture attained by both the poet and the audience become more important than ever, for cultural background alone will determine not only the form, but the inception of the work of art.

It is obvious that both the German *word-tone poet* and the German audience would lack the qualifications necessary for the Latin method of creation. The sense of form lacking in them must be imposed upon them externally; that is, through a principle independent of their free will, for, as we have already seen, form is not a part of their basic aim.

On the other hand, the longing of the Latin artist is identified with the potential existence of form, and the virtuosity which the Latin develops in every branch of art is the necessary expression of that longing. Thus the form is left to the caprice of the artist, and the only guiding principles to be obeyed are those laws which control the technical aspects of the medium.

Each individual part of the musical play has its own particular technical requirements, but these individual requirements all spring from the necessity for harmony between them, so that the arbitrary nature of the production is reduced to a minimum and is absolutely dependent upon the degree of virtuosity in the artist.

A work of art created in this way can emerge only from a culture whose outstanding characteristic is virtuosity. Latin culture fulfills this requirement remarkably well. Furthermore, in furnishing the artist with a means of expression, virtuosity alone automatically secures for him an audience, which, in Latin culture, is inseparable from the artist. Thus we see that the musical play is the integrated form of art best suited to the Latin race. It is based on harmony, is aristocratic in nature, and requires the highest degree of virtuosity.

German Drama and the "Musical Play"

We shall now try to define the musical play, as it appears on the stage, as accurately as possible, and then compare it with the German drama. This comparison, which leads us back to the theory of production as a means of expression, and to the effect of this theory upon theatrical technique, as described in Part I, will enable us to see how much practical value this aesthetic speculation has in reality.

The only fundamental concept we have deduced from our observation of the normal relationship between the score and its production is the relatively automatic transference of the score into the stage space without the initiative of the stage director, or even of a specific idea of the staging on the part of the dramatist. Through a consideration of Wagner's dramas and their production defects, we arrive at an indispensable corollary to this basic principle: the word-tone poet *must be conscious* of the transfer effected by the music; he must know the method thereof, as well as its consequences. If he fails in this, he not only deprives himself of an invaluable medium of expression, but in doing so, substitutes for it a kind of vision incompatible with all his other expressive media, thus weakening his whole concept.

Generally speaking, Richard Wagner cannot be taken as a typical example. His genius superseded all technical faults and, fortified by the trials of exceptionally unfavorable circumstances, he was able to overcome certain difficulties, without, however, removing them from the path of his successors. It would be presumptuous to suppose that his work would have been perfect if he had known the principle of the scenic hierarchy. Yet the violence sometimes done by the poet in him to his power as a musician (particularly noticeable in the *Ring*) derives primarily from the poet's desire to invest his drama with the only scenic existence Wagner ever understood, and that was a realistic one.

But the degree of suggestion the word-tone poet can attain by liberating himself from realism is far from being an absolute quantity, and depends entirely upon the individual. Socrates maintained that leisure is the greatest good. This is true only when we know how to use it. "For," says Schopenhauer, "one's leisure is

worth exactly what one is worth oneself." A highly developed individuality knows of course no greater pleasure than to be itself, and
the opportunity for such self-consciousness is made possible only
through leisure. An empty head or empty heart seeks by every means
to avoid the ennui of its own society, for such leisure is only a
burden, or a pretext for countless deplorable excesses. It was in
leisure that Wagner conceived the score of the *Ring*. Another man
might have conceived the ideal of the enslavement of his fellow men.
Freedom in production will therefore be fruitful only in so far as the
dramatist is worthy of it and knows how to use it. This is why we must
eternally regret Wagner's unconsciousness of the possibility of such
freedom.

Each specific creation requires a special talent in the dramatist if his freedom is to be used to advantage. What kind of talent is
needed by the German dramatist, and what kind by the creators of
the musical play? And will their freedom be of the same kind?

The unified work of art has a twofold existence: one is
ideal; the other material, and therefore subject to circumstance and
limitations. Hence the first part of this study has been only a technical
analysis of the theory of word-tone drama and is not necessarily
more applicable to the German dramatist than to the Latin artist.
Unlike the theory, the actual phenomenon is always somewhat irreg-
ular, and so are the conditions of its existence. This irregularity is
what is implied in the term "relative."[1]

The idea of the *integrated work of art,* the art which appeals
to all of man's faculties, will be the same for the German as for the
Latin. But since the two personalities are vastly different, in order to
captivate all the faculties of each, the appeal must be quite different.

Because of the freedom granted the dramatist through the
hierarchy of production there evolves a form of production which is
infallibly a part of the idea of the word-tone drama. In the actual
realization of the idea on the stage, the degree of infallibility of the
form depends upon the cultural background of the author. It is

---

[1]The existence of Bayreuth is in itself the symbol of an Idea, but its Festivals are
detached from the Idea in order to participate in the relative life of the phenomenon. It is the simultaneity of the two manifestations which creates the strange
grandeur of the experience, as well as its disturbing complexity.

obvious that for the German this form must be as independent of the dramatist as possible; whereas, for the Latin the form of the musical play has its source in the artist himself.

The idea, as it exists between these two extremes, could only hope to find a balanced realization by having the genius of the two races simultaneously combined under one controlling judgment.

Although it can be said, of course, that the freedom of both is identical, in the sense that it is related to the most intimate longings of every artist, still, from a practical point of view, it varies according to the particular prerogatives it bestows upon the dramatist of each culture. The German is free to express the inner longings of his soul in so far as that expression can be visibly realized. The Latin is free to create and then to sustain harmony as far as the methods he employs to that end allow. Thus, both are limited by an element uncongenial to their nature: the German by the *mise en scène,* and the Latin by the musical expression.

From this situation, we may easily deduce the kind of suggestion offered by the new freedom and the qualities needed to make it useful. In both cases indeed, their freedom will be subordinated to a *higher* principle, which on the one hand will save the form from the banal capriciousness of the artist and from the dictates of a modish society, and on the other, will free the poetic-musical expression from those heterogeneous realistic elements which have devalued its significance. Thus released, the artist brings into play the purest essence of his being, for his desires are in harmony with the very conditions necessary for their fulfillment. The first demand made on the dramatist, therefore, is that he cultivate the best part of himself. Instead of producing such depraved monsters as many of our contemporary painters, poets, and musicians have become through the exclusive exercise of the "artistic" technique, the integral work of art evokes and develops the balance of faculties and talents, laying the foundation for this balance on the nobility of the spirit.

The Search for an Environment for the Integral Work of Art

But, alas, where in our great cities can the integral work of art find a refuge in which to demonstrate its existence? Bayreuth cannot be re-created; those who would attempt it would only succeed in proving their inability to understand it.

No, we shall not be able to convert by means of the idea. *Today the integral work of art must clear the way for itself by technical means, for in the midst of our corrupt artistic institutions, it is technical form alone that can create the refuge which the idea attempted explicitly to establish at Bayreuth.*

Once upon a time, in ancient Greece, the beauty of the body *expressed* the beauty of the soul; love and the virtues seemed inseparable, and the work of art grew out of daily life as a simple efflorescence. The Greek, as he went about under the porticos embellished with statues, felt the intimate harmony which bound him to them; in the songs of his poets he recognized the very rhythm of his existence, and on the steps of the amphitheatre he realized the supreme fact of his *social life*. Already a brilliant figure, the Greek sought only to see his own image reflected everywhere; for him, the work of art was the *environment* from which his whole life radiated.

But a gradual transformation has changed the order of things: body and soul have created separate lives for themselves; life being thus fragmented, their indivisible radiation is therefore no longer possible, and fades into obscurity. The life of the imagination, which for the Greek was simply a synthesis of his own existence, has become the only means of regaining that lost harmony. In this sense, the creating of an imaginative world for us is the supreme act of the *Personality*.

The roles are thus reversed. Instead of providing us with an *Environment*, the work of art must attempt to create a setting for itself *within us*.

Does not the huge number of books in our libraries, the pictures in our museums, in exhibitions, or simply in their varied grouping on the walls of our homes, as well as our crowded concert programs, the routine in our theatres, affirm this fact? And if, blessed by fortune, a few exceptional men manage to create around themselves a viable atmosphere for a work of art, what price this achievement? Deaf to all demands except their own aesthetic desire, they live like hermits, divorced from humanity—and their creation is nothing more than the incarnation of an offensive dilettantism.

Drama, as performed, is the most evanescent of all art forms. One cannot see it in passing as one can a picture or a statue or a building, nor can one scan it at leisure, like a poem. Its existence depends upon several individual wills whose mutual agreement alone can make a production possible; and this production can never be a definitive one: once achieved, it must be begun all over again, and so on, continuously.

What the painter or the writer creates in the privacy of his studio and presents directly to the public, the dramatist must transfer to the stage. If his work is to be presented to an audience in its finished form, it must be in production—the most fugitive of all art forms. In our culture, already negative in its attitude toward art, there is no situation more disadvantageous than that of the dramatist; nor is there any artist who ought to wish more passionately for a refuge for his work.

But of all the unhappy dramatists, the word-tone poet is the most miserable, for by adding music to drama he is exposed to all sorts of misunderstandings. On the one hand is opera, which he renounces with good reason; on the other the spoken play which cannot serve him. However, if he gives up production of his work, and permits it to be performed in a concert, those misunderstandings suddenly disappear. This distinctive characteristic has so far led to nothing. Why, indeed, is the audience of a first-class concert in a much better state than the audience of an opera (lyric drama, or some other fabrication)? Why is an overture listened to with peaceful contemplation in a concert hall, whereas, at the opera, it is performed for people preoccupied with everything else but the music? Could it not be that in the transplendent opera house, the *technical methods* employed have created an atmosphere unsuited to any kind of contemplation whatever, while the hall dedicated to concerts leaves the responsibility for contemplation to each listener's soul?

But this is achieved in the concert hall by the use of *technical* effects, for in itself a concert hall is nothing definite.[1]

Is there then a method of concealing the soul from itself, of depriving it of its responsibility by perverting its taste, of making it see the same picture white one day and black the next? When fashion and the frivolities of worldly life do not interfere, can one still lead the soul where one wishes?

It seems to me that the example of concert hall and opera house is conclusive, permitting the statement that the use of *technical* devices in itself exercises a decisive influence upon the audience's state of mind, independent of the nature of the work performed.

Therefore, if a work of art is forced nowadays to find its only suitable refuge in our souls, the artist should have no more vital concern than to prepare within us a climate favorable to what he has to say. Today the use of techniques has not only an artistic importance, but a decided social significance as well.

We must not descend from a theoretical refusal to compromise to a practical inflexibility regarding the state of our culture. The Bayreuthian compromise was an heroic one, and its continued existence is still necessary; but its paradoxical nature resembles that of certain arguments whose truth is only extremely relative. These arguments are dangerous weapons, to be handled with care when the obstacles which once determined their use are removed. For the moment, man may well be saved by means of an artificially purified atmosphere; he finds the effect invigorating and out of the miasmas to which he is accustomed he draws new conclusions. But he must seek the reacting force within himself: the artificial atmosphere is but an illusion, and in time its effect becomes unhealthy, for today fiction is too powerful a force to risk attaching it for any length of time to the realities of life itself.

Having ascertained the influence at Bayreuth of the environment upon a work of art and its audience, it remains for us to

---

[1] We know that a theatre always seems to take on considerably more dignity when a concert is being presented there.

discover what effects the technical procedures themselves have had. We shall find these effects of a much more complex and a far more lofty nature than we could possible have imagined.

Richard Wagner's only effective weapon against the lifeless scenic conventions of our theatre was the score of his drama. The score came into conflict with the stereotyped methods of the production staff. This should have been realized in order to free it from the inertia of those methods. Unfortunately, no one understood the problem. Obviously, we are not concerned here with the artistic egoism of the production staff; such candor is appropriate to genius but would serve only to make us thoroughly ridiculous. Certainly the production reform I am discussing here will ultimately require the participation of living people, but it can begin with the reform of the inanimate elements of production. Rather than insisting upon speaking in our own language to people who do not understand and will always answer in another, we must compel ourselves to translate inwardly our intentions into the dialect of those whose help we need. A good diplomat always arranges it so that those who do the most to carry out his wishes think that they are only following their own desires. The realization of a work as complex as the word-tone drama requires such diplomacy.

By beginning with a consideration of the inanimate elements of production, we shall not need to reveal the main motive underlying the whole discussion. After all, when one gives a workman the technical drawing he is to execute, one does not appeal to any but his personal interests; so we can exploit even the fashion to achieve our ends, provided—and this is most important—that we appear to be armed with nothing but a technical plan.

The atmosphere created at Bayreuth is not necessarily an infallible help to us; for the individuals who seem to need it the most are usually those whose spirits are the least subject to time—in other words, who are least able to get into a mood at a given hour. So all of Bayreuth eludes them in their weakness. Such an environment does stimulate an already existing state of mind, and can even awaken it—but cannot regulate its duration or its course.

The influence of purely technical methods, since they remain

184 ·

more or less at the service of the audience, will thus have the advantage of permitting each member of the audience to choose the moment most favorable to him—or, at the very least, will not run the risk of destroying a happy frame of mind by a conflicting suggestion.

My reader will undoubtedly recall certain evenings spent at the theatre in which everything seemed calculated to turn him away from any kind of aesthetic enjoyment whatever; and where, in spite of this, he still experienced genuine pleasure—because from the very first, no one demanded any particular state of mind from him. Harassed by the stifling rush of modern life, we tend to live more and more within ourselves and are grateful to the artist who knows enough to take this into consideration. Were we to be given an environment—as at Bayreuth—it would be necessary to force ourselves into a mood frequently hard to attain, and in so doing we weaken (if not destroy) our receptiveness to the work of art being presented. We must therefore find a way of uniting the work and its environment in one idea alone. However, it is obvious that this can happen only if we concern ourselves with the form of drama itself.[1]

In this sense, our big cities offer every resource necessary for an integrated art form. They do more. They force the sensitive man into the greatest reserve by violently cultivating his aesthetic sensibility, thus making him more open than others to the influence of technical methods, and hence better equipped to bring them into harmony with the rest of his being. Moreover, the inhabitant of a large city hardens himself to resist the thousands of clichés of mediocrity with which he is assailed every day; and while he has become accustomed to pay no attention to them, he is only too anxious to preserve a few powerful impressions. These impressions are, in fact, what determine the *atmosphere* for the work of art.

Upon his arrival in a great capital, the provincial novice is at first overwhelmed by the brilliant display surrounding him. How can he ever begin to relish these multiple pleasures! His whole being is torn this way and that—it wants to embrace everything—and

---

[1] It should be understood that I have to a certain extent considered Bayreuth from the point of view of its weaknesses, which, unfortunately, lie within ourselves.

is astonished to find that it can retain nothing at all.

He carefully observes the faces and the bearing of those who are plunged into this overheated atmosphere, and sees in their features a calmness and in their attitude a precision which have no relationship to the "drama" in which they are playing a part.

The newcomer finally realizes that this "drama" consists of a strong network of roads, all quite different from each other, crowded with human beings who are there to pursue the satisfaction of their personal desires. The charm of such polyphony is to be found precisely in the obstinacy with which each one of these voices clings to its part.

Since the big city embraces all human inclinations, it is as capable of neutralizing them as it is of pushing any one of them to its furthest limits; it is midway between nullity and plenitude.[1]

Thus, the inner life is a challenge thrown in the face of nothingness and a guarantee of success for every manifestation of humanity, for the inner life establishes for itself alone what we call an environment. And that is what explains the compelling interest that our young provincial has for some of the heads he encounters: each one of these heads embraces, not only a distinct individuality, but also the needed environment for the life of several other individualities—and their features bear a *characteristic mark*.

In Paris, capital of the Latin culture, this mark has an extremely plastic form and reveals more clearly than in any other city the nature of its source (for the principle of classification does, after all, confirm the fact that the work of art finds its home within ourselves). In German countries this is less apparent, and one must delve more deeply to discover its distinctive features. Thus, the German audience is a heterogeneous one and thus more difficult to classify: its art is essentially democratic.

The atmosphere created by the German individuality lacks the Latin flexibility, and besides the German would not know what to do with it. For him, the principle of classification is little more than an entirely superficial imitation of Parisian life and can be

---

[1] The type of depression one experiences only in large cities must result from the fact that the soul dwells momentarily upon the first of these possibilities.

maintained only by the use of techniques foreign to the work of art itself. The result of this is that for the German a work of art is more truly national as it becomes more universal in character. Wagner was very conscious of this when he built his Festival Theatre.

Nevertheless, the big city ought now to provide an atmosphere for the German drama, but the German, in contrast to the Latin who realizes his aims through a very specific technique alone, can do this only by universalizing the scope of his art. For this reason music must be his point of departure.

The music will determine how the various elements of production are to be used, and these in turn will then influence the musical expression. The peculiar integrity of this form will of necessity influence the soul of the spectator, and, because it does not fit into any existing artificial classifications, will reveal to that soul the possibility for an aesthetic pleasure that is completely satisfying. The German mind will thus create, in the midst of the most deplorable imitations, an environment for integral art.

"The Artist-Musician"

In Germany, the musician—first and basic factor of German drama—is not hard to find. Consequently, all reforms in production will not be directly concerned with the composer's vocation but can be concentrated on other elements. The case is not quite the same in Latin countries. In Paris, there are composers with a thorough command of their profession who would be completely incapable of grasping the idea of the musical drama. For the majority of them, music, in spite of everything, is merely a superficial game of form, and the character of their creations is in no way altered by virtue of scholarly commentaries upon them—any more than the vintage of a wine can be changed by what is written upon the label. The Latin musician (in the usual sense of the word) is an artistic anomaly. The characteristic shade of disregard which the Parisian writer directs towards the musicians of his country is not unjustified, for, in dedicating himself *exclusively* to music, the Latin produces something purely personal and usually mediocre; he does not participate in the development of his contemporaries and thus finds himself, more or less consciously, obliged to exploit the ignorance of the bourgeois or the futility of society—and so his pretensions are always slightly absurd.[1]

The cultivated Latin who still wishes to avail himself of music has two ways out of his dilemma. Either he will seek *in the form of the music itself* the development of his people's virtues, or these virtues will, as they appear in *other branches of art,* strongly influence his musical aspiration. In the first instance, he diverts music from its proper function, removing from it the form revealed by the Wagnerian idea; and the fictitious object he creates for it finally is aimed only at the intelligence of complaisant colleagues. When this happens, the composer loses popularity in order to create musical mathematics, the tediousness of which cannot be equaled.

In the second case, the composer is an *artist* who understands instinctively that music is an art of expression. Unlike the German, he does not discover the object of this expression exclusively and unquestionably within his soul, but seeks to deduce it from all other artistic manifestations. But these other art forms cannot capture his attention unless they possess a very decided "artistic" character —that is, unless they occupy the highest place in the hierarchy of Latin art.

Because he *desires* music, he will be acutely aware of its absence, but the high virtuosity displayed in works which delight him will not strike him as being an adequate compensation for the absence of musical expression: therefore, he will bring it to the same excessive refinement to which his soul has been accustomed elsewhere. Thus in his desire to fill the void, he creates an independent work of art. Because of his particular virtuosity he can endow music with the same perfection as that brought by the painter or the writer to their works.

And this is only natural, for if it is impossible for the need

---

[1] This is why, in German countries, certain theatres receive these products so warmly —obviously, nothing is sham enough for such places. Not content to debilitate themselves all season with borrowed feathers, they seem to have a continuing predilection for seeking out the most mediocre foreign trash in order to adapt it for their own use. Could it be, after all, a need for harmony that drives them to this?

for harmony to operate on all the factors at once (this can occur only in musical drama), the Latin artist attempts to replace it by a need for *equivalence* between the resonance which non-musical works produce in him and that with which his own work must be endowed by the music.

In the same way as the "mathematician," such an artist loses all popularity. On the other hand, his work is "artistic" to the highest degree, so that he can still be assured of an audience capable of enjoying his efforts. Unfortunately, music cannot long survive this kind of excess—as I have said, it almost becomes a vice, so that the already limited number of people who enjoy this form is reduced even more.

To extricate music from this dilemma, the poet is now brought in as assistant. At this point, the artist must of necessity compose music adequate to these poems which have been carefully wrought with the most patient affection. But—the poem is a masterpiece by itself. How can it be further exalted by combining with it sounds that are foreign to its composition?

Without suspecting it, the modern *poet* has met the *artist*-musician halfway; brimming with musical desire, he has concocted outlandish works upon which has been lavished everything that words can suggest, by means of sonority, juxtaposition, and, above all, by the *intricacy* of their meaning. These subtle intentions, demanding as they do of the reader a kind of interior translation, force him to that activity which the Latin so enjoys: he completes the work for and in himself.

It is this very activity the artist then seizes upon and expresses in music. His music most seductively supplies what the poet had required the reader to provide; at times the music goes so far that it virtually assumes the role of the reader of the poem—the hearer is positively involved *in* the work of art.[1]

I cannot analyze here the rapport thereby established between the word and the musical sound. This rapport is at once too complex and too evanescent. It must be confessed, however, that these artists are very little influenced by the Wagnerian method; their great

---

[1] Some of M. Claude A. Debussy's compositions carry this to extreme.

respect for the poem they compose impels them to put every bit of their unbelievable virtuosity at its service. Their music thus becomes "French," in the philological sense of the word. This results in a kind of beauty to inspire the greatest confidence for works to come.

Obviously, the idea of musical drama could develop beyond any question from such distinguished foundations. And it is not without interest to attempt to discover what change this idea would effect in its production.

The musical "mathematician" remains of no concern to us. He longs to be German, without possessing the indispensable gift for this, and French, without drawing upon the highest qualities of his race for his work. His products are bastard—even the best of them are worthless except as collectors' curiosities. They have nothing to do with *living* art.

Quite the opposite is he whom I shall call the *artist-musician* (as opposed to the German *word-tone poet*). Despite his modest pretensions and the aesthetic impossibility of embellishing his work with commentaries with which others are so prodigal, he alone represents the most advanced stage of Latin culture. Instead of following the mainstream, of yielding to evolutions already long in the making, he knew, most of the time unconsciously, for he is first and foremost an artist, that the fertile principle lay in the work of Richard Wagner. He assimilated what the Latin genius could absorb from it; then, unfalteringly he set to work, dominated by an irresistible impulse. This proves his artistic judgment to be so sure and of such rarefied taste that there are perhaps no works of art in Latin countries comparable to his. Other artists develop to the best of their ability elements already in existence; he enriches his culture by means of a new element.

The Object of Music in Latin Countries

The artist-musician's work eloquently demonstrates the fact that the essence and the beauty of "French" music are the result of a profound respect on his part for an *artist inspired by musical desire.*

Consequently, musical desire, even without the professional skill, is the indispensable condition for all "French" music. *Such music cannot exist independently; rather it is the efflorescence of a desire which also extends to all the other branches of art.*[1]

Previously we have seen that when this musical desire seeks to express itself in some form other than music, it endows the resultant work of art with a suggestive character that requires a kind of internal reorganization. The play of this reciprocal activity proves that the author and his audience sense the presence of an Unknown—and since they are both too artistic to dare to replace this Unknown by means of simple technical expedients, they feel it is best left alone; hence it is relegated to an undefined place in the creation. *This interplay is the object of music for the Latin.*

In composing his music, the artist-musician makes manifest the Unknown; he fills the place *reserved for that alone.* Thus the roles of both the poetic and the visual aspects of production in the musical play are clearly defined. The space left instinctively by the painter, the sculptor, and the modern poet in their works for the purpose of allowing the audience to enjoy the charm of an unexpressed music gives to the products of art a form eminently suited to their unification.

The simplification of detail necessary for a simultaneous action of all these factors is already three-fourths accomplished—*and with the full assent of the audience.*

This is truly a triumph of form! Just as astronomers determine in the infinity of the heavens the place of a yet invisible star, so, because of a highly cultivated sense of form, the Unknown can be anticipated and its place approximately charted.

The law regulating the activity of Latin artists is as infallible as the one determining the calculations of astronomers: both prophesy the coming of a star they have not yet seen.

Enter the artist-musician, the artist who possesses the light and knows how to focus it—and suddenly all eyes *will see.*

The musical drama will become the center where all talents will converge. Out of the conditions and intensity of expression result-

---

[1] Here I would remind the reader of the particular definition I have given the term "musical desire" in relation to Parisian artists.

ing from this union will come a new form for each individual art.

For the Unknown, now revealed, will transform the mere suggestion into positive expression, so that the unspecified place previously reserved for it suddenly becomes *measurable,* thus effecting a vital change in the relationship between the author and *his* audience.

The artist did not exaggerate the importance but he did the extent of this mysterious and unknown element; by refining his technique in the service of an ever more complete suggestion, he seemed doomed to founder in a void—and the ever more febrile curiosity of his audience encouraged him along those lines.

At this crucial moment, music, *in a form that he could appreciate,* gives the artist back to himself: it reveals to him the new prestige of forces neglected through excessive refinement; and now, with his "musical desire" finally satisfied, he opens himself to a fresh source of energy and vitality.

The Ideal Norm for the Artist-Musician and for the Poet-Musician

The main theories derived from the idea of word-tone drama —and this includes the reforms in technical theatre as well—which we established in the first part of this book, will serve as the ideal norm for both the artist-musician and the word-tone poet.

The idea placed between the creations of both artists unites them and tends to attract them to one another. Only through this idea can their need for harmony be completely satisfied, so that the idea alone can protect each artist from dangerous digressions.

The distance separating them from this common ideal is dependent upon the variable qualities of personality: the *richer* the inner development of the German, the more motives he will find for the externalization of his drama. The more *deeply* the Latin artist's desire develops, the better he will learn to confer upon the actor alone the right to control the scenic picture.

From a theoretical grasp of the idea will necessarily result a progressive step toward a practical refusal to compromise. The artist-musician, admirably supported by his colleagues in the other isolated branches of art, will strive mainly to perfect the *techniques* of production: the respective value of each element of production and the means of uniting them will pose no problem for him—for he will be guided by his powerful instinct for form.[1]

On the other hand, the word-tone poet will make a special study of the respective values among the production factors; then he will be able, almost without restriction, to apply the theories of the *mise en scène* as a means of expression; in other words, the transference of music by means of the hierarchy of production. But for the Latin, these theories will, at least to some extent, be dependent upon existing technical methods.

Nevertheless, for one, as for the other, the only worthwhile treatise on the integral work of art will always remain the theoretical and speculative demonstration of the word-tone drama—anything else would have only a temporary value.

Still, we have seen that such a demonstration is not a matter for debate—in its most detailed aspects, it is founded upon laws and facts quite independent of the personal taste of the artist; therefore, its theoretical value is absolute for one who *desires music*.

---

[1] Everything that can be communicated by means of today's *mise en scène* the Parisian has achieved, and considerations of a different nature now make him perpetuate the scenic convention.

—APPENDIX—

INTRODUCTION

Such a solidly entrenched convention as the modern-day stage cannot be suddenly overturned — especially since it applies almost universally to most of the plays of the current repertory, and suits the superficial tastes of a public interested only in the temporary distractions of the theatre. There are, however, some first-rate plays, old and new, which, merely because they are in the minority, should not always be dragged into that commonplace world. Dramatists must often be aghast at the banal settings that are imposed on their works; and they must sometimes ask if the complex and costly machinery of the stage really could not provide something less repugnant to the eye and place at the disposal of the dramatist less crude materials. The answer is "no," and since those who give it are those in charge, the dramatists are forced not to believe them but to give in to them.

Since there is an insufficiently strong impetus to effect these much-needed reforms, and since there is no one to defend those authors who are dead, perhaps it may be possible—from a different approach—to introduce some provisional improvements in the art of staging.

The dramas of Richard Wagner are presently enjoying an extraordinary success, but one which, unfortunately, has little to do with the composer's own aims. This popularity, and the money which it brings to certain box-offices, fills theatre managers and their technical staffs with profound respect and so disposes them favorably toward Wagner's genius. Why not, with the excuse of faithfulness to Wagner or of turn-of-the-century staging, take advantage of such favorable conditions to attempt some little reform in the staging of Wagner's music-dramas? Indeed, the public reaction to a new mode of production would be much easier to gauge in dramas which the public does not feel it has to judge but rather can admire with confidence; and, artistically, the staging would develop strictly from the drama itself. Furthermore, one would have the advantage of being able to accustom the eyes of the spectator to a kind of harmony, which he would not perhaps appreciate at once, but which would become the more evident when compared with the other offerings of the day.

I shall not refer, at this point, to the Bayreuth stage which has been treated in its own chapter. Since its equipment is basically not different from that of our own stages, it can easily undergo the same adjustments in scenic technique. Such adjustments are too exclusively technical to be described here; moreover, the first part of this study—in establishing the ideal to be pursued—has noted clearly what factors are in need of reform. But, very briefly, here are some of the things we have in mind.

Painted scenery must renounce its sovereignty, if not in fact at least in appearance; the lighting will confirm the subordination of painting by giving up most of its obligations to painting and concentrating on the development of its own devices. The use of footlights must be reduced to a minimum and, even sometimes, completely eliminated. Practicability will be the most important factor among the scenic elements and as a result will rule temporarily out of use certain of the stage devices. Finally, the actors will have to familiarize themselves with the new state of things, and seek to approach it by an ever more complete and conscious sacrifice of their own wills to the harmony of the whole. As we know, all this excludes the pursuit of scenic illusion.

There is only one serious obstacle to a reform of today's staging. The tiny area reserved for the theatre wings (by which I mean the offstage areas invisible to the audience) makes very difficult an increase in three-dimensional pieces of scenery and their rapid shifting. So it is here that one must insist on the most decisive changes. Those who inspect a theatre for the first time are usually amazed at the clumsy machinery which is used back stage and the infantile, primitive character of some of the devices. Why is it, they ask, that science provides industry with masterpieces of design and precision, while the theatre so highly extolled as an artistic institution has only children's toys with which to entertain its audience? This is indeed strange, but it is easily explained by the over-emphasis placed on painted scenery. If this expensive element is put in its proper place, the resultant considerable savings can be applied to a more worthy object. The present concept of practical scenery makes a reasonable handling of costs impossible. However, this element— second only to the actors in the hierarchy of expression, requires in in its construction very special care; yet, the opposite is what happens. The square boxes, the folding frames, the sections of flooring, all the grotesque practical pieces in our theatres, are proof of the modern producer's complete ignorance of the importance of this element. Yet every technical resource should be mustered to hasten the development and easy handling of three-dimensional scenery; and the rejection of stage illusion gives the engineer a very considerable freedom in this respect.

But the hierarchic principle can be applied only at the command of the music; it is music only which can bring it into being. One may therefore wonder what usefulness a scenic reform on this basis could have for dramatic works in which music plays a minor role or is absent altogether.

The main vice of modern staging is *convention* (justified apparently by painting) and it paralyzes the whole technical realm. Convention is always obstinately opposed to any change; its only value lies in its rigidity. On the other hand, to attack it arbitrarily would only create in its place a convention of another kind. Therefore, if we wish to make our stage production an elastic, workable machine that can obey the demands of the dramatist, whatever they may be; if we want to outlaw conventional staging, we can do so only by opposing to it a dramatic form whose perfectly legitimate elements *necessarily* bring with them a new principle of staging. And this new principle, emanating only from the work of art itself, will have in it nothing of what is called "convention." The technical world of the stage, subject only to *natural* laws, will find itself free like a living organism. Certainly, it is music alone which makes the *mise en scène* a means of expression, but the fact that the latter can attain this superior position proves that it can realize all the aims of the dramatist, and in its lower position can give him intelligent assistance.

By using music to effect a reform in staging we secure the only means at our disposal today; and since the dramas of Richard Wagner are the only ones we have in which music incontestably holds its rightful place, my proposal is, I feel, quite justified.

The *Ring* and *Tristan* are, in their staging, opposite extremes in Wagner's work. *Tristan* lends itself completely to the expressive principle in its staging; however, the *Ring,* as we have seen, must make use of compromise to compensate for its technical defect. I have therefore singled out these two dramas as examples. But the size of the *Ring* allows me here to indicate only the most cursory ideas for reforming its staging.[1] *Tristan,* however, will be treated in more detail, although still quite generally, since the complete scenario of a Wagnerian drama requires a treatment beyond the scope of this study.

---

[1]These views are part of a complete and detailed study which the author plans to publish with numerous illustrations.

THE STAGING OF TRISTAN AND ISOLDE
Translated by Walther R. Volbach

The performance of this drama is in itself an ordeal for our nervous system, but it is still further aggravated through the failure of the production to alleviate the overpowering dramatic tension and through the inability of our imagination to compensate for the probable defects of the performance. These are so grave that we close our eyes in order not to see the gross inadequacy of the stage; only the *presence* of the characters obliges us to open them again. And yet, if we study the drama's musical score in search of the scenic elements, we find nothing worthy of being realized with more precision than was exercised by the author in his brief notations. The place and period of the action could well suggest to us a thousand things. The excitement left in our memory by the musical expression seems to force upon us a sumptuous production worthy of the music's intensity. So we plan this and plan that—in the end we discover that, for all our efforts and the experience still vibrating in us, we have not touched the core of the drama, that the dramatic action which was to determine the theatrical form persists in remaining alien to it.

As a matter of fact it eludes theatrical form and will forever elude it because the dramatic action is *entirely within.*

In conflict with the outer world, Tristan and Isolde choose death voluntarily. Death deceives them and throws them back into life to which they no longer belong. It is not this life which the stage director must present to the audience; the author had no intention of conveying it to us and, moreover, the duration of the inner action would not have permitted him to do so.—At the beginning, the conflict is presented to us as it is reflected in the souls of Tristan and Isolde. Later on, the external world holds no conflict any more. Death, summoned by them, merely frees them of empty phantoms. How can such action be performed at all? But *Tristan* is rightly a piece for the theatre, a theatrical work that has to be *performed.*

The audience at a performance relates everything it sees on stage quite naturally to the action. This visual aspect has been reduced by the author to a minimum, leaving the stage director several possibilities. Thus the spectator may hear an action communicated to him with the unique precision of poetic-musical means while he looks at a setting completely unrelated to the inner drama. If this seems *a priori* a favorable solution, in practice it is not. It destroys the equilibrium—the basic principle and virtually the justification for the word-tone drama's existence—and delivers the drama to a chaos of sensations.

Hence, it is indispensable to set the expressive precision of the inner drama against a visual form capable of giving it full expression on the stage. In *Tristan* then the task of the stage director is not to seek the necessary harmony in the drama, since the drama has nothing to do with it. On the other hand, he cannot establish an immediate, that is a positive, contact between the inner action and the audience unless he finds a method directly derived from the dramatic intention. What method can be drawn from a drama indifferent to its performance?—Unquestionably the *utmost* reduction of decorative elements.—Beginning with act two, the empty phantoms surrounding Tristan and Isolde . . . these are the ones which the stage, supported by the music, must show while music strips the characters themselves of all reality. The necessity of escaping these phantoms through death will be sufficiently explained by the mere fact of their representation.

In emphasizing thus the indifference of the stage toward the dramatic action, we compel the spectator to *take part* in this action. The exclusively inner function of the poetic-musical expression becomes for him a necessity: the equilibrium is re-established through the production.

In *Tristan* Wagner permits us to experience the emotions of his hero and heroine more fully than in any other drama. Though our eyes participate in the experience, they remain nevertheless aloof from this life: on the one hand we are observers; on the other, we are blind supernumeraries.

The main principle for the production of *Tristan and Isolde* consists, therefore, in *making the audience see the drama through the eyes of the hero and heroine.*

This definition is not of course to be taken literally, but it describes well the purpose which must underlie all endeavors to realize this masterpiece on the stage.

One must begin with the greatest scenic reduction in order to make sure that only the bare necessities are provided for those scenes which do not admit of so complete a reduction. Therefore let us start with act two.

Act Two

When Isolde enters she sees only two things: the absence of Tristan and the torch (the last trace of act one), the reason for his absence. The mild summer night gleaming through the tall trees has lost its meaning for Isolde; the luminous view is for her eyes only the cruel Space that separates her from Tristan. Yet, in spite of her extreme impatience, a fire in the depths of her soul transforms all the forces of nature into a wondrous harmony. The torch alone remains indubitably what it is: a signal agreed upon to warn away the man she loves.

By extinguishing the torch Isolde removes the obstacle, wipes out the hostile Space, arrests Time. — With her we are shocked at the slow death agony of these two enemies.

At last, everything comes to an end. There is no time any longer, no space, no singing nature, no menacing torch — nothing at all. Tristan is in the arms of Isolde.

Then the time, that is no more, maintains for us, the audience, a fictitious existence, music. — But what about Space? What remains of it for us who did not drink the death potion?

Like the two leading characters we see nothing and want to see nothing but their presence. What burns in their hearts appears to us, as to them, superior to their visible forms, and the fictitious existence of the music carries us deeper and deeper into the mysterious world where their union is consummated forever. — A single anguish grips us: we still see them. Vaguely we realize that it is our painful privilege to *see* those who are no longer of this world; and when the cold phantoms of our life appear suddenly with wide open eyes to assert their right upon these chosen ones, we feel like their accomplices.

How will the stage director contrive to let the spectator participate wholeheartedly in the performance without resort to conscious thought?

After the preceding analysis, perhaps I need not justify the following ideas point by point.

The appearance of the stage when the curtain opens: a large bright torch in the *center* of the picture. The rather limited space of the stage is illuminated by a diffuse light, just enough to make the characters clearly distinguishable without entirely depriving the torch of its somewhat blinding brightness, nor above all, destroying the shadows projected by this brightness.

The forms determining and limiting this space are only dimly seen. The quality of the light gives an impression of outdoors. One or two lines of the barely visible setting suggest trees.

The eye becomes gradually accustomed to this view and then perceives distinctly part of a building which can be entered from a terrace. During the entire first scene the characters, Isolde and Brangaene, remain on this terrace, leaving between them and the downstage area a space where one senses that there is some kind of depression in the ground.

When Isolde extinguishes the torch, the setting takes on a uniform chiaroscuro in which the eye loses itself, unarrested by any line or object.

Isolde rushing to meet Tristan is plunged into a mysterious darkness increasing the impression of depth which the setting gives to the right half of the stage.

During their first outburst of joy they remain on the terrace. At the height of the music (vocal score, p. 112, ff of the orchestra "mine"[1]) we see them walk toward us: they gradually leave the raised

[1] Page numbers refer to the vocal score, prepared by Hans von Buelow, Breitkopf & Haertel, Leipzig, also Schirmer, N.Y. Tr.

level of the terrace and by way of a ramp that is barely visible reach a sort of platform downstage. This platform, the ramp separating it from the terrace, and the other ramp leading downstage form an acting area full of variety for the succeeding passionate outpourings.

Thereafter, when the lovers at last satiated by these emotional exchanges unite in a single thought — when the death of time seems to become ever more evident for us, they finally reach downstage (p. 136-137) which has, as we notice only now, a shelter at the foot of the terrace. All the mysterious space grows still more uniform; the form of the building is lost in the same darkness as the upstage area; even different levels of the floor are no longer really visible.

Is it the vague and undefinable recollection of shadows created by the brightness of the torch, or is it the path the two lovers have just traversed before our eyes, that makes us sense deeply how things are closing in to enwrap and delude them?

During Brangaene's song the light fades still further; the characters are seen less clearly.

Lastly the surge of passion is revived, grows, and threatens to overpower the entire scene when suddenly (p. 162 with the first ff by the orchestra) a pale light glimmers upstage right.[1] King Mark and his followers rush in. Daylight slowly increases, cold, colorless. The eye begins to see the entire setting in its full severity, when Tristan, with a supreme effort, returns to life by challenging Melot, who has betrayed him to the king.

In this ghostly setting only one area remains dark, spared from the rising dawn: the shelter in front of the terrace.

To clarify this account and to explain the attached design I shall give an exact description of this setting.

The *terrace,* crossing the stage diagonally, begins stage center left, stretches to the right farther upstage, and disappears in the darkness of the background. It is raised at least two meters above the stage floor. The left part of this terrace, up to one third of the stage width, is supported by a *wall.* This wall forms a left angle and, dropping directly downstage, carries the setting to the proscenium.

From the left third of the stage to the extreme right of the setting, *two ramps* lead downstage from the terrace with a rather large platform between them. The ramps are angled slightly toward the extreme corners of the stage.

The *first wing area,* properly speaking, is quite restricted through this arrangement, for it is bound by the angle of the wall supporting the terrace and cannot extend beyond the lower ramp, which extends far beyond stage center.

The *building,* with a door giving access to the terrace, stretches from the torch, thus about center stage, to the left wing where it follows at some distance the bend of the terrace wall and encloses the downstage

---

[1] The stage directions are from the audience point of view. Tr.

area completely.

Stage right remains undefined. In a very general manner we discern the simplified outlines of some tree trunks which bound the setting and whose barely indicated foliage masks the flies.

A bench is at the foot of the terrace; the angle of the wall inclined like a support serves as its back. The bench, thus located on the *left* in the first quarter of the stage width, provides a contrast to the ramps descending from the terrace and seems to face the entire undefined part of the setting without doing so completely.

The torch is attached to the wall of the building between the door and a narrow outside staircase whose contour dominates the dark background. The torch is on a rather long shaft so that most of the spectators may see its bright light set off against the background and not against the building.

The color of the scenery is in general neutral. The walls and a part of the floor seem overrun by moss and ivy. The combination of platforms must be toned down by painting and distinguishable only through the movements of the characters.

The vague outlines which enclose the setting at the top do not represent the usual regular branching from a central trunk; instead they slope over the left side like an arbor, while on the right they rise as freely as possible so that each half of the stage may maintain its particular character: the left, that of a shelter beyond which no one can penetrate; the right, that of an opening into the unknown.

The following examples will demonstrate how the characters are to make use of this setting.

Up to page 100, Isolde and Brangaene remain at center and at the right side of the terrace. With the words, "Thy act, oh foolish girl," Isolde reaches the left side of the terrace and sings (page 101 and 102) standing at the edge of the wall, thus directly above the shelter downstage. She returns to the center only to seize the torch. — I have already mentioned that with the ff on page 112 Tristan and Isolde leave the terrace and move downstage very gradually to the platform. With the cue, "To sunlight," on page 116, Tristan takes a position at the extreme left of the upper ramp center stage, at the spot which will be occupied by Isolde on page 133 for her "bright bonds of empty splendor" and by Melot during the whole last scene. Tristan standing here sings toward the right. On page 122 he gradually reaches the lower ramp, then on page 123 he returns to the platform, and on page 124 to the upper ramp, while Isolde, with her "Oh daylight's slave indeed" on the same page, makes place for him on the lower ramp by turning her back to the extreme left of the stage as if to forbid Tristan's crossing to it. — With his "my day was ended quite," Tristan, turning slightly left, steps forward on the platform facing the audience, to be with his "Oh hail the potion" on page 130 at the top of the lower ramp as close to the audience as the ramp permits. Isolde remains on the platform and on page 133 "in bright . . .," is at the extreme left of the upper ramp stage center. Tristan stays on the lower ramp close to the audience turning slightly to Isolde, *i.e.* to the left, for his "Oh now were we to-night devoted." They slowly approach each other on pages 134-135, and come downstage left, 136-137, an area they do not leave until the end of the act.

Kurvenal rushes in to warn Tristan of the betrayal; he does not go beyond the terrace. Only after the entrance of King Mark and his retinue does he move to the *lower* ramp. The King himself remains on the platform between the two ramps until the end of the act; his attendants are grouped on the terrace. Melot stands center stage at the extreme left of the upper ramp and the audience sees him between Kurvenal and the King, though a little to the rear of the latter. Provoked by Tristan, he leaps on the platform and from there to the ramp on which Tristan then collapses.

The spatial arrangement, because the floor is covered with platforms, steps, and ramps, assumes the leading role in the setting of act two. Unquestionably lighting must emphasize those three-dimensional elements, keeping unobtrusive the two-dimensional canvas pieces around the stage, but its role as regards the performer is in a way negative. By contrast, in act three light becomes all-important for the production; floorplan and elevation are solely and uniquely subservient to it, and painting is reduced to whatever place is permitted by the scenic arrangement.

Act Three

When Tristan awakes he does not at first know where he is; when told, he does not understand; the name of the castle, his estate, leaves him completely indifferent. The sad melody that awoke him does not offer him the least tangible clue. Trying to express his feelings, he can think only of a sensation of light that disturbs and pains him and of a sensation of darkness escaping him but which he would like to retrieve. He associates Isolde with these two sensations, because, at Tristan's awakening, Isolde has been returned to the light. On this bright day he must "search, seek, find her" — and yet it is this daylight that keeps him away from her, like the menacing torch of act two. When he learns that she is coming, that she is actually drawing near, the castle's existence suddenly makes sense; it dominates the sea, from it one can descry on the horizon the ship carrying Isolde. In his feverish yearning this idea takes form: Tristan, who is unable to see even the sea from his sick-bed, "sees" the ship.

The melody that awakened him is now going to speak to him in more explicit terms than all the hallucinations.

Yet his longing persists deep within his soul; his affliction makes it more bitter; the light of the sun nurtures it relentlessly; no relief is possible, no recovery. — A paroxysm of despair plunges Tristan anew into night. He loses consciousness.

It is not the sad and universal lament that brings him back, nor the insolent hostility of the day. No, a wondrous ray penetrates the depth of the night: Isolde has come, she is very near.

After the divine vision, comes reality.

The piercing sun, the blood of the wound, are now only manifestations of joy; may they flood the castle: "She who must heal the wound forever . . . she approaches . . . her voice resounds . . . brilliant . . . But in order to meet her the torch must be extinguished . . . ." Tristan sways and falls lifeless in Isolde's arms.

The beautiful clarity of daylight — which became their supreme illusion — slowly sinks below the sea's horizon throwing a last blood-tinged halo around the reunited lovers.

So the part played by lighting is clearly prescribed for the act. As long as light is only a source of Tristan's suffering, it must not fall on him directly. But as soon as he really sees it and associates it with blissful visions, it comes and illuminates his face.

On the whole this sums up the task of the stage director and it must ultimately determine the use of painting and the spatial arrangement.

In order to achieve the effect I have described, it is necessary to limit the light, leaving much of the space in the dark. Under these circumstances, one appears relatively free in designing the setting. Nevertheless, since everything which will assist the lighting must be carefully considered and since to assist the lighting is the sole function of the setting in this act, there cannot be many ways to design the place indicated by the dramatist, and I cannot be accused of the arbitrary exercise of my imagination, if I give a fairly definitive form to the setting.

The buildings of the castle must cover the left side and the background of the setting, like a screen around a patient, then turn from the rear slightly to the right. The downstage right wings are assumed to serve as the other end of the screen, some of whose panels are presumably cut out to let the audience see the stage. — The two ends of this screen form a kind of wide bay open to the sky, and are connected with the floor by a wall.

Only what is strictly needed to mask the flies and to motivate the shadows which fill the courtyard should be added to this simple construction. But to give life to the light striking the floor, the platforms are arranged in the following manner: the foot of the left wall is buttressed in its entire length, which, in a simple way breaks its monotony. From the base of the buttress the floor drops somewhat, then rises to form the roots of the large tree under which Tristan is lying. From the roots the floor drops again, but this time more deeply, and so creates, between the tree and the wall on the right, a kind of path, hollowed through being trod upon — a path that extends from the door in the background to the downstage area. The inside approaches of the wall which looks out to the sea are slightly raised. Thus the stage presents an incline from left to right and the light, falling from the right and increasingly slanting, will eventually strike the base of the buttress.

Since *utter* simplicity has to be maintained in the enclosure of the luminous bay, everything that stands out against the clear sky will be carefully selected. — The raised area from which Kurvenal can scan the horizon is on stage right in the panel covering the first wing, so that, though not perceptibly breaking the general line of the setting, it, nevertheless, isolates Kurvenal in an expressive silhouette. Of course, the ocean cannot be seen at all; nothing is visible between the wall and the sky, and the perfectly blue sky is cloudless.

In accordance with the specific function of light here, Tristan lies facing the bay that opens toward the sky; he is surrounded by as few properties as possible, for *real pieces* would mar such a simplified setting. — Between large tree roots Kurvenal has placed some cloaks on which to lay Tristan. On the improvised and barely perceptible couch the ailing man is stretched out.

The character of the picture being thus sufficiently indicated, we need not go into further details, but turn now to the score to see quickly how light is to be used.

The attached design gives the general effect to be achieved by the lighting during the first half of the act.

On page 215, the light, turning increasingly more golden, begins to touch Tristan's feet; on page 218 it reaches up to his waist; on page 221 it touches his face; on page 223 Tristan is fully lighted; on page 225, the beam extends to his surroundings. During pages 233-236, the stage attains the maximum of light which is relatively low, for the section of wall restricting the view of the sky upstage throws a deep shadow over a large part of the courtyard, especially over the door and its approaches. Starting with page 236, the lighting takes on the hues of sunset, then rapidly decreases its intensity during pages 238-242 until, on pages 245-248, the turbulent action occurs in relative darkness and the audience cannot distinguish its details, while the downstage areas are hit directly by a light which grows redder and redder . . . .

The platforms at the foot of the wall serve well for the fighting (pages 138-149). Kurvenal, when wounded, steps into the light and falls down close to Tristan. None of Mark's or Kurvenal's men leaves the dark area. — The greatest care must be taken in handling the shadows created by the characters in the last scene. This means that Mark and Brangaene, their backs turned toward the spotlight, must become dark silhouettes without throwing any shadow on the two principals. — Kurvenal has fallen into the shadow cast by Tristan. — Beginning with page 254, the light continues to fade, plunging the setting into an ever deeper twilight. The curtain closes on a quiet and uniformly lighted picture in which the eye can distinguish only the last touch of the waning sun which faintly colors Isolde's white dress.

It is understood that the scenic description of this act in the score must be regarded as a brief dramatic commentary rather than as a literal request to the stage director; for, in it we see clearly how Wagner turned from the actor to the dramatic contents as the mainspring for his scenic arrangement. Here the master apparently sought a theatrical form outside of his poetic-musical expression . . . .

In the last two acts lighting and the spatial arrangement have all but eliminated painting. The actor does not display a great deal of *visible* activity; for the most part his presence is enough. In act one we find that the external life, and the conflict incited by it, will appear tragic in the *theatre* only if the cruelty of this life is shown to us. On the other hand, if, in the following acts, we claim the right to reduce the visual role to the simplest expression, we must in the first act not only present the ruthless reality, but we must present it as merely a drama whose existence can be denied by the hero and heroine.

In this respect the setting of the first act is one of the most felicitous.

Act One

In the subdued light of her tent, Isolde, hiding her head in cushions, longs to escape the hated reality. An echo of this detested life strikes her. Beside herself, she jumps up; she feels personally offended by the sailor's song. The shelter which is no shelter weighs upon her; she stifles within the canvas walls. Since reality imposes itself thus upon her, she, Isolde, is going to oppose it, willingly face it and feast her eyes on it: at her command the curtains of the tent separate.

There is the wide open space filled with an invigorating breeze. Isolde gazes and gazes, and painfully fills her eyes with this wonderful light which has for her, however, only one meaning: it supports and verifies Tristan's betrayal. His presence makes her sense the reality of the world into which he has cast himself: thus she keeps her eyes fixed on him. Soon she is unable to endure this passive attitude any longer and, as it is impossible to escape what she sees, she wants to participate in it. The conflict is imminent. Through a cruel dramatic trick Isolde must witness it, powerless and silent. Finally the tent curtains are closed again at the very moment when, for us, the spectators of Isolde's drama, this twofold performance becomes intolerable.

Music seems to be muted before the overpowering reality. In the grip of an otherwise masterful hand, music did not know what to make of this brilliance. In the quiet intimacy of the half-light inside the tent, it can burst forth unrestrained. No matter how the tide of the outer world sometimes batters against the sides of the tent, its curtains will not open again until Tristan and Isolde have disavowed the world of reality and their sole obligation will be to act and to act at once. This wrings from them outcries of supreme distress, but they will no longer feel the significance of their action.

The curtains of Isolde's tent thus symbolically separate in the fullest meaning of the term the visual aspect of the outer world from the expression of inner life. The conflict which constitutes the dramatic action is then directly realized before our eyes in a plastic form justified by the dramatic expression, and complete, from the bare necessities of place to the most subtle demands of sound.

All that remains for the stage director to do, is to contrast the two areas satisfactorily and, with all his resources, make the most of their excellent arrangement.

In Isolde's tent, which means during most of the act, everything that occurs expresses the inner life of the drama. Brangaene, it is true, plays the classic role of the *confidante,* but her role is transformed by the music. It is no longer the last resort between the improbability of a monologue that is too long and that of too confidential exchanges among the leading characters; music gives her voice an importance far surpassing that of an unnatural interlocutor. Brangaene's powerful presence is not out of order in a place dedicated to the expression of inner life, in the shelter of those draperies which open and close like eyelids before the light and the vistas of reality.

The illumination of this area will be quite uniform, with no shadow whatever. The use of footlights, though at very low intensity, will permit the characteristic planes of the faces to be distinctly seen. — By contrast, the outdoor area will be brightly lighted and its reality emphasized through a variety of shadows thrown against the tent. Within the tent light will reveal the furniture and other three-dimensional pieces but will de-emphasize their plastic form. In the outdoor area the whole setting, almost completely three-dimensional, allows the actors to blend with the inanimate elements of the picture and thereby gives light the utmost expressiveness. The minor role of painting in this setting is thus unmistakably indicated.

If these conditions are strictly observed, the specific pictorial arrangement matters little. However, the conditions themselves entail certain conclusions as to details. For instance, sea and sky should not be visible when the tent curtains are closed; and when, at the beginning of the act, Brangaene lifts a corner of the side wall to look at the sea, the spectator sees merely an infinitely small part of the horizon, perceiving the outdoors only through the bright light that grazes the singer's feet without penetrating enough to throw a heavy shadow on the tent floor. The place of action is easily indicated by some characteristic lines of ropes. The text is from the outset so explicit about the place that the stage would appear grossly overloaded were it burdened with useless maritime items. (Note: unfortunately this is invariably the case in the production of this act.)

When the tent curtains part for the first time (page 13-14), the light from outside, falling almost straight down, does not pass beyond the threshold of the tent. On page 80 when they open again, the outside light is less bright (it is late afternoon), but the rays are more slanted; it covers the floor of the downstage area as with a large bright golden cloth. The shadows of the characters fall toward the audience. All that is seen is two groups of people: those who are to be received, and those who face them waiting for the king. Those in the first group (in particular Tristan and Isolde), hit by a slanted ray from upstage, are seen by the audience as shadowed silhouettes; the second group is not placed directly between the spotlight and the spectator, and consequently is much more brightly lighted and fully visible.

In conclusion let me briefly state the role of the *mise en scène* in *Tristan and Isolde*. In act one it presents to the audience in a tangible form the conflict which is going to relegate the drama to the souls of the two principal characters. Illumination plays the same negative role for Isolde's tent as it does for the setting of act two. But outside of the tent it makes the audience understand the full extent of the sacrifice and thus prepares us for the effect which the next setting must create immediately.

In act two, the decorative element is reduced to a minimum. Nevertheless, the drama in order to find some visual expression prescribes, by virtue of the actors' playing, a telling combination of platforms; but lighting, subservient to a higher purpose, undertakes to lessen their effect as much as it can.

In act three, lighting reigns supreme and determines everything else on stage. In the course of the dramatic action, shadows and light take on the significance of a leitmotif which, once stated, can, as it develops, radiate endlessly. The pathological condition of Tristan gives renewed intensity to these two ideas. And the audience, totally immersed in the destructive action which consumes the souls of the two lovers, could not follow a performance that would divert from it. Such a production would be painful to the spectator because he needs a visible rhythm to offset in some measure the extraordinary fury of the musical expression. Lighting alone can *continually* offer the necessary rhythm which is motivated by the poetic-musical text.

This brief review demonstrates how important it is for the production of *Tristan and Isolde* to determine the general aspect of the stage; for, if the director understands the reason for the sacrifices demanded by this drama and accepts them, he gives proof of enough culture to save him from gross errors in taste.

THE STAGING OF THE RING
Translated by Walther R. Volbach

Richard Wagner has inserted in his scores numerous scenic directives which must be given serious consideration. Yet, for all their profusion, they are far from providing a complete picture of the *mise en scène* and are fragmentary in their treatment of the characters. Besides, their authenticity is not always a proven fact, nor is their place in the poetic-musical text always clear. Nevertheless, they are all the master has left us on this subject, except for some essays which treat of production very generally, without reference to any particular score.

From his unpublished manuscripts about staging, we know only too well that Wagner was groping for a scenic form, so that if the directions are a record of past productions they are only of relative value, because the master considered those productions merely a tentative beginning in the new domain of "scenic dramaturgy."[1] But if, assuming the impossible, they are complete plans for staging, not based on actual productions, they must contain, along with valuable suggestions, the mark of the technical defect which has been discussed in the preceding chapters. The mere fact, incidentally, that Wagner would consent to the publication of his scores without including a thorough treatment of stage business in each one of them is consistent with his relative silence in his essays regarding the stage form of his dramas in general.

Therefore, the wealth of the master's instructions on the interpretation and the proper relationship of libretto and music is matched with a complete lack of any *corresponding* expression of his ideas on scenic art; all the production books which may be attributed to Wagner will not fill the gap in his writings on the visual aspect of production.

There is still the so-called tradition. Yet it must share the fate of the writings on staging, for it depends on the same incomplete and defective elements and, furthermore, its authenticity, based not only on the memory of witnesses but, above all, on their good or bad judgment, cannot be relied upon.

As a consequence, the value of the only directions we possess — those inserted in the score — remains dependent on a general intention whose meaning is unknown to us and which, moreover, must sometimes be suspected of opportuneness. What remains then, if, on the one hand, the poetic-musical text is conditioned by a scenic conception defective from a technical viewpoint, and, on the other, if the suggestions in this

---

[1] Richard Wagner, *Schriften*, Vol. X, *Das Buehnenweihfestspiel in Bayreuth, 1882.*

text have only a relative significance?

What is left is the *unity of intention,* as I shall call it. And this unity alone will justify the entire *mise en scène* of Wagner's music dramas. — In what does this unity consist?

Since the author alone is responsible for the word-tone drama, he determines its proportions in time as well as in space through the score — and in particular — through the musical time-values. Therefore he cannot achieve a unity unless the *entire* production is in harmony with his original conception. In Wagner's dramas this unity is lacking and must be provided. To this end, each of the scores has to be absorbed as thoroughly as possible, then compared with the others in search of the author's intentions. One must strive to bring them into accord with the scenic annotations in the poetic-musical text and, finally, under the influence of these preliminary studies, conceive an independent stage form for each of the scores. This last step will perforce carry the mark of individuality of the person who makes it. Accordingly it should be purged as much as possible from too personal elements. This is the really crucial part of the operation and it requires, above all, the greatest respect for the author. But respect by itself would be unproductive; love is indispensable to guide our judgment and to save it from divergences, which could result either from fanatical admiration or from too much license, not the superficial love we have for the author of fascinating works, but rather the deep and *entirely personal* feeling instilled by a man like Richard Wagner in anyone keen to understand him. — Respect will teach us the sacrifices we have to make in our own personal vision in order to approach the master's principal intentions; — love will allow us great freedom of choice in the pursuit of harmony and intensity on the stage.

Thus prepared, *unity* cannot fail us; and its nature is absolute in the sense that nothing except the unity *produced under the same conditions* by another personality can replace it. It is, however, probable that, after various attempts of this kind, a standard unity will be devised, for the divergences which naturally appear in secondary motifs will be easily reconciled, while the essentials, since they have a single origin, will be very similar.

Hence, the *unity of intention* is, as I have stated, the first condition for the production of Wagner's dramas. Serving as substitute for the original unity which they lack, the unity of intention tends to establish not an idle tradition, but a definite stage form.

The work of preparatory assimilation can of course not be indicated here; I shall present ideas drawn from the advanced and mature project.

In my statements about *The Ring* in the preceding part, I have intentionally neglected to point out the particular form of *The Rhinegold.* This prelude—or as Wagner calls it "The Eve" to the trilogy of *The Ring* —occupies a very special place in the Master's work and constitutes a unique phenomenon of its kind in the history of the theatre.

Let us first consider that the prelude of a gigantic drama must contain an action distinct from the parts following it. Otherwise it would be just a first act, its arbitrary isolation notwithstanding.—Moreover, the use of music on such a scale necessarily evokes a multitude of developments which must be properly managed. Consequently, because of its position, the prelude will offer the least development, content to state the elements of dramatic expression whose combinations will determine the course of the succeeding parts.

It is obvious, even without knowledge of the score, that these two conditions are splendidly fulfilled in *The Rhinegold*.

However, before we go into details of the score, another condition, general and essential to the production, has to be taken into account. The prelude of a drama in which the phenomena of nature play so predominantly a realistic role must include, either a category of very different phenomena, or the same, but in some kind of hieratic form that will justify the extreme and constant realism of the succeeding parts. In other words, a drama based on these premises can only have a mystic origin which its prelude must clearly express.

How has Wagner, from this point of view, conceived his "Eve"?

The significance of *The Rhinegold* is its somewhat esoteric quality. Its presentation is in a way analogous to images used by the sages of a country to communicate their doctrine to popular understanding. Although their images are not purely symbolic, they nevertheless contain in a certain stage of development the key to the hidden sanctuary. Never are they wholly illusory, and thus they communicate to very different degrees of intelligence. By means of these images, contemplative minds can dimly glimpse the Ineffable.

Those who have the good fortune to attend a performance of *The Rhinegold* at Bayreuth—that is to say in the only desirable atmosphere in spite of the basic and painful flaws of the production—experience the unprecedented emotion caused by the consistent revelation of the Ineffable in no less consistent contact with the beautiful masks which cover it. We know, however, that the subjective ideality of the word-tone drama assumes such a character. Then what distinguishes the ideality of *The Rhinegold* from all the others?

I repeat, it is its esoteric nature: that is to say, here the musical revelation, which in *The Rhinegold would correspond* to that of the other *Wagnerian dramas,* is somehow only a first stage of knowing: the specific form of this prelude, in its fable as well as in its poetic-musical expression, does not exhaust the contents of the dramatic intention. And yet, strangely enough, these media, combined as they are in the production, suffice to let us have a glimpse of the revelation concealed in the music. In short, the pristine character of the stage fiction in *The Rhinegold* calls for a *musical fiction* of transcendent radiance.

The impact of this combination on the audience must be mainly attributed, I think, to the awe-inspiring respect which seizes us when so colossal a work as *The Ring* begins. Indeed the magnitude has a bearing on the mood of the spectator who rightly assumes that the poet-musician will not keep his attention for such a length of time unless he has a series of extraordinary impressions to communicate. And the elemental character of the musical motifs confirms his opinion: he feels that in this prelude are laid the foundations needed to sustain a gigantic edifice and that, therefore, its significance extends well beyond its abrupt form.

In this frame of mind and by virtue of *The Rhinegold's* particular fiction, we reflect the work twofold: as a work of art in itself and as the *beginning of all the action* of the trilogy. This second image is naturally unlike that evoked later by the numerous consequences of such a beginning.

At this point I shall be accused of trying to analyze, in a rather clumsy manner, that which just is not analysable. I cannot deny it but neither do I presume to touch upon a domain which can be reached only by intuitive feeling. The aim I am pursuing authorizes me, however, to try through a demonstration, though necessarily and voluntarily quite imperfect, to make my readers understand the origin of my vision for producing *The Rhinegold*, and to justify this vision as being derived from within the work itself not from mere personal whim.

In a production of *The Rhinegold* all non-essentials must be omitted because the spectator instinctively feels that chance is a part of the development, not of the introduction, and the introduction must permit him to devote his full attention to what I superficially call the second stage of knowing whose ineffable secret is held by *The Rhinegold*. For this reason the stage form of the succeeding parts has some influence. The spectator's power tacitly to lavish on these later parts the magic of a revelation which they cannot furnish alone depends on the rapport that can be established between their stage form and the specific vision of *The Rhinegold*. The indefinable memory of *The Rhinegold* must remain vivid in the audience's mind during the rest of the drama, not as an abstraction which, incidentally, would be impossible, but as a tangible past whose image will rise unconsciously while the whole mind seems deeply absorbed in the dramatic development.

The production of *The Ring*, therefore, falls into two distinct but interrelated parts: 1. *The Rhinegold*; 2. *The Valkyrie, Siegfried* and *Götterdämmerung*. Any compromises we may have to make with the latter, will have a bearing on *The Rhinegold* and hence the nature of these compromises must be discovered before we can create the *mise en scène* for *The Rhinegold*. Then we shall be able to see whether the essential character, inherent, as we have pointed out, in the prelude of the immense drama, is compatible with the necessary contrast between the two theatrical forms.

The degree and character of realism in the conception of the word-tone drama is governed by the restrictive law that places the sign in opposition to the expression. Disregard of this law will necessarily weaken the very conception of a drama in which realism plays a predominant role. For the integrity of the production it will be imperative to sacrifice, sometimes part of the sign, sometimes part of the expression. This will result in a subdued intensity for all the passages of the poetic-musical text where these opposing elements come in direct contact for any length of time. To keep this grave inconvenience to a minimum, some scenic stratagem will have to be devised for preserving the highest degree of intensity possible in both elements. Accordingly, the character of the stage realism must appreciably be transformed. This is only possible through a more or less *expressive* form of production. If, for instance, *The Rhinegold* needs this form in order to be sufficiently distinct from the other parts of the drama, the scope of its expressiveness will be reduced by the different character of the realism that follows.

In *The Rhinegold* Wagner has created a harmony similar to that in *Parsifal* but by very different means. The variety of the spectacle, a variety which in *Parsifal* is intimately connected with the characters' mode of existence, is in *The Rhinegold* somewhat detached from their existence and seems indeed to become expressive in itself. But it must be noted that the elemental nature of the poetic-musical media does not, in this case, sanction the complete independence of the spectacle. The predominance of factors pertaining to intelligibility of the word over those of the musical expression entails a realistic sequence in time, a close relationship of cause and effect. Thus, whatever ideal fluidity there is cannot be the direct result of a certain degree of expression but simply of the obligation to offset, for the audience, the too realistic sequence in time by an appearance of scenic omnipresence.

In this task Wagner has fully succeeded: we witness a series of interdependent acts and yet, in the final glow that ends the marvelous "Eve," we preserve an impression of a harmony comparable to *Simultaneity*: instead of turning the pages of the score one by one, we have glanced over one vast picture. The degree of scenic expression needed to counterbalance the modified realism of the succeeding parts indeed reduces the realism to be used in *The Rhinegold*. But this happens to correspond to its special structure, for its poetic-musical combination does not require a high degree of scenic expression; and as signification is always at a minimum in the word-tone drama the production is not enhanced by increasing the sign but rather by reducing it. Yet the fluidity and elemental nature of the visual aspects in *The Rhinegold* can give the reduction itself an expressive quality which will so powerfully oppose that of the succeeding parts that it may appear superior and so force itself on the imagination. The hieratic form, which seems to us appropriate at first sight for the prelude of a drama with an exterior setting such as *The Ring,* is thus confirmed by the drama itself. And no form could be more favorable to the use of the devices required in the parts which follow, nor better distinguished from those parts. Hieratism is of an *exclusive* nature.

I must explain, however, the meaning I attach to the term *hieratism*. One speaks of the general character of the production and specifically the form to be given to the phenomena of nature found in *The Rhinegold*. Three elements are successively represented in it: Water, Air, Fire. It is self-evident that they must appear in their *typical* aspect; the contents of *The Rhinegold* and its position at the beginning of *The Ring* permit no uncertainty on this point. On the other hand, if such elemental motifs are left to themselves they will furnish more or less accidental combinations which, though not altering their character, will narrow their aspect. Here the hieratic spirit intervenes. Only in abstraction can we grasp the supreme harmony contained in every event of nature. Nevertheless to give us an image it is necessary to translate the group of motifs into a language we can understand, just as priests render the mystery intelligible by investing it with proper emblems to satisfy our need for form. The principal purpose which determines the choice of these emblems is to preserve the symbol from any arbitrary deviation, to keep it beyond the fluctuations of taste.

For this reason the composition of the emblems is invariably based on a definite idea that will justify it. Hieratism is, therefore, eminently conservative, setting limits to individual wishes. The presentation of the elemental motifs in *The Rhinegold* must likewise avoid all personal fancy, all that is open to argument, and impose them in a form which excludes all that is accidental. This constitutes a kind of hieratism, or, if preferred, of stylization, although the latter term implies a process too arbitrary for our purpose.

On these general premises we shall be able freely to compose, on the one hand, the *mise en scène* for *The Rhinegold,* on the other, that for *The Valkyrie, Siegfried* and *Götterdämmerung,* assured that we do not trespass upon their respective spheres.

Let us now examine the mutual relationship of the four parts, for each of them differs from the others by its own distinct character, whose origin is rooted in the dramatic intention that holds them together.—This intention is epitomized in Wotan, the god. It is Wotan who provokes the course of events; without Wotan the *drama* ceases to exist. All the events that unfold are the fulfillment of his divine will. Since it is thus a question of relationship, it is imperative to bring all the events back to their point of departure, *i.e.* Wotan's will, and to present them in accordance with the fluctuations of this will. Consequently we have two fundamental conditions; to wit, his will is always present and the events are invested with a spirit imposed upon them by his will.

The heart of the drama is that the events instigated by the god contradict the inner purpose of his activity, that he becomes conscious thereof—and that, unable to stop them or change their course, he gives up trying to control them and, in spite of himself, plays the passive spectator awaiting the denouement which must bring about his ruin. From this point of view, the drama is divided into two parts. The first presents the *active* mind, the second the *passive* mind of Wotan; the one embraces *The Rhinegold* and *The Valkyrie*, the other *Siegfried* and *Götterdämmerung*.

The second part shows clearly how *not to will* does not bring freedom. Activity, above all for a god, ceases only through his total ruin: by relinquishing control over his creatures, Wotan does not give them their independence; rather he exposes them to the perils of the existence he created for them and thus *deliberately* refuses them his aid. It is at this point then that the drama as such attains a high degree of intensity; —for Wotan is actually more closely connected with it than ever; by renouncing his will, he consents to everything and identifies himself with the creatures he has abandoned. This is why *Götterdämmerung* can be presented without the presence of the god.—

Indeed, the more imminent the catastrophe, the more does the action, such as it is, implicitly *include* him whom it threatens. Music has enabled the poet-musician to give us this strange synthesis. The essential drama as established in the previous parts puts such rich material at his disposal that, thereafter, he is able simply to indicate the events for the spectators. The stage action then serves him only as continuity and is opposed to the intensity of the musical expression which alone contains the essential drama. The extraordinary power of *Götterdämmerung* is thus the direct consequence of the whole drama's colossal dimensions. Without such a development the expression which in the last part becomes purely musical would be unintelligible.

From a theatrical viewpoint this arrangement is very unusual. The stage life, though it receives the time pattern and harmony from the music, seems nevertheless independent of the music's expressive intensity which, in turn, is out of proportion to the formal significance of the scenery; though inextricably united, they are unlike in value. And it must be so because this variance alone can communicate to the audience the poet-musician's intention. The task is to make his intention so clear that even the least prepared can sense it immediately and indubitably. It is obvious that the score does not permit any modification whatever, so the production must vary its principle to mark the change from the preceding parts. Therefore, if we want to convey the independent course of the inner drama—the leading action—we must establish a precise stage form commensurate with the life of the earlier portions, then suddenly substitute a visibly different form for *Götterdämmerung*: the orchestral music will retain the familiar vision, and the collateral dramatic action which serves the music as continuity will discover in the new surroundings a means of asserting itself independently of the musical intention.

The drama sufficiently warrants this procedure: when we leave the heroic world to enter the arbitrary society of mere mortals, Wotan no longer appears on stage. The *mise en scène* can easily indicate the descent but it will have to emphasize it in order to avoid any misunderstanding.

Scenic characteristics must be found for the heroic as distinct from the human world. The production of Wagner's *Ring* can only rather indirectly be based on the mythical source from which it springs. Its significance is not symbolic; on the contrary, it is *typical* and thereby attains a preciseness which raises it well above any effect of myth. Its significance is of such a nature that we long to dress the characters as we please and place them in environments similar to ours. The only way to accomplish this is to keep the setting and the costumes as rudimentary as feasible. Such a scenic picture is not opposed to the manifestation of the world of heroes but rather should express it with great clarity. The arbitrary world of men will be treated arbitrarily and, since for that purpose it will not do to load the setting with superfluous details, a different principle must be used in staging it.

Thus the scenic character of *The Rhinegold* at the beginning of the drama and of *Götterdämmerung* at the end of it must differ from that of the intermediate parts. The character of *The Rhinegold* has already been determined. That of *Götterdämmerung* will depend on the particular expression exacted by *The Valkyrie* and *Siegfried;* for an arbitrary form, not absolute in itself, evidently exists only in opposition to another form. In spite of their manifest parallelism, *The Valkyrie* and *Siegfried* are definitely distinct from one another: *The Valkyrie* is still dominated by the active will of Wotan, whereas *Siegfried* is just the drama running its course without *direct* intervention of Wotan's will. The very substance of *Siegfried* has more the form of a "spectacle" than has *The Valkyrie.* I mean that the personality of Wotan, always tending to identify itself with the scenic action, brings together in *Siegfried* the two poles of the drama in order to unite them in a simultaneous expression in *Götterdämmerung.*

The poetic-musical equilibrium and the very characteristic scenic abundance in *Siegfried* (primarily in the first two acts) undoubtedly derive from the fact that the identity of the two poles is not yet achieved: Wotan is still visible and we see him observing himself as though in a quiet pool. Later on, the work of destruction will sweep him away in an irresistible flood; we shall then hear the powerful voice of the god but shall no longer be able to see his face.

What I have called the element of musical *omnipresence*—which in *The Ring* is concerned with the appearance of Wotan—is in *Siegfried,* the extremely realistic train of events notwithstanding, placed in so perfectly harmonious a relation to the *episodic* element that the staging problem is here resolved by the same realism which elsewhere makes it unsolvable.

The Valkyrie is less fortunate. From many viewpoints this music drama may be considered the most difficult of Wagner's works to stage.

Its popularity is based on the particular charm of certain episodes on which our theatres, by means of numerous cuts in the score, put exaggerated emphasis. As a diversion, its audience is given a sequence of incestuous adultery, a family quarrel, lovers in great danger, and the like. Since these scenes are rather enchanting in themselves, their inner purpose is overlooked. But why, of all the master's dramas, must this one alone be so completely distorted by our theatres? The appearance of the Wanderer in *Siegfried*, no matter how mutilated, remains unalterable: the mere fact of Wotan's presence conveys the sublime thought of the dramatist. By contrast the invisible god in the first act of *The Valkyrie*, the god's proud stature in the second act, when, driven and cornered by his own will, he senses that the world escapes him, his desperate and final intervention in the third act are motives so complex, that to comprehend them it is imperative for the audience to devote all its attention to the language of the poet-musician. Here the stage director needs almost infinite tact to be in some measure worthy of his duties.

The technical defect in the Master's scenic conception which I have pointed out is here exposed. The realistic principle of the production has violated the drama and, from one end of *The Valkyrie* to the other, one feels the relentless struggle of the poet-musician against an element which resists his powerful will.

Indeed the scenic realism gives the episode an importance that can become incompatible with the omnipresence of the music. The happy combinations of the episodic element and the music in *Siegfried* and *Götterdämmerung* are relatively accidental; *The Valkyrie* serves to prove this. It demonstrates, unfortunately only too brilliantly, that the word-tone drama cannot be based on realism, that it merely allows realism as a means of expression whose *optional* use—as well as that of "scenic illusion"—depends on a superior principle. In *Die Meistersinger, Siegfried* and *Götterdämmerung,* Wagner has carried this realism into his dramatic intention; in *The Valkyrie* realism carries away the master. It makes the misinterpretation of the work excusable to a certain extent—and recriminations in this respect are unfair; for, just when we need all our visual faculties to recognize the inner action, the dramatist so dazzles us that he uncovers in vain the depths of his thoughts: to see these we have to close our eyes. In the first act of *Tristan,* Wagner shows us gradually and very carefully the attitude he expects of us—but in the impressive spectacle of *The Valkyrie* we are not aware of such an intention.

It is impossible to fathom the genius that could write the score of *The Valkyrie* under these conditions, and compel the rebellious elements to go beyond the limits of their power.[1] Therefore the stage

---

[1] The second act particularly presents a strange example. In this act Wagner achieves by a special arrangement of the events what the rigid form of the work otherwise forbids. No doubt this procedure is *indirect* and, in this sense, opposed to the essential character of the word-tone drama. But confident of his power Wagner could afford it. Thus, for instance, the entrance of Siegmund and Sieglinde, because it immediately follows the scene between Wotan and Brunhilde, arouses in the spectator's mind a solemn protest which a more flexible scenic technique could have evoked long before and maintained without effort.

director's task here is artificially to restore, in favor of the poetic-musical text, the scenic equilibrium so greatly impaired by the realistic principle. He will try to keep the various settings, all of which are in *The Valkyrie* exclusively assigned to the episodic segment of the drama, extremely simple. They will then approximate the form necessary for the passages where the inner drama develops, in a way, outside the setting. Such an arrangement, as it reduces the material reality of the production, will bring the characters to the fore and at the same time permit the music, now unhampered by the production, to resume the place required by the drama. In addition, the settings, specifically those for the second and third acts, will be so composed that the arrangements for the episodic action converge on those designed to increase the intensity of the musical expression, and any direct contact between factors must be carefully avoided; this means that the characters use the area reserved for the musical expression exclusively at the moments of supreme concentration. When the singers express the inner drama by means of declamation they are more or less detached from the setting; hence the foreground area will serve them well. From there by the thousands of nuances at the poet-musician's disposal, they reach the purely scenic life.

In a setting based on this principle, *The Valkyrie* clearly shows its dissimilarity to *Siegfried;* for, during the first two acts of *Siegfried* the inner drama is not immediately expressed: Wotan—the Wanderer who carries it conveys it to us solely by his presence upstage and this presence is expressive only in relation to the very absorbing episodic action. Thus, though parallel, the general arrangement of staging for *Siegfried* is exactly the reverse of that for *The Valkyrie.*

The last setting of *The Valkyrie* is used again in *Siegfried* and in *Götterdämmerung* and so not only represents for the eye the connecting link between the three parts but also leads it (the eye) time and again to the most sensitive moment of the drama. This gives the setting the value of a dramatic role and it has to be treated as such, without however permitting the conclusion that it must be especially rich in pictorial effect. Quite the contrary! More than ever the performer dictates the setting. The large number and varying character of the scenes performed in this setting require the design of a geographical relief, as it were, whose several areas fit precisely the poetic-musical action and form in their perspective a whole which is expressive in its simplicity, including only such details as are required by the action.[1]

We see that *The Valkyrie* differs from *Siegfried* in the "simplicity" required for its settings, whereas the measured harmony of the elaborate settings in *Siegfried* contrasts with the despotic excess which in *Götterdämmerung* must emphasize the independence of the musical expression from the spectacle.

---

[1] Illusion, of course, will not enter as a decisive principle in the three-dimensional construction of the setting. I cannot dwell here on the exclusively technical problem of the allowance to be made for speedy shifting and shall reserve it for a treatise on the *mise en scène* of *The Ring.*

In *The Ring* the stage form constitutes therefore a kind of crescendo: its point of departure, the sacramental hieratism of *The Rhinegold,* leads gradually to the exorbitant cumulation of accidental phenomena in *Götterdämmerung.* And let us add that the final catastrophe restores the elements of *The Rhinegold* and insures the scenic unity of the drama.

The unmanageable realism from which *The Ring* suffers can thus be transformed into an expressiveness which, by its calculated modulations, diffuses through the entire tetralogy an ideality, which is the very essence of the word-tone drama.

THE DESIGNS

The sketches which are added here to illustrate the preceding part make no claims to artistic perfection. The settings of the word-tone drama exist meaningfully only during the performance. Outside the context of the performance, they can only be reproduced in a purely technical fashion. They are to the production what the notes of a musical score are to the music, or they might be thought of as analogous to the instruments of the orchestra or the mere physical presence of the actor. Nevertheless, in order to make these sketches somewhat more enjoyable, and thus create a favorable impression on the reader, the author has tried to put them in bolder relief by employing "pictorial elaborations" which partially restore life to them. It should not be difficult, however, for an artist to extract the basic idea which underlies these extra details.

The author feels that he is exposing himself to misunderstandings by publishing these sketches without adding to each of them a detailed explanation. This, however, would lead far beyond the limitations of this study. Therefore he asks the reader to consider these designs as the product of respectful and devoted study of the dramas for which they are meant, and not as an expression of the artist's purely personal taste or of a transitory mood.[1] Therefore, they can neither be understood nor judged without being carefully examined in the light of the musical score. The following brief explanations have the sole purpose of facilitating for the reader the reconstruction of the drama.[2]

The Ring of the Nibelungen

A sketch for each of the four parts shows how the scenery gradually develops from the sacerdotal simplicity of the *Rhinegold* into the overflowing abundance of the *Götterdämmerung.*

---

[1]The sketches for the *Ring of the Nibelungen* belong to a complete and conscientiously executed scenario which the author plans to publish at a later date.
[2]Details and examples to supplement the present study are found in my *La mise en scène du drame wagnérien* (Paris, 1895).

(as seen from right to left by the spectator)

Rhinegold. Scene II

On the backdrop, the lower levels of Valhalla are traced. They rise up to the borders and disappear there, so that the Castle of the Gods need be of no clearly recognizable type of architecture. The castle must be situated in the center. The spectator imagines the Rhine between the backdrop and the extensive, easily convertible foreground where the action takes place. The crevice in the ground to the right leads to the dwelling of the Nibelungen; the cavelike depression on the left is reserved for the appearance of Erda.

The same scene.

After Freya's abduction, pale autumn colors are created by the effects of the lighting. Valhalla is invisible, wrapped in fog; the world at the foot of the Castle of the Gods can be seen only in blurred outline.

(I have already pointed out above that it would require too much space to explain the method by which in the new production the scenery and the pieces of the setting representing the sky can be replaced, for the explanation is possible only in purely practical terms.)

Valkyrie. Act III

The general arrangement of the scenery must produce the vivid impression that one is on a mountain peak. If the full trunk of the fir tree were reproduced, that impression would be destroyed; therefore, the presence of the tree may only be suggested. The Valkyrie come in from the right over the slope whereby they can make an uninhibited and graceful entrance; then they disperse (according to the detailed and carefully worked out scenario) over the entire mountain top; when Wotan appears, he remains in the center of it. Especially in the scenes with Brunhilde he goes down to the platform, which leads to the foreground, and remains there. Only at the climax of his dialogue with Brunhilde does he come truly to the foreground, after which he returns to the platform. Brunhilde is lying asleep to the right on the boulder. Wotan disappears behind the narrow path that leads to the highest peak, in fiery light. Siegfried appears (in the following part) at the same spot where Wotan disappeared. He remains for a long time at the right on the boulder where Brunhilde is asleep; then both move only for a short while to the foreground and climb up to the center of the mountain top. Siegfried exits with Grane by way of the depression behind which the last fir tree tops become visible in the center. When Brunhilde is alone she sits on the stone step which leads to the cave—with Waltraute, she remains on the platform which separates the mountain top from the foreground. The foreground is used only for Waltraute's tale. Thereafter, both go back to the platform. Siegfried appears as Gunther (*Götterdämmerung*) at the peak, which dominates the chasm situated in front of the highest rock.

Siegfried. Act I

This setting must represent an interior which, narrow and paltry in itself, is so constructed and arranged, being a residence of a little

220 ·

person who sits at home all the time; this is the home of Mime—and a dwarf, furthermore a very timid one, would not reside in a spacious cave. Siegfried with his handsome, tall posture does not feel at home in such surroundings, and the audience must feel vividly this uneasiness. Therefore, it is necessary to restrict the stage by dark and colorless layers of earth and rock. The light, falling through the doorlike opening in front on the uneven cave floor, should be warmly colored; the light which comes in through the invisible opening in the background, having trickled through the foliage, must have a greenish shimmer. When Mime or Siegfried are working at the anvil, they face the cave entrance (not the audience). Siegfried enters through the front opening to the right—then throws himself down on the stone which, immersed in sunlight, is situated at the foot of the middle cave pillar—then he hurls himself upon the rock in the right foreground. The different tools on the left belong to Mime and are in proportion to his dwarf dimensions. The Wanderer comes from the center of the background and sits down on the corner of the bench which encircles the hearth. He goes off through the front opening on the right.

While Siegfried is standing near the fire, he holds the handle of the bellows in his left hand and looks at the audience. Mime moves busily around in his small kitchen between the cupboards carved out in the rock and the long flat rock on the left which serves him as a table. While he is busy at the hearth, he stands on the bench on which the Wanderer sits.

Götterdämmerung. Act III, Scene I

This scenery must show geological layers so that the earth thus represented and the scattered pieces of rock render the Rhine daughter scene plausible. First, Siegfried remains standing close to the large rock overhanging to the left; later he moves farther down to the right. At their second (serious) appearance the Rhine daughters gather around in front of the large rock in the middle—then before they disappear they swim swiftly back and forth between the cliffs on the right and almost touch the foreground,—Gunther sits down on the left, next to the isolated birch tree, Siegfried and Hagen rest on the other side of the birch tree toward the center. The depression in the ground in the middle of the stage foreground serves to add variety to the grouping of men stretched on the ground and to emphasize their position in relation to Siegfried (not to the audience). Hagen is searching for herbs above the strong tree trunk on the left; then he climbs down again and, in order to hand the drinking-horn to Siegfried, remains standing in the grass-covered steps on which the hero is resting. From here he will later make his jump to kill Siegfried. The latter collapses in the depression in the center of the stage.

In this picture the distribution of light and shadow must be sharply accentuated, in order to make Siegfried's exclamation meaningful also for the eye: "Descend! Here it is fresh and cool."

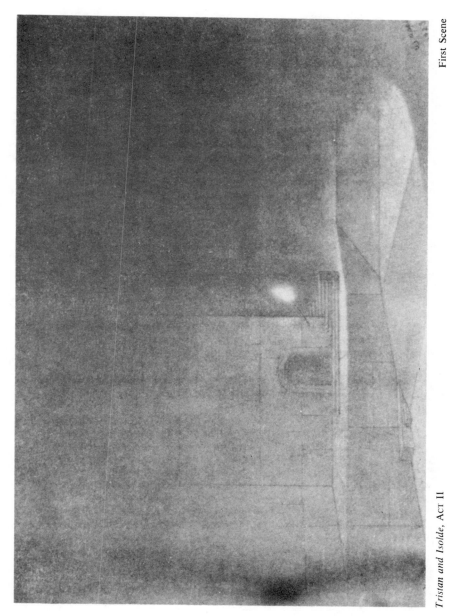

Tristan and Isolde, ACT II

First Scene

Tristan and Isolde, Act II

"Frau Minne kenntest du nicht?
. . . des kühnsten Muthes Königin?"

Tristan and Isolde, Act II

After Isolde has extinguished the torch.

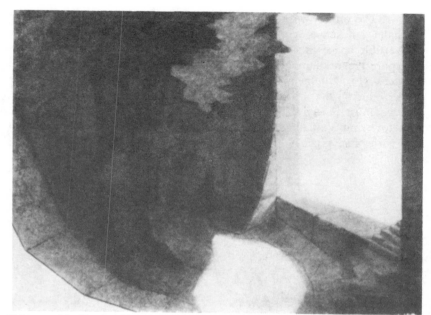

Tristan and Isolde, ACT III   Opening

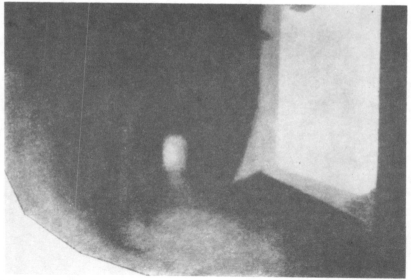

Tristan and Isolde, ACT III   Close

The author wishes to remind the reader that, especially in the Valhalla landscape, color plays an important role. The very large, convertible space in which the action takes place gleams in that fresh and pure green characteristic of Alpine meadows. Only the two rugged crevices (for Nifelheim and Erda) show bare earth and rocks. The background — the world dominated by the Castle of the Gods — is for the most part a large wooded area seen from a bird's-eye view. The towering Valhalla rises majestically, though artificially, above all this variegated green.

The Ring: Rhinegold, Valhalla   After Freya's exit.

The Ring: Rhinegold, Valhalla   First Scene

The Ring   Rock of the Valkyrie

The Ring: Valkyrie, Act III   Opening

The Ring: Valkyrie, ACT III   "Der Sturm kommt heran! Flieh', wer ihn fürchtet!"

The Ring: Valkyrie, ACT III   "Weh! wüthend schwingt sich Wotan vom Ross!"

The Ring: Valkyrie, ACT III   Wotan: "Wollt ihr mich höhnen? Hütet euch, Freche!"

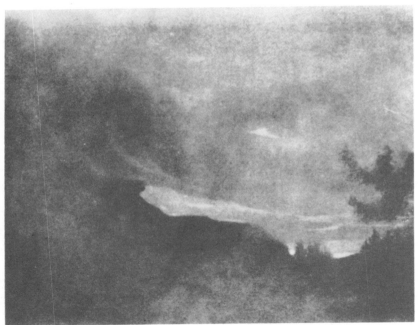

The Ring: Valkyrie, ACT III   After Wotan's arrival.

The Ring: Valkyrie, Act III   Close

The Ring: Siegfried, Act I

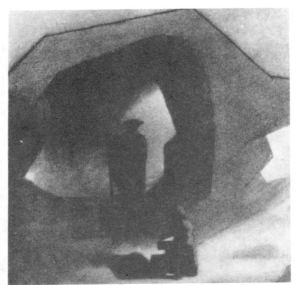

The Ring: Siegfried, Act I   Wotan: "Heil dir, weiser
                                        Schmied!"

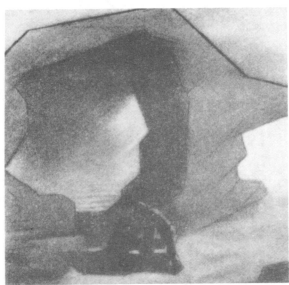

The Ring: Siegfried, Act I   Mime: "Fühltest du nie im
                                        finst'ren Wald . . ."

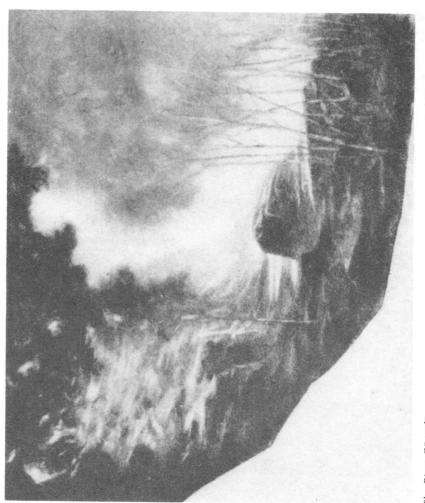

The Ring: *Göiterdämmerung*